John M. Sublett
3337 E. 45 St.
Tulsa, Ok. 74135

D0856065

WHO KILLED THE CONSTITUTION?

WHO KILLED THE CONSTITUTION?

The Judges v. The Law

by

William Eaton

REGNERY GATEWAY
Washington, D.C.

Library of Congress Cataloging-in-Publication Data

Eaton, William, 1927–
    Who killed the Constitution?/by William Eaton.
       p.   cm.
    Includes index.
    ISBN 0-89526-560-5 : $16.95.   ISBN 0-89526-776-4 (pbk.) : $10.95
    1. United States—Supreme Court.   2. Judicial review—United
States.   3. Political questions and judicial power—United States.
4. Separation of powers—United States.   I. Title.
KF8742.E18   1988
347.73'26—dc19
[347.30735]   88-4207
                                                                                      CIP

Published in the United States by
Regnery Gateway
1130 17th Street, NW
Washington, D.C. 20036

Distributed to the trade by
National Book Network
Lanham, MD

10   9   8   7   6   5   4   3   2

To Renee

ACKNOWLEDGMENTS

THIS BOOK COULD not have been completed without the encouragement, assistance and goodwill of many friends and associates. For generous financial support in its publication my thanks to Pat Donovan Jelley, Philip M. Jelley and the L. J. Skaggs and Mary C. Skaggs Foundation; to Daniel J. Popeo and the Washington Legal Foundation; and to Jaquelin Hume.

The principal research burden was borne by "Chip" Barber, who has an unerring instinct for finding exactly the right material. Details and supplemental research were faithfully produced by my assistants, Ann Sebastian and Susan Almeida, who also typed and retyped endlessly with good cheer.

Michael P. McDonald applied imagination and diligence to editing the main body of the work, adding greatly to its clarity and organization. Harry Crocker and Denise Berthiaume contributed the final editorial touches and production expertise.

For reading the manuscript and furnishing valuable thoughts for improvement I am indebted to Richard and Arlene Heath, Dr. Norton Seeber, Henry C. Stockell, Jr., Professor (now Judge) John T. Noonan, Jr., Louis Barron, Francis Canavan, SJ, Dr. James McClellan, and Col. Charles Stockell.

James P. McFadden, Joseph J. Brady, Robert Bork, Jr., and Dr. J. S. Holliday offered extraordinarily productive suggestions and support.

Most especially, for her loving patience, devotion and good cheer, which kept the fires burning through adversity and a pressing work schedule, I thank my wife, Renee Grignard Eaton.

CONTENTS

FOREWORD

by Senator Charles E. Grassley

[T]he judiciary, from the nature of its functions, will always be the least
dangerous to the political rights of the constitution; because it will be
least in a capacity to annoy or injure them. . . . The judiciary . . . may
truly be said to have neither force nor will, but merely judgment. . . .
                Alexander Hamilton, *The Federalist*, No. 78 (1788).

AS I PARTICIPATED in the Senate Judiciary Committee hearings on the
nomination of Judge Robert H. Bork to serve on the Supreme Court, I often
wondered what Hamilton would have thought of those proceedings if, by
some magic, he could have been with us. Hamilton, of course, presented
the classic argument for judicial review in *Federalist 78*, an argument that
was restated by Chief Justice John Marshall fifteen years later in *Marbury v.
Madison*.

I concluded that Hamilton, and the other Framers, would have been
shocked.

They founded this nation on the then-revolutionary notion that the
people can and must be trusted to govern themselves. Fundamentally, they
believed that the most reliable protection for human liberties and rights is
decentralized government, a national government of limited powers, and
with most issues of social policy left to the exclusive control of the
individual states and the people themselves. Electoral self-government and
federalism were thus to be the twin pillars of the Constitution.

The legislative and the executive branches would each be held in check
by the judiciary. Congress and the President would also have the power to
check each other. Even the inferior courts would be constrained due to the

Supreme Court's review power. The Framers thus drafted a written constitution not just as a check against the runaway majoritarianism of the elected branches, but also as a restraint on the unelected judiciary.

But who would check the Supreme Court? The only answer is self-restraint. Former Chief Justice Stone identified this duty of the Justices when he wrote in *United States v. Butler*, "that while the unconstitutional exercise of power by the executive and legislative branches of government is subject to judicial restraint, the only check upon our own exercise of power is our own sense of self-restraint."

Or as Judge Bork put it during his confirmation hearings: "The judge must be every bit as governed by law as is the Congress, the President, the state Governor and legislatures, and the American people. No one, including a judge, can be above the law."

Strict fidelity to the text, language, and history of the Constitution is, of course, the approach most likely to avoid the dangers of judicial arrogation of the legislative and executive function. Justice Curtis cogently warned of the dangers inherent in any other approach, when he penned his dissent in the infamous *Dred Scott* case in 1857:

> When a strict interpretation of the Constitution, according to
> the fixed rules which govern the interpretation of laws, is
> abandoned, and the theoretical opinions of individuals are
> allowed to control its meaning, we have no longer a Constitution; we are under the government of individual men, who
> for the time being have power to declare what the Constitution is, according to their views of what it ought to mean.

To say that judges must "follow the written law" rather than their personal bias is not to say that a "crabbed" version of liberty, or other expansive concepts, is the result. To the contrary, when deciding constitutional cases in the "gray area," the judge's responsibility is to discover the Framers' values, defined in the world they knew, and apply them to the world we know. I do not suggest that this formula always yields an easy result, or even a result I will always agree with, but it is a perfectly respectable way to grapple with the tough cases that come before the court.

The result is not a constitution that is a worthless, yellowed parchment, but a charter filled with vitality for today. Consider the expansion of the First Amendment protection to the electronic media, and the Fourth Amendment to electronic surveillance.

For more than three decades, however, the judiciary has lost its moorings to a written constitution. During this time, virtually every major change in fundamental social policy has been made not by the democratic representatives of the people, but pursuant to the personal preference of the unelected, and unaccountable, Supreme Court.

A new generation of Justices seems to have forgotten that they are appointed, not anointed. These Justices, including some who currently sit on the Court, have demonstrated an impatience with the democratic processes upon which our nation was founded, and has flourished. Instead, they would abuse Hamilton's and Marshall's limited power of judicial review to impose their own view of wise public policy. They would prefer to act as scientists who use a kind of "judicial alchemy" to transform the words of the Constitution into meanings contrary to its plain meaning or intent.

Hamilton would have been particularly amazed to hear many of my colleagues remark that their vote on the Bork nomination was the most important one they would cast as Senators. How could this be? As Senators, we vote on far more substantial matters, such as whether to declare war, how to allocate the federal budget, and how to spread the burden of taxation, to name a few. We were not, after all, selecting a king or an emperor, but merely passing on the fitness of a judge who was universally acknowledged as the generation's foremost practitioner of judicial restraint.

My colleagues' statements, alas, merely served to underscore the fact that the Supreme Court has become the most important lawmaker of American government. The fact is that the law many of my colleagues prefer is not found in the Constitution or the statutes. Instead, these legislators prefer judges who will give their political views victories in the courts, should they be unable to marshal majorities in the legislature.

In this book, William Eaton carefully and comprehensively traces the origins and spread of judicial activism. He skillfully chronicles the damage inflicted by a generation of activists who managed to transform the judicial role from one of umpire to partisan.

Who Killed the Constitution? is a book for the ages. It recasts the debate as not whether judicially created laws should be "conservative" or "liberal," but whether judges or legislatures should make the laws.

The book holds great promise to enhance our understanding of democratic society and an impartial judiciary. Indeed, *Who Killed the Constitu-*

tion? should be required reading for every law student in America today, for only if a new generation of lawyers understands the excesses of judicial activism can we return to the true balance of powers the Framers so carefully created.

My enthusiasm for this work is founded in my fundamental belief that an informed nation—conscious of both the responsibilities and limitations of each branch of government—is essential if we as a people are to preserve the value of the democratic governance that has been the basis for our unbroken freedom and prosperity. I commend Dr. Eaton for educating us.

And this was what we foresaw . . . that neither cities nor States nor individuals will ever attain perfection until the small class of philosophers . . . are providentially compelled, whether they like it or not, to take care of the State, and until a like necessity be laid on the State to obey them.

Plato

To consider the judges the ultimate arbiters of all Constitutional questions is a very dangerous doctrine indeed, and one which would place us under the despotism of an oligarchy.

Thomas Jefferson

I.
IN PURSUIT OF
LAWLESS JUDGES

1.   An Outline of Abuse

THE UNITED STATES Constitution, penned in elegant eighteenth century script, and signed by the Founding Fathers, has been preserved as executed. The original is displayed to the public under heavy glass in a hermetically sealed case in the National Archives, on Pennsylvania Avenue in Washington, D.C. Under constant guard, it can be lowered mechanically, case and all, into a vault beneath the floor when not on view, or in an emergency. This system has successfully preserved the document from physical deterioration and decay, as well as from theft or vandalism. But few systems, however well conceived, are foolproof.

Supposing that, on some infamous afternoon, the attention of the guards was momentarily diverted elsewhere—a shadow flashes against the wall, there is the whispering movement of a powerful object through the air. The guards, weapons drawn, turn back in horror to see a gigantic gavel crash through the glass cover, shattering the sealed case to splinters. In the wreckage great patches of the aging document lie mutilated, parts of it almost beyond recognition.

In wielding the power of judicial review, this is essentially what the United States Supreme Court has done to the Constitution over the last century or so.

The Founding Fathers understood thoroughly the corruptions of power and the temptations of office. They feared most of all the tyranny of *unchecked* government power. And so they fashioned a system of checks and balances to operate against the *institutions* of government to which particular powers are granted.

In Article 1 the Constitution grants "All legislative Powers" to Congress. But those powers are to be checked by presidential veto, by the judiciary, and ultimately by voters at the polls. The amending power is guarded even

3

more carefully. Article 5 provides that Amendments are to be initiated only by a two-thirds vote of both houses of Congress, or upon petition of two-thirds of the States. Ratification requires approval of three-fourths of the States, either by their legislatures or by conventions called for the purpose, as Congress may direct.

The Supreme Court has severed legislative power from Article 1, and has transferred such power to itself. That is troublesome enough. What it has done to Article 5 is truly revolutionary.

On subjects which have caught its fancy, the Court has simply negated the requirements of that Article, and has set itself up as a kind of continuing constitutional convention. A majority of five or more of the nine *appointed* Justices has become accustomed to doing, on its own authority, what the Constitution requires be done only with deliberation and difficulty through *elected* officials in Congress and the States. There can no longer be any doubt but that the Court has done this consciously and deliberately.

Thus, the belief that the Court has stood steadfastly as the faithful guardian of the Constitution, and the unfailing protector of our liberties, is a myth. Rather, in respect to its duty to defend the Constitution, the Court is a case study in judicial schizophrenia. In one era, the Court has been the mild and beneficent Dr. Jekyll, the dispassionate curator of constitutional stability and fundamental law. In the next, it has been the marauding Mr. Hyde, tearing at the vitals of the document whose protection is its principal legitimate function. These oscillations have been occurring, with an accelerating tilt towards judicial tyranny, for well over a century.

In 1857, on the eve of the Civil War, the Court went out of its way to defend slavery, stated that the Negro was of an inherently inferior race, and held that, even if free, Negroes could never be citizens. Some forty years later the Court held that segregated public facilities for blacks, if found by a court to be "equal" to those of whites, were not unconstitutional, *per se,* thereby grafting onto the Constitution the infamous "separate but equal" concept of race relations. For some decades after the turn of the century the Court told the country that it was constitutionally impermissible for either Congress or the state legislatures to outlaw sweatshops, set maximum hours of work in hazardous occupations, and in other ways regulate abuses in the mines and factories of the new industrial society. Most of these decisions vetoed or prohibited actions attempted by state or federal government. These decisions were *legislative* in nature, rather than judicial, were not authorized by the Constitution, and in effect *amended* the Constitution.

In 1954 there began an even more audacious era of judicial amendment. In this era the Supreme Court has required that children be bused miles away from their neighborhoods to school, that every legislative body in the country except the United States Senate be reapportioned, that voting systems be changed, and that state prisons and hospitals be restructured as lower federal courts might determine; it has held that there is a constitutional right to have an abortion, that free speech includes pornography, and that the guilty must go unpunished where there may be technical flaws in the gathering of evidence.

This most recent era differs from prior eras of unauthorized judicial action in that, instead of merely vetoing legislation of Congress or the States, the Court has *invented* a whole *legislative program* of its own, and imposed that program upon the country. Some of the most enthusiastic supporters of this program have hailed the Court in this new role as a "Revolutionary Committee," and the description is apt. There having been no constitutional authority for any of this judicial legislation, the Court simply rewrote the Constitution to conform to what it wanted to do.

The constitutional system of checks and balances *breaks down* when the powers granted are transferred *away* from the agencies of government where their abuse can be corrected by constitutionally provided means. The President cannot veto the Court's legislation; the people cannot vote the Court out of office; the Court certainly does not police itself; while Congress and the States gaze in naked disbelief as the Court amends the Constitution again and again, in the hope of legitimizing its own transgressions. The decisions in which these things were done have carried the Court far beyond the Constitution, and threaten the very concept of a rule of law.

In all of these decisions the Court has moved ever nearer to the condition which Jefferson feared, and Plato longed for. We have come perilously close to creating Plato's Philosopher Kings, "providentially compelled . . . to take care of the State whether its citizens like it or not."[1] Or, to describe what has happened in Jefferson's words, we are in danger of being placed "under the despotism of an oligarchy."[2]

If all of this is such a massive usurpation of power, and so patently unconstitutional, one is entitled to ask, how did it happen? How is it that the Supreme Court could get away with it? Part of the answer is that these occurrences have been incremental, so that their full import is not easily perceived. All of the decisions in which the Court has been guilty of legislating, or of amending the Constitution, arise from its exercise of the power of judicial review, which we shall examine in the following chapter. Exercise of that power allows the Court to judge the constitutionality of the acts of the executive or legislative branches of the federal government, and the acts of state governments. Acts found to be unconstitutional are declared null and void. The power of judicial review is a sweeping power, so that what the Court has done has often appeared to fall within that power. Nevertheless, construed within the constitutional framework, the power of judicial review is a limited power—and a power whose limits the Court has willfully transgressed.

A second explanation of the Court's ability to indulge these excesses is that, in the rather elaborate scheme of checks and balances devised by the framers, there is a curious omission. The Constitution provides for no direct *institutional* check upon the accumulation and exercise of excessive judicial power. No other agency of government is specifically authorized by the Constitution to *check* and *correct* unconstitutional decisions of the Supreme Court.

In inquiring into this apparent omission, we shall see that the reason for it was that it never occurred to the founding fathers that the Supreme Court would ever assume or exercise the kind of legislative and amending power which it has come to claim. There had never been a court of law, up to the time of the framing of the Constitution—nor has there been one in any other country since that time—which had exercised such powers. Hence there appeared to be no need to provide a constitutional safeguard against such a possibility. With no other agency of government designed to check its abuses, the Court has been free to choose whatever policies struck its fancy, and to amend the Constitution by judicial fiat in order to justify its new departures.

Another part of the answer as to how the Supreme Court gets away with usurpation of the legislative and amending powers is that it has not always gotten away with it. As we shall see in due course, when the Court has exercised these political functions of government, there has nearly always arisen a political counterattack on the Court, forcing the Court to back away from its unconstitutional practices. But this has provided only temporary relief, and has kept the Court within the constitutional traces only until some new majority could form, with a different social philosophy, and begin to impose its views in a new area of concern.

The various social and political philosophies advanced by the Court from time to time are not the *primary* concern of this book. Whether it is a good idea to promote slavery, to deny government the power to regulate the economy, to allow every woman the right to an abortion, or to require that "one man" shall have "one vote" are wrenching social issues, and it is a fact that the Court has oscillated wildly over the years between the "liberal" and "conservative" approaches to such issues.

But our main concern is with a *process* of government, of which the Supreme Court was designed to be but one part, although a very critical part. The judicial power is peculiarly suited to protect individual rights, and to see to it that the other branches of government do not exceed the powers granted to them by the Constitution. The constitutional system itself is basically a device by which to limit the power of government, while at the same time allowing government enough power to govern. The balance between freedom and governmental power is not easy to maintain, but it is essential that it be maintained if we are to continue to enjoy liberty under law.

The danger in the Supreme Court's usurpation of legislative and amending powers is that the Court will become more and more like other agencies of government, the legislative and executive. It will become merely another *political,* policy-making agency, and will be perceived as such. It will then lose the capacity to act as, and be perceived as, an independent agency above the political fray. If it does, it will also lose its authority to have its decisions respected and obeyed. As more than one constitutional scholar has observed, the Court would never have the strength to prevail in the face of widespread public repudiation of its legitimacy.

In order to acquiesce in court decisions, and to comply with their requirements, the people must believe that the court system, and the Supreme Court especially, is governed by a rule of law, not a rule of men. We must believe that the judicial system insulates us from the whims of individual judges, from their prejudices, and from their areas of ignorance. We must believe that the courts preside over a system of justice which is impartial, judicious, and unbiased if their authority is to be maintained.

On a deeper level, we must believe in the constitutional system itself, if our privilege of living in a condition of liberty under law is to prevail. If a constitution is to be a constitution, it must represent something more than passing judicial fancy. There must be a permanency about it, a dependability. A constitution, if it is to have meaning, is a solemn document. The American Constitution was adopted after prolonged, often bitter, but remarkably articulate debate. The amending process was designed to assure similar, and equally solemn, consideration if the document were to be changed. But the Supreme Court has decided, from time to time, that it cannot wait. And so five or more votes on any day the Court announces its decisions have come not only to override the restraints of the Constitution, but to threaten the processes of government which have been embodied in that document: processes provided with the intent of assuring a free society, governed by elected representatives.

The extent of the Supreme Court's transgressions, particularly since the advent of the Warren era, is amazing, and at first difficult to believe. But the evidence is there, and it is clear. This book is addressed to thoughtful Americans, be they students, government officials, or concerned citizens, who sense that something has gone terribly wrong with our courts, and who would like to understand what it is, how it happened, and what might be done about it.

While this book is not addressed to constitutional scholars as such, it has attempted to present a perspective of the issues involved, particularly concerning the nature and origins of constitutionalism, which might be of interest to the academic as well as the general reader. It could also serve as an effective antidote to the activist jurisprudence many students in law, political science, or history are exposed to these days.

However that may be, it is well to note that there is a complex, often arcane, scholarly debate in progress concerning these developments, wherein the antagonists have found themselves grouped under the clumsy nomenclature of "interpretivist" or "noninterpretivist." An "interpretivist" is one who believes, simply, that judges should hew rigorously to the expressed meaning, or the ascertainable intent, of the Constitution and its Amendments, or to conclusions closely reasoned therefrom, in interpreting those documents.

Those who place themselves in the "noninterpretivist" camp (the simplest analysis of the appellation they choose exposes their transgression) hold, for various and often astonishing reasons, that judges are *not* bound by the terms of the Constitution, or by close reasoning therefrom, in their exegesis of that document and its Amendments. Rather, they are free to impose values (even a revolutionary agenda amounting to a new social ethos) in the name of the Constitution—but unrelated to it. The noninterpretivist movement would appear to be propelled by an elitist distrust of ordinary citizens, and by distaste (if not contempt) for the results of the legislative processes of constitutional democracy.

The interpretivist-noninterpretivist fray, as any scholarly approach would recognize, deals in the main with secondary sources. That is, it deals with what scholars and commentators are *saying* about what the Supreme Court, and other courts, are *doing;* and (frequently of greater interest to the scholars and commentators) what the scholars and commentators are saying about what their fellow scholars and commentators are saying about what the courts are doing. It is not the purpose of this book to tread those murky waters.

Rather, we shall deal, insofar as possible, with the primary sources of constitutional interpretation. These are the expressed views of the Supreme Court Justices themselves—their majority, concurring, or dissenting opinions—written in deciding the landmark cases which have shaped the Constitution. Critics may well complain about this choice, and about the absence of any further, or more detailed, discussion of the interpretivist-noninterpretivist dispute in the terms the disputants themselves have chosen. Fair enough, and the author, as a former academic, must confess to a certain sympathy with that critique. Why skirt the "turf" of one's intellectual opponents? Why not meet "noninterpretivism" head on? There are at least five reasons for the course chosen.

The first is that, while that crippled rubric, "noninterpretivism," is of recent origin, the decisions of the Court with which we shall be concerned range over its entire history, and all bear the same stamp of licentious disregard for constitutional order. Thus, they may fairly be called noninterpretivist in spirit, if not so labelled in their own era. They all display, as Professor Richard E. Morgan recently said of one representative noninterpretivist, "nothing more than colossal impudence." If these instances of judicial transgression, set forth one after another, convince the reader that the Court has, indeed, gone astray, then it is a matter, as the law might have it, of *res ipsa loquitur*—the thing speaks for itself.

The second reason follows from the first, and the author wishes to be quite frank about it. It is the premise of this book that, as to the matters discussed herein, the actions of the Supreme Court in handling our constitutional documents have been so wrong that they cannot be defended on any ground. To present the case for such a thesis fully and fairly, as obviously controversial as it is, it is necessary that it be developed on its own terms. Once the case is made, it must stand in the full light of day, and be tested however one may wish. If the premise proves persuasive, however, "noninterpretivist" reasons why the Supreme Court, and the judges of other courts, state and federal, have no obligation to try, in good faith, to follow the Constitution are irrelevant. To follow any other course would be to risk obscuring, in a fog of turgid disputation, the otherwise stark structure of illicit power upon which, as this thesis has it, the Supreme Court has come to rest its decisions.

This raises a third, and equally important, reason for proceeding in the manner indicated. The dominance of the "noninterpretivist" approach has become so commanding in the law schools, in intellectual circles, and in the media (even if not there identified as such), that it is imperative that the "interpretivist," traditional, and what we shall call "good faith" approach to understanding the Constitution, be presented simply, starkly, and without equivocating embellishment. This is an urgently required antidote to the nearly ubiquitous presence of the "noninterpretivist" philosophy, and should be welcomed in a spirit of free inquiry.

Next, we shall urge that the vital principles at stake are not complicated. They can be easily grasped by attentive analysis of the Court's own work. Comprehension of these principles is most readily attained by addressing the subject as directly, and in terms as fresh and incisive, as can be managed.

Finally, there is a crucial distinction between the Court's opinions, and commentary on those opinions, which makes it imperative to concentrate on the former at the expense of the latter. A commentator, however logical, however compelling his view may seem, can only hope that people will listen and consider. The decision of a judge, whether logical or illogical, whether put eloquently or crudely, is an action which requires institutions and individuals to comply, on pain of fine or imprisonment. The question is not which opinion, that of the commentator or the judge, might be *preferable*. Our concern is whether the decision of the judge, mandatory as it is, is *legal*.

The reader, having now been apprised of the ongoing "interpretivist-noninterpretivist" imbroglio, will have no difficulty in identifying to which camp any particular decision, quotation, or analysis presented in this book should be assigned, if retention of that frame of reference is desired. Those who might wish to pursue the academic details further could do no better than to see Professor Richard E. Morgan's penetrating and witty analysis of noninterpretivism in his recent book, *Disabling America; The "Rights*

Industry" in Our Time.[3] For the rest, the polysyllabic onslaught is over, and we now turn our attention to the primary sources of consideration, the Supreme Court's opinions.

This book is motivated by a conviction that the Supreme Court has allowed itself to be lured into a profoundly non-judicial role. There is no intent to damage the Court; rather, the purpose is to stir a realization of how deeply the Court has, repeatedly, damaged itself and the country. Judicial power is now so far out of control that an effective remedy may well require political means as extraordinary as the usurpation to be corrected. Our pursuit of lawless judges is not to do them in, but to expose them far beyond the constitutional boundaries from which they have escaped, and to consider how they might be returned to their proper function within a government of constitutionally limited power.

2. The Pit, the Smoke, and the Oracle

THE HUSHED PRECINCTS in which the United States Supreme Court carries on its often mysterious business are lodged behind a splendid marble colonnade, a design which originated in the temples of ancient Greece, some twenty-five hundred years ago.

The modern copy in Washington may be more symbolic than accidental, for there was in ancient Greece, housed in a similar temple, an institution which was not so very different from the Court. It was the oracle of Apollo, located at Delphi, now a short drive northwest of Athens. The ruins of the temple are still there, in the spectacular setting of a huge natural amphitheatre, formed by a massive stone ledge near the base of Mt. Parnassus. The view below is over a carpet of gray-green olive trees towards the little town of Itea, on the Gulf of Corinth. Above, the sheer walls of Parnassus tower over the ruins. In the temple's inner sanctum, the Mysteries were pursued.

Questions to the oracle of Apollo were submitted in writing, and were answered by the priestess of the temple in a most arresting manner. She prepared herself by drinking from a sacred spring, and by chewing the sacred laurel leaf. She was then led into the dusk of the temple and seated upon a magnificent tripod of gold, set on a pillar of three serpents, interwoven in bronze. The tripod had great symbolic meaning, having been contributed by all the cities of Greece in dedication to Apollo for the seemingly miraculous victory of the Greeks over the Persians in 479 B.C., a battle which saved Greek civilization as we know it from barbarian destruction. The tripod still exists, in Istanbul, where it was taken by the Emperor Constantine. In the temple at Delphi it was set over an opening in the floor under which there was a dark pit, in the depths of which fires smoldered, while a mysterious substance was sprinkled upon the embers. Smoke drifted upwards, wafted about the priestess, and bathed her in

12

intoxicating fumes. Full of the holy water, chewing the laurel, and breathing the fumes, she received her questioners, and rendered opinions on the most troubling matters of the Greek world.

An obstacle did arise, in that the priestess answered the questions in wails, groans, mutterings, and ejaculations of joy or fear, but never in coherent language. Fortunately, there were at hand holy men who had made an art of understanding and interpolating these inarticulate utterances, so that the wisdom of the priestess was not lost. Thus captured, it was rendered by the priests into poetic language, supposedly in iambic pentameter, similar to the meter later used by Shakespeare. Such are the sounds of ancient Greek that almost anything rendered into iambic pentameter has a canonical ring about it.

The Greeks were master dramatists, and the drama surrounding their most sacred oracle was calculated to be intense. One can easily imagine that even awaiting the stroke of Fate in the great tragedies of Aeschylus or Sophocles could hardly have been more breathtaking than the awesome interval between the questions put to the priestess of Apollo, and the rolling cadence of the priests' prophetic replies. In such a circumstance, one would be prepared to believe almost anything.

There is about the Supreme Court in Washington, as spectators gather eagerly on decision day, a not dissimilar aura of mystery and expectation. Passing through the colonnade, and down the solemn corridors, one is ushered into a chamber palpitating with expectation, hinged at the edge of what is known, awaiting a link to that which is to be. The black robed Justices, filing to their places behind the massive bench, sitting imperiously above the crowd, evoke a Delphic sense of dramatic awe. If there is an absence of smoke rising through the floor, that is sometimes compensated for by the amount which seems to linger from arguments of counsel before the Court, while various opinions of the Court itself have borne a high resemblance to the groans and cries of the priestess, lending a distinct aura of enigma to their meaning. As to what the Justices might chew, drink, or inhale in preparation for these seances, we have no information.

The power of Apollo was in prophecy; the power of the Supreme Court is in judicial review. Prophecy is as ancient as superstition or religion, while judicial review was invented on the American continent at the time of the Revolution. In its inception, judicial review was a limited and legalistic concept, a product of logic designed to serve a carefully defined purpose. As it has developed, however, judicial review has come to be as freewheeling as the imagination of a drugged priestess, and as licentious—though seldom as poetic—as anything her priests ever concocted.

Judicial review depends upon the existence of a written constitution. In its essence, judicial review is the power of a court of law to determine whether an act of another branch of government, the executive or the legislative, violates some provision of the written constitution. If the courts find that it does, judicial review provides them with the further power to declare that act null and void, and to order the agency of government charged with carrying out the act not to do so.

The American power of judicial review was articulated, and attached to the Constitution, as an unintended result of the first major attempt in our history to use the courts for political purposes. The presidential election of 1800 was one of the most bitterly contested ever. When the Jeffersonian Republicans defeated the Federalists, the Federalists viewed the results as something like Doomsday, or at least the end of the Republic. Federalist newspapers referred to Jefferson's followers as "the worthless, dishonest, rapacious, the vile, the merciless, and the ungodly." So intense was their hatred of the Jeffersonians, and so manifest to them their own virtue, that the Federalists considered no tactic too abominable if it could be used to undo the results of that election. One device which they seized upon was to create numerous new federal judgeships, so as to pack the courts with Federalist sympathizers. The judiciary was to be the Federalist sanctuary, fortified and secured against the supposedly radical views of Jefferson and his Republicans. Of course, Jefferson was, contrary to Federalist fears, devoutly committed to limited government, as were his Republican followers, the direct forebears of the Democrats of today.

Amongst the Federalist "hordes," as the Jeffersonians viewed the new judicial appointees, was one William Marbury, appointed as a Justice of the Peace for the District of Columbia. A lapse in the protocol of his appointment led to perhaps the most significant decision which the United States Supreme Court has ever rendered. Marbury's commission had to be signed by the Secretary of State, and then delivered to Marbury, in order for it to become effective. The outgoing Federalist Secretary signed the commission, but forgot to deliver it before his party left office with the inauguration of Jefferson in 1801. Marbury thereafter brought suit against the new Secretary of State, James Madison, to compel its delivery.

The form of the suit was to ask for what lawyers term a writ of mandamus. The writ of mandamus is a formal order running from a court to a public official or other individual, requiring or mandating that he take certain action. It is a writ of ancient origin in the common law, which judges have been accustomed to issue for centuries upon showing of proper cause. But Marbury's request was for no ordinary writ, and it was brought in no ordinary court.

Marbury sued Madison directly in the Supreme Court of the United States, as the court of original jurisdiction. The term jurisdiction defines a court's authority to hear and decide cases. Original jurisdiction refers to the court in which a case is initially tried or heard. Appellate jurisdiction defines the power of a higher court to hear an appeal from the trial court. Ordinarily the Supreme Court does not exercise original jurisdiction. In the three-tiered federal court structure nearly all cases are originally heard in the federal district courts. They may then go to the circuit courts of appeal, and possibly thereafter to the Supreme Court. There are, however, a few cases in which the Supreme Court does have original jurisdiction. Therein lay the basis of Marbury's suit, and of the remarkable decision which resulted.

Article III, Section 2, of the Constitution provides that,

> In all Cases affecting Ambassadors, other public Ministers
> and Consuls, and those in which a State shall be a Party, the
> Supreme Court shall have original Jurisdiction. In all other
> Cases . . . the Supreme Court shall have appellate juris-
> diction, both as to Law and Fact, with such Exceptions,
> and under such Regulations as the Congress shall make.

Congress had provided, in the Judiciary Act of 1789, that in addition to the original jurisdiction set forth in Article III, Section 2, the Supreme Court should also have original jurisdiction to issue the writ of mandamus in specified cases.

Marbury's case came to the Supreme Court in 1803. The passage of two years since the inauguration of Jefferson had done nothing to reduce the intense animosity between the Jeffersonians and the Federalists. It was evident that, had the Federalist Supreme Court ordered the Jeffersonian Madison to deliver the commission, he would have refused to do so. The Court's authority would have been repudiated, and the Federalist Justices would have looked foolish. There would have been nothing they could do to enforce such a decision. The country would have had an early and famous reminder that, in the end, it is only voluntary acquiescence upon which

courts of law can depend for their authority. Judging by the more deviant of
the Court's excursions outside judicial boundaries since then, that might
have been the better lesson from the case of *Marbury v. Madison*.[1] The
actual lesson was quite the opposite.

When the Federalists had packed the courts in the waning hours of their
administration, they had done a thorough job. The packing went all the
way to the top. Even the Chief Justice who wrote the opinion in *Marbury*
had been one of the "midnight appointments" designed to contain Jeffersonian anarchy. As it happened, he had also been the outgoing Secretary of
State who forgot to deliver the commission to Marbury in the first place—
John Marshall. Today a Justice having such an involvement in a case before
the Supreme Court would disqualify himself, but the fact that Marshall did
not do so seems not to have occasioned great comment at the time.

The first task facing Marshall as he formulated his opinion was to do
something on behalf of his Federalist friend Marbury. So he scolded
Madison roundly, told him that his action was wrongful and illegal, and
complained that he should have given Marbury his commission. That was
about all Marshall could do for Marbury, knowing that an order to deliver
the commission would be defied. Such "lecturing" is what lawyers call
obiter dicta, or free advice, as it might be termed in the vernacular. The
phrase refers to statements of a court which have nothing to do with the
actual decision of the court, or with the reasons for that decision. It is a sort
of letting off of steam in which judges sometimes indulge when they have
feelings or opinions which go beyond the case at bar, but which they simply
cannot contain. Having unburdened himself, Marshall turned to his real
purpose in the case.

To Marshall, the issue involved both the constitutional status of the
Supreme Court and the constitutional powers of Congress. He examined
Article III, Section 2, carefully. He observed that it was only in cases listed
therein that the Supreme Court was granted original jurisdiction. In "all
other Cases," he noted, the Supreme Court was to have appellate jurisdiction. Marshall concluded that this amounted to an exclusive grant of
original jurisdiction to the Supreme Court by the Constitution. He therefore reasoned that it was not within the power of Congress to enlarge that
grant by providing for additional original jurisdiction in the Court. It
followed that the portion of the Judiciary Act of 1789 which purported to
enlarge the Court's original jurisdiction by empowering it to issue the writ
of mandamus sought by Marbury was beyond the authority of Congress. It
was therefore null and void. In short, it was unconstitutional.

Marshall had thereby claimed for the United States Supreme Court the power of judicial review. In the classic sense, as formulated by Marshall, this power is essentially rather simple. It is the power and authority of the Court to examine an act of the legislative or executive branch of government in order to determine whether that act is in violation of any provision of the Constitution. That is what Marshall did in *Marbury v. Madison.* In this understanding of judicial review, the power to initiate policy remains with the legislature or the executive. The Court merely exercises a judicial veto in the event that an act of one of the other branches of government goes beyond the power granted to that branch by the Constitution, or is in conflict with some provision of the Constitution.

Marshall thus established for the Court a supreme power, and he did it through a supreme irony. In politely declining for the Court an attempted modest addition to its powers, Marshall in actuality added to its arsenal one of the most potent weapons ever wielded by a judge. And he did it in the most hostile atmosphere imaginable for the expansion of judicial power. He did it by ingeniously conceiving a manner of announcing the new power which the Court could enforce by its own authority, without executive or legislative assistance, which most surely would not have been forthcoming. The coup was carried off by simply refusing to issue the writ which Marbury wanted, thus denying him the commission, which the Jeffersonians had already refused to deliver anyway. Marshall had won by doing nothing. But it was his reasons for doing nothing which left the Jeffersonians fuming helplessly. Marshall had declared an Act of Congress unconstitutional, and there was nothing they could do about it. They were as impotent to respond to Marshall as Marshall would have been had he directed that the commission be issued and Madison had refused. Marshall had left open no road for repudiation or defiance.

But Marshall was not content simply to announce his decision and then sit back and chuckle at his own ingenuity. He was a judicial statesman of the first order, and sought to entrench his holding through reasoning as irrefutably stated as possible. The main problem Marshall faced was the fact that there is nothing in the Constitution which explicitly grants to the Court the power of judicial review. Nor is there anything in logic which indisputably requires that it must be the Supreme Court, rather than the President or Congress, which should determine the constitutional limits of power.

Marshall based his reasoning on the nature of the judicial process. He pointed out that it is the duty of courts to find and to apply the law in cases coming before them. He observed that, if both a law and a constitutional provision were to apply to a particular case, and if they were to be in conflict, the Court would necessarily have to determine which was to have precedence. Marshall characterized this determination as "of the very essence of judicial duty." In such an instance, he said, the Court must consider the Constitution to be "a superior paramount law, unchangeable by ordinary means, or it is on the level with ordinary legislative acts, and, like other acts, is alterable when the legislature shall please to alter it." The logic of Marshall is crisp, and to a considerable extent persuasive. But the rub comes, when the Constitution must be compared to a statute or to some other act of government, in determining exactly what the Constitution means. We shall presently see what a deceptive quest that can be.

Curiously, Chief Justice Marshall failed to refer either to the debates during the constitutional convention, or to the debates at various ratifying conventions in the original thirteen States. The question of judicial review had been specifically raised in those debates. James Madison, who was to become the Secretary of State involved in *Marbury v. Madison,* had stated at the constitutional convention that, "A law violating a Constitution established by the people themselves, would be considered by the judges null and void." A similar view had been expressed by other delegates at Philadelphia. The same opinion had been expressed even by Marshall himself, speaking before the Virginia ratification convention.[2]

Whatever omissions there may have been in Marshall's argument, the principle of judicial review had been firmly established, and was destined for a role in American history which Marshall could only dimly have envisioned. Marshall himself outlasted not only Jefferson, but the three Presidents who succeeded him, James Madison, James Monroe, and John Quincy Adams. Yet during the whole of his long remaining term as Chief Justice, Marshall did not again venture to exercise the power of judicial review which he had claimed for the Court in *Marbury v. Madison* in respect to any other act of the federal government. In a later chapter we shall see why this may have been.

When Andrew Jackson inherited the party of Jefferson, and changed its name from Republican to Democratic, he also inherited Jefferson's animosity towards Marshall. When the eighty-year-old Chief Justice died in 1835, it was with manifest pleasure that President Jackson named his successor, Roger Taney. It was to prove a choice of momentous consequence. For Marshall had provided Taney with a power as awesome as the prophesies of

Apollo, and Taney had the will to bend that power towards purposes in which he passionately believed. Taney was destined to launch in earnest the judicial invasion of the legislative and amending powers of the Constitution, based on the power of judicial review. That invasion began on the eve of the Civil War.

II.

FRUIT
OF THE
POISONED TREE

The device which the Supreme Court has used to pry itself loose from constitutional restraints has been the expanding wedge of judicial review, which the Court has fashioned into a weapon of immense and unanticipated impact upon our system of limited representative government.

The harbingers of contemporary judicial "creativity" are to be found in decisions of the last century, particularly in the terrible questions arising out of African slavery and its painful aftereffects. On the eve of the Civil War the Supreme Court pronounced the institution of slavery to be inviolable, a decision which ushered a dividing nation more swiftly towards the brink of war. Decades later, at the turn of the century, the Court enunciated the deceitful and absurd "separate but equal" doctrine, and thus retarded for yet more decades political and social integration of blacks into American society.

In the meantime the Court was leaping into the turbulent economic and social struggles of a rising capitalist industrial society. It issued sweeping decrees which crippled efforts of government at all levels to take political action in order to deal with novel conditions created by the new economic order, a "conservative" interference in political and social matters quite at variance with the Court's "liberal" bent of more recent times.

3.   A Slave and the Forbidden Fruit

IN THE CHAMBERS of the United States Supreme Court on March 6, 1857, packed rows of spectators rustled in their seats awaiting the entrance of the nine Justices. A rising sense of foreboding filled the room, for a decision of momentous importance was about to be announced. The slavery question was sweeping the nation towards civil war. Growing ranks of abolitionists insisted, at the least, that slavery be prohibited in the nation's new western territories, an indictment of their way of life which slave-owning southerners refused to accept. The buzzing spectators sensed that the Supreme Court's decision that day might change the course of history, but none guessed that the legacy of that decision would stretch far beyond the issue of slavery to the function of the Court itself.

The crowd gathered in the Washington courtroom sensed in its bones that the nation could not resolve the fearful issue of slavery. By the Missouri Compromise of 1820, Congress had "forever" prohibited slavery in most of the territory acquired by the Louisiana Purchase of 1803. That compromise did not last. By 1854 it was replaced by the Kansas-Nebraska Act which gave each new territory the right to decide the slavery question for itself. Now, in 1857, a Missouri slave named Dred Scott had forced the Supreme Court into the raging center of national dissension.

The buzzing hushed, and the anxious crowd rose to its feet as the nine members of the Court—five from the South, four from the North—took their places behind the imposing bench of supreme judicial authority. As the crowd settled respectfully back into its seats every eye in the room was fixed on the figure at the center of the bench, Chief Justice Roger Brooke Taney, a man past eighty, of failing health, thin and emaciated. The only sound in the room as Taney opened the pages of the Court's decision was the rustling of paper in the frail old hands. Then, in a voice as ethereal as

23

his appearance, the Chief Justice began to read aloud his momentous decision to the incredulous gathering. He read for three hours, and what he read thrust the Supreme Court itself into a role never contemplated by the authors of the Constitution.

The audience in the courtroom strained forward to catch his hollow whisper as the Chief Justice expounded the case of Dred Scott, the slave who claimed to be free. Scott, they knew, had been taken by his master from Missouri into free territory covered by the Missouri Compromise, and later returned to Missouri. There he had sued in state court, claiming that residence in free territory had made him free. The Missouri Supreme Court had held that, whatever claim he might have had elsewhere, once he returned to Missouri he was in a slave State, and remained a slave. Scott had then sought to press his claim in the federal courts, leading to the decision which Taney was about to announce.

Negroes, the Chief Justice told the spectators, "were not intended to be included under the word 'citizen' in the Constitution, and he could not bring suit in federal court . . ." Although the Declaration of Independence promised that "all men are created equal," Taney announced as the majority opinion of the Supreme Court that "it is too clear for dispute that the enslaved African race were not intended to be included . . . [because] they had for more than a century before been regarded as beings of an inferior order, and altogether unfit to associate with the white race, either in social or political relations . . ." The Court's decision meant that no Negro, even if free and living outside a slave State, could ever claim the right to be a citizen.

The case, *Dred Scott v. Sandford,* [1] could have been decided without ever imposing, or even considering, such a far-reaching damnation of the black race. Taney had agreed with the Supreme Court of Missouri that Scott remained a slave once he had returned to a slave State, which he had. It is clear enough that, as a matter of law in 1857, a person who was a slave, and living in a slave State, could not claim the rights of citizenship. This is all the Court had to say in order to justify its holding that Scott remained a slave. It did not have to go on to deny forever the possibility of a freed slave becoming a citizen. But the old Chief Justice, the fever of his cause dancing upon his ghostly countenance, did not stop even there.

As his faltering voice dropped to an even more remote whisper, he delivered the blow which would reverberate over the decades as an eruption of judicial arrogance, and as a model of judicial usurpation. Congress,

Taney read, had had no authority to prohibit slavery in any new territories, as it had attempted to do in the by then superseded Missouri Compromise. To do so, he stated, would be to deprive the slaveowner of his property—the slave—in violation of the Fifth Amendment's due process clause.

That clause provides that no person shall be deprived of life, liberty, or property without due process of law. As we shall see presently, the due process clause was never intended to have any application to legislative acts. It was intended only to govern the procedures of the courts. In reaching this decision, Taney also repudiated the provisions of Article IV, Section 3 of the Constitution, wherein Congress is granted the power to "make all needful Rules and Regulations" governing the Territories.

Taney declared, retrospectively, that the Missouri Compromise, in seeking to limit the spread of slavery, was unconstitutional to make doubly sure that Dred Scott, and others in his position, could never claim any of its benefits. In changing the accepted understanding of the due process clause of the Fifth Amendment, as he did to accomplish his purpose, Taney in effect amended the Constitution in violation of the amending process set forth therein. And in retroactively repealing, by judicial fiat, the congressionally enacted Missouri Compromise, he invaded the legislative powers vested by the Constitution in Congress. This momentous decision was rendered by a vote of five to four, and would have permanently robbed four million slaves and their descendants of any chance of citizenship.

The *Dred Scott* decision marked only the second time in its history that the Supreme Court had declared an Act of Congress unconstitutional. It was the first use of the power of judicial review to nullify an Act of Congress since 1803, when Chief Justice Marshall had created that power in the case of *Marbury v. Madison.*[2] But if Marshall had been audacious in his enunciation of such a power, it is doubtful whether he ever imagined that judicial review would be used to wreak such havoc as was destined to flow from the *Dred Scott* case.

The power of judicial review was designed to allow the courts to strike down as unconstitutional acts of government in conflict with specific provisions of the Constitution. It is a power generally regarded as legitimate, so long as the Court adheres faithfully to the Constitution in its exercise. What Taney did, instead, was to change the meaning of the Constitution, and then to use that changed meaning to destroy congressional legislation with which he disagreed.

Not surprisingly, the arrogance of Taney's *Dred Scott* decision stirred up a firestorm of anger and denunciation. Historian George Bancroft, in a memorial tribute to President Abraham Lincoln, observed caustically that Chief Justice Taney "without any necessity or occasion, volunteered to come to the rescue of the theory of slavery." Abolitionist Senator Charles Sumner attempted to sabotage the placement of a memorial bust of Taney in the Supreme Court Chamber after his death in 1864, urging instead that Taney's name be "hooted down in the pages of history."[3] In one of his famous debates with Stephen Douglas, Lincoln himself advised his audience to prepare for "chains of bondage" if such decisions as *Dred Scott* were to be accepted.[4] Lincoln pursued the theme in his first inaugural address, warning again against the potential tyranny of an uncontrolled Court.[5] Years later Theodore Roosevelt described Taney as "a curse to our national life,"[6] while constitutional scholar Carl Brent Swisher, commenting upon the *Dred Scott* case, reflected that "no decision in American history has done more to injure the reputation of the Supreme Court."[7]

It may well be that it was the ghostly voice of the old Chief Justice, as much as the guns at Fort Sumter, which fired the opening salvo of the Civil War. Yet, though he was denounced, and even vilified, over the substance of his decision in *Dred Scott,* few of Taney's detractors perceived the truly monstrous nature of the decision. It was the precedent Taney set for the Supreme Court as an institution of government, not his futile attempt to save the dying institution of slavery, which was Taney's devastating legacy. Taney taught his successors on the Court that they could tinker with the Constitution to their own liking, and then pass off the results as constitutional law, even though the "law" which they thus imposed had just been invented by the Court for the occasion at hand.

Despite Taney's efforts to save it, slavery was abolished by war, by the Emancipation Proclamation of President Lincoln, and finally by the Thirteenth Amendment of the Constitution. And the Fourteenth Amendment granted the citizenship which Taney's decision in *Dred Scott* had sought perpetually to deny former slaves, even if they became free.

In substance, the *Dred Scott* decision had been reversed by political and military power. But the decision had left an infection of unprecedented virulence within the Court itself. In reaching across forbidden boundaries for the rationale of its decision, the Court had taken its first luscious bite of the fruit of the poisoned tree of forbidden power.

4. Louis Lochner's Bakery

WITH THE SLAVERY question settled, and the country reunited, the industrial energy generated by the Civil War began to produce a continent-wide chain of mines, mills, factories—and sweatshops; and along with these developments, new political and economic issues. Dangerous and exploitive conditions in many industrial enterprises resulted in growing pressure for remedial measures, and in State after State, legislation was passed to regulate the worst of the abuses. Those subject to regulation began to turn to the courts for redress from the new social legislation.

Meanwhile, on the Supreme Court, after a long period of quiescence following its *Dred Scott*[1] debacle, a new and strong-willed majority had begun to form, one which yearned to savor once more the fruits of expanded judicial power.

Among the entrepreneurs of the new industrial system was a man named Louis Lochner, who ran a business which, if a bit removed from the ancient Delphic Oracle, bore certain evocative similarities. Subterranean fires glowed through the dark of the early morning hours, men sweated in the pits, smoke arose, and heady vapors filled the air. But the end product of Louis Lochner's work was nothing so fragile—or divine—as priestly prophecy. It was bread, rolls, and pastry, delivered up at dawn for hungry customers.

As was common at the time, the workers in his bakery labored twelve to fourteen hours a day, six or seven days a week under hot and dangerous conditions, much like those encountered in mines and factories everywhere. When the State of New York enacted legislation restricting employment in bakeries to ten hours a day, and sixty hours a week, Lochner brought suit to prevent enforcement of the law in his establishment.

Lochner argued that the law violated "Liberty of Contract," the idea that

27

free men have the right to contract among themselves for goods, services, or labor without government intervention. This view derived from the day's dominant *laissez-faire* philosophy, as articulated by Herbert Spencer. According to his theory, the grimiest puddler in a steel mill was on an equal footing with Andrew Carnegie in making his bargain, and each man exercised the same unfettered right to contract in his own best interests, whatever his station in life might be.

The case of *Lochner v. New York*[2] reached the Supreme Court in 1905, when the Court again closely split its vote, as it had in *Dred Scott,* in a fundamental decision about what the Constitution meant—this time about how it was to be applied to legislation regulating economic interests. The majority opinion, written by Justice Rufus Peckham, left no doubt about the Court's philosophical underpinnings. Peckham wrote that, "Statutes of the nature of that under review, limiting the hours in which grown and intelligent men may labor to earn their living, are mere meddlesome interferences with the rights of the individual." Far worse, he continued, if such legislation were not struck down the country would be "at the mercy of legislative majorities." To save the country from the horrors of legislative majorities it was placed at the mercy of Supreme Court majorities—in this case a majority of five to four. Rarely, if ever, has the Court been more candid in expressing the condescending elitism which animates its intrusion into the realm of democratic policy formulation.

In tackling *Lochner,* however, the Court faced a difficult problem. To get rid of the noxious New York law, the Court had to find that its regulations violated some provision of the Constitution. But what provision might that be? Nowhere does the Constitution refer to any concept remotely resembling the Liberty of Contract dogma which Louis Lochner wished the Court to impose, and which the Court heartily agreed should be imposed, for the good of the country. Lacking a constitutional hook upon which to hang its virtue, but expressing imaginative genius equal to that of the entrepreneurs it wished to serve, the Court proceeded to invent one.

As Taney had used the due process clause of the Fifth Amendment to justify his stand against congressional prohibition of slavery in the territories, so Peckham used the due process clause of the Fourteenth Amendment to strike down the effort of New York State to regulate the new industrial society. Taney's problem had been action by the federal government, to which the Fifth Amendment applies; Peckham's problem was action by a State, to which the Fourteenth Amendment applies. That

Amendment, designed to guarantee the freed slaves citizenship and other civil rights, provides, in Section 1, that, "No State shall . . . deprive any person of life, liberty or property without due process of law." The Fifth Amendment provides a virtually identical guarantee against federal government action.

The concept of "due process of law" had the same meaning in 1866 for the framers of the Fourteenth Amendment that it had had in 1789 for the framers of the Fifth Amendment. Not only was the phrasing nearly identical, but the legal history of due process was well and similarly understood by the framers on both occasions. After the Court's remodeling of it in *Lochner v. New York* in 1905, however, due process was never the same again.

Founding father Alexander Hamilton explained clearly and succinctly the meaning of due process of law, speaking to the New York Assembly in 1787, as the constitutional convention was about to convene. The words, he said, have "a precise technical effect," and apply only to "the processes and proceedings of the courts of justice." To make his point unmistakable, he added that the concept of due process of law "can never be referred to an act of the legislature." In other words, Hamilton believed that no *legislative* act could ever be held by a court to violate due process of law.[3] Yet, in the *Dred Scott* decision, the Supreme Court had used the due process clause of the Fifth Amendment as a basis for declaring the Missouri Compromise unconstitutional, with the purpose of permanently denying Negroes citizenship as well as access to the processes of the courts.

In the debates surrounding the adoption of the Fourteenth Amendment, the framers of that Amendment repeatedly stated their intent to remedy the outrage of the *Dred Scott* decision, and to provide the Negro with the rights that decision had denied to him. In discussing their intent regarding the due process clause to be included in the Fourteenth Amendment, the framers reiterated the intent expressed by Hamilton concerning the due process clause of the Fifth Amendment. Speaking of Hamilton's view, Raoul Berger, formerly of Harvard Law School, in his illuminating book, *Government by Judiciary,* asserts that "no statement to the contrary will be found in any of the constitutional conventions, in the First Congress, nor in the 1866 debates" which led to the adoption of the Fourteenth Amendment.[4]

The concept of due process as uniquely applicable to court proceedings runs as far back as Magna Carta, signed in 1215, which sets forth the essence of due process. From Magna Carta to the Fifth and Fourteenth Amendments, the concept had always referred to *judicial* processes required before any person should be deprived of "life, liberty, or property" by a *court of law.* Nevertheless, in *Lochner v. New York,* as though excited by Taney's example in *Dred Scott,* the Supreme Court completed the transformation of the concept of due process of law into something which Hamilton, the framers of the Fourteenth Amendment, and everyone else for over six centuries had never remotely conceived that it might become.

Due process, as it has traditionally been applied to court proceedings, is often termed "procedural due process." In *Lochner* the Court invented an expanded interpretation, one which would thereafter allow due process of law to be used to judge the content of *legislation,* as well as the legitimacy of judicial proceedings. That newly minted concept, dealing with the substance of legislation, is now commonly referred to as "substantive due process," to distinguish it from traditional "procedural due process" concerned with court procedures.

But the Court in *Lochner* was still not home free. There remained the problem of tying Liberty of Contract to the Court's audaciously created concept of substantive due process. To hold invalid legislation affecting wages, hours, and conditions of employment as violating the due process clause, there had to be shown some connection between that clause and Liberty of Contract. How, finally, was Liberty of Contract to be joined to the Constitution?

The idea of Liberty of Contract derives from so-called "natural law." Its thesis is that in the "natural" order of things, people are free to deal with one another, in commercial affairs or otherwise, without government interference. Natural law is not a new idea in American history. The Declaration of Independence is full of natural law concepts, such as the "self-evident" truths that "all men are created equal," and that they are "endowed by their Creator with certain inalienable rights." As ideals such concepts are stimulating, and can lead to great advances in political freedom. But the difficulty with natural "law" is in defining precisely what it is in concrete *legal* terms. What is "self-evident" to one may be "out of sight" to someone else. Natural law inevitably has about it an aura of the ethereal, if not the godly. It is a quasi-divine concept, a good example of which is the once asserted "Divine Right of Kings." It was in part to escape those who ruled by such a "divine right" that the American continent was

populated. Natural rights, or divine rights, perhaps blissful in contemplation, depend upon who is doing the divination, and for what purpose.

In *Lochner v. New York* the masters of divination were five Justices of the
Supreme Court who wanted very badly to find the state laws regulating
hours of work in bakeries to be unconstitutional. Let us speculate as to how
they did it.

Prodded by his dissenting brethren, and embarrassed at his faltering
steps, we may imagine that Justice Peckham cast his eyes towards heaven.
There, to his infinite delight, the Justice perceived Liberty of Contract,
swinging on a star, sparkling in a crystalline sphere, just as Herbert
Spencer had prophesied. Such beauty, such grace! Who could resist her? If
such a vision could only be captured and joined to . . . due process of law!
Ah! There is was. Enraptured by the vision, Justice Peckham bundled
Liberty of Contract down to earth and married her off with priestly, if
hasty, benediction to plain old due process. It proved a fruitful union whose
first issue, as though immaculately conceived, appeared almost at once.
Substantive due process was born into the world. Suitably blessed, confirmed, and anointed with oil, the progeny was carried directly up to Louis
Lochner's bakery. There it gurgled and cooed in Delphic effusions, which
the Court was more than happy to elucidate. Louis Lochner's sweating
workers were informed that the New York law which purported to limit the
hours of work for which they had freely and openly contracted was, by
natural right and law, henceforth and forever unconstitutional.

The oddest thing about this little invention is that it really is no exaggera-
tion. No one knows to this day what sensible connection there ever was
between Liberty of Contract, a concept of *laissez-faire* economics, and due
process of law, a legal concept designed to govern court proceedings. The
truth of the matter is that Justice Peckham, after the manner of Chief
Justice Taney before him, had the votes on the Court to say that it was so,
whether it was or not, and to make what he said stick. It was a decision of
which Taney might have been proud, if not a bit envious, his own transgression having been somewhat crude by comparison.

But the due process clause of the Fourteenth Amendment applies only
against the States. Presently Congress began passing laws similar to those
of New York, also designed to regulate the burgeoning industrial system. If
Liberty of Contract were to do her job, she simply had to become biga-
mous. So she was married to the due process clause of the Fifth Amendment as well. Not only that, but she brought along her progeny, substantive

due process, as part of the bargain, in a kind of early day constitutional commune. Now the federal government, as well as the States, found social legislation struck dead under the heavenly aegis of this pristine creature of natural law, Liberty of Contract.[5]

For some three decades the Court used these principles, and on occasion other constitutional devices as well, to strike down scores, if not hundreds, of state and federal attempts to regulate industrial abuses similar to those which New York had found to exist in Louis Lochner's bakery.[6] Whatever constitutional variations might have been employed after the Lochner case, the determination of the Court majority remained the same—to prevent government "interference" in the economy. For over three decades, by such devices, the Court stood like the legendary Dutch boy at the dike, refusing to let a single drop of social legislation dampen the dust of the mines or freshen the heat of the mills.

The constraints imposed by the nay saying Court became ludicrously paralyzing during the Great Depression of the 1930s. Attempting to cope with national economic disaster, President Franklin Roosevelt's New Deal found itself tied up in a judicial straightjacket. Legislation to assist agriculture and industry was struck down time and again by the Court on principles deriving from the *Lochner* case. The first Agricultural Adjustment Act, the National Recovery Act, and many similar programs felt the judicial axe. The President and the Congress—the political branches of the government charged by the Constitution with the formulation of national policy—were helpless in the face of an economic dogma imposed by the Court without constitutional authority.

By the mid-1930s, criticism of the Supreme Court came to rival the outrage which had followed the *Dred Scott* decision eight decades earlier. Nevertheless, a majority of five Justices—the same tenuous margin by which *Dred Scott* had been decided, and by which Lochnerism had been fastened onto the Constitution—clung tenaciously to the idea that our elected government should not, and could not, interfere in the economy.

It was only after Franklin Roosevelt's landslide reelection of 1936 and his threat to "pack" the Supreme Court by adding new members, that the Court's stranglehold was broken. The Court's usurpation of political power under Chief Justice Taney had been a one-shot affair. That of the Lochner era lasted for some three decades. In each case public reaction, and a vigorous counterattack on the Court by the political branches of government in order to reclaim their legitimate constitutional functions, had forced the Justices back into the traces of the constitutional framework. But only for a time. In neither case was the cure permanent, for the reason that the true condition of judicial encroachment was not addressed. The usurping propensity of the Court was not subject to institutional restraint by any other agency of government.

In one case, the results of a pro-slavery distortion of the Constitution were nullified; in the second case it was a conservative, *laissez-faire*-oriented perversion of that document which was, at last, driven to defeat. But no constraint was fashioned to anticipate or prevent the future emergence of some new mutant of the same species.

Following the demise of *Lochnerism* in 1937, the Supreme Court was relatively quiescent for a few years. But the pendulum was quietly swinging once again. Successor Justices, slowly incubating a new moral fervor at least as passionate as that which had animated their brethren in *Lochner* and *Dred Scott,* were preparing to resume the battle to aggrandize judicial power—and with a vengeance. The Court's next great onslaught against the Constitution was to be conceived of the same painful cause which had so inflamed Chief Justice Taney, the treatment of blacks in America. To pick up this thread of the story we must return briefly to the waning years of the nineteenth century.

5. Louisiana Train Ride

ON A FINE day in June of 1892 a man named Plessy attempted to take a ride on the East Louisiana Railway. While his effort got him nowhere on the railway, it did get him into the constitutional hall of fame next to Louis Lochner and Dred Scott.

Plessy, a citizen of the United States, bought a first class ticket, got on the train, and sat down. The conductor came along and told him to move to "a coach assigned by said company for persons not of the white race." Plessy's racial status, according to the Supreme Court's summary of facts in *Plessy v. Ferguson,*[1] was "of mixed descent, in the proportion of seven-eights Caucasian and one-eighth African blood." Plessy refused to move, was "forcibly ejected" from the train, and was subsequently convicted for having criminally violated an act of the General Assembly of the State. His case, which reached the Supreme Court in 1896, involved another clause of the Fourteenth Amendment, the equal protection clause: "No State shall . . . deny to any person within its jurisdiction the equal protection of the laws."

The Louisiana statute, which the Supreme Court agreed Plessy had violated, required the State to provide separate, but "equal," railway accommodations for the white and colored races. The Court rejected Plessy's argument that this law violated the equal protection clause of the Fourteenth Amendment. It found that "in the nature of things" the Fourteenth Amendment "could not have been intended to abolish distinctions based upon color, or to enforce social . . . equality, or a commingling of the two races upon terms unsatisfactory to either." The Court pointed out, as the "most common instance" of "the nature of things" in 1896 the fact that separate schools for white and colored children had been commonly accepted, not only in the various States, but by Congress in the District of

34

Columbia. Hence, there was nothing particularly novel about requiring similar "social distinctions" between the races on a railroad.

As surprising, and even offensive, as it may now seem, these observations and conclusions reflected accurately the intent of the framers of the Fourteenth Amendment—that separation or integration of the races in social or educational contexts be left to the States. There was no intention that the "equality" provided in that Amendment require that the races ride in the same railway cars or attend the same schools. To this extent the *Plessy* decision was sound constitutional law. All the Court had the constitutional authority to do was to say that such matters had been left to the States. But the Court did not stop there. Rather, it produced a gratuitous discussion about "equality" which violated constitutional boundaries by rewriting the Fourteenth Amendment in order to satisfy its appetite for social "justice," as then perceived by the majority. The result was creation of that gross hypocrisy, the "separate but equal" doctrine.

It was the opinion of the Court in *Plessy* that, if the "colored race" felt the Louisiana law to be a "badge of inferiority," it was "not by reason of anything found in the act, but solely because the colored race chooses to put that construction upon it." It is difficult to believe that the Court's majority could have made such a statement with a straight face. Justice John Marshall Harlan, dissenting in the case, observed that the purpose of the legislation, "under the guise of giving equal accommodation for whites and blacks," was, instead, "to compel the latter to keep to themselves." "No one," he taunted the majority, "would be so wanting in candor as to assert the contrary."

But with no apparent embarrassment, the majority did assert the contrary. By holding that separate facilities *might* be equal, the Court invited federal district judges in future years to find that separate facilities *were* equal. This allowed trial judges virtually unchecked discretion in deciding when "equality" was present, and when it was not. This result rested in part on a crucial distinction between law and fact which appellate courts make when reviewing the decisions of trial courts.

When a trial court decides a case, it makes both a finding of fact and a ruling of law. The purpose is to see whether what happened in the real world, the *facts* of the case, is to have any *legal* consequences: whether any law has been violated or any legal right affected. In the "separate but equal" cases, the job of the judge was to find whether the separate facilities were, in fact, equal. If the finding was that they were equal, there would be no legal, or constitutional, consequence, because no law would have been violated, and no legal rights affected.

Appellate courts in the federal system do not ordinarily question the findings of fact of trial courts. Rather, they determine whether the trial court correctly applied the law to whatever facts it may have found. In the "separate but equal" cases it was the habitual finding of fact of federal district judges that separate facilities were "equal." What developed as a result was a system characterized by a great deal of separation and very little equality.

There is another important legal distinction, inherent in the *Plessy* case, which was to become crucial in segregation cases a half century later. The distinction is whether segregation, if found to exist, is *de facto* or *de jure*. Segregation which is *de jure* is that which is brought about through the operation of law, whether state, local, or federal, which requires segregation. It was *de jure* segregation which was involved in the *Plessy* case. State law had required the separation of the races in railroad cars in Louisiana.

De facto segregation, on the other hand, may result without any government action. An example would be segregation resulting from housing patterns. Local schools in black communities would be predominantly black, in white communities predominantly white. As a constitutional matter, the difference is critical. The Fourteenth Amendment prohibits only "state action," and is not directed against the results of private, or non-governmental, actions or conditions. It was long believed, therefore, that the Amendment could not be used to correct or test *de facto* segregation, but only *de jure* segregation. Of this, more later.

The *Plessy* decision raises one further question of legal and constitutional authority. Whenever law is interpreted, or declared, by a court, one must necessarily inquire into the "sources" of the law being pronounced. If there is something new in what a court is saying, where did it come from? How did the court happen upon its discovery? Law is supposed to be stable and dependable, yet new rules of law from time to time appear. It is important that these new rules of law be based upon sources which are recognizable and acceptable. Sources which can be considered legitimate. In the common law system the two primary sources of law are statutory law and judge-made law. The difference between the two was involved in the *Plessy* case, and goes to the heart of the matters considered in this book.

Legislative bodies at all levels of government, from Congress to the local school board, express social policy in the form of statutory law. Within the limits of its authority a legislature can change the law it has formerly made without embarrassment, because it is authorized to do so by virtue of its representative capacity and its political nature. Legislative bodies are expected to change their laws and ordinances as changing conditions require. Judge-made law, often referred to as common law, is quite a different matter.

Many elements of the common law derived from commonly accepted traditions and practices. Judges came to recognize these customs, in deciding cases at bar, as authoritative and controlling. They were thus incorporated into "the law." In the common law, for example, three days delay in payment, called days of grace, were allowed on bills of exchange. This was because the judges found that this custom had long existed among merchants, and so adopted it as part of the commercial law. It was said that, in a similar manner, custom often became law when it was honored as having originated at a point so remote in time that "the memory of man runneth not to the contrary."

The general theory of the common law is that judges "find" law, and then declare what the law "is." Once such law is found, it remains theoretically fixed and unchangeable, as it supposedly always had been while waiting to be found. Hence, though it can be said that the common law judges "made" law in a sense, they did so only at a glacial pace, over a very long period of time, often centuries. As a result, the expectation of judge-made law is continuity and stability. That is what lends legitimacy to the common law process. Rapid adaptation to changing conditions is expected of legislative bodies, but not of courts.

The "sources" of law cited in *Plessy v. Ferguson* are, in a sense, similar to the sources to which common law judges might have looked over the centuries. The Court referred to "established usages, customs and traditions of the people" between the Civil War and the time the case was decided. Those conditions were illustrated by court cases in which the States had been allowed great leeway in adjusting racial relationships. It was upon the basis of such considerations, as the "source" of its finding, that the *Plessy* Court concluded that the Fourteenth Amendment "could not have been intended to abolish distinctions based upon color."

The curious thing is that the Court's opinion made no reference whatsoever to the 39th Congress, in which the Fourteenth Amendment originated. Nor did the Court in any other manner discuss the intent of the framers of that Amendment in regard to the meaning of its equal protection clause. Yet, the conclusions reached by the Court in *Plessy*, particularly those relating to "established usages, customs and traditions of the people," undoubtedly did reflect the intent of the framers. In these respects, the Court's decision was sound constitutional law.

The point at which *Plessy v. Ferguson* ceased being sound constitutional law, or even persuasive common sense, was in its adoption of the hypocrisy that the "separate" facilities under consideration, and similar separate facilities, could in any meaningful way have been considered "equal." It is one thing for the Court to leave racial matters to the States, even where the State of Louisiana claimed that its railway facilities, though separate, were equal. It is quite another thing to cast the same separate but equal doctrine in constitutional cement, as an appendage of the equal protection clause of the Fourteenth Amendment. But that is what the Court did in *Plessy v. Ferguson*. The effect of the decision was to focus the question of racial relations upon a false doctrine, and the result was stultifying.

The turn of the century era in which *Plessy* was decided was one of great social ferment, and substantial social reform. It was an era in which the States, as New York had attempted to do in regulation of bakeries, adopted a great deal of legislation designed to curb the worst abuses of the new industrial system, and to remedy other social abuses. Legislative attempts to prohibit child labor, and to adjust wages and other conditions of employment abounded. The tide of social justice was running high. These reform movements might well have embraced racial relations as well, had the racial question not been frozen into the "separate but equal" dogma spawned by the *Plessy* decision. That dogma was as gratuitous and unnecessary to the disposition of the case in *Plessy* as Taney's defense of slavery had been to his disposition of the *Dred Scott*[2] case, and was equally lacking in constitutional authority.

Thus, the most unfortunate aspect of the case may have been its effect in damming up all movement towards racial justice behind the walls of the separate but equal doctrine. But as the decades passed, the pressure became more intense, and after World War II it became increasingly evident that the doctrine could no longer hold. When the dam finally broke, the consequences for separation of powers and constitutional government were disastrous.

III.
A MANTLE OF ARROGANCE

The past three decades have witnessed the transformation of the United States Supreme Court from a court of law into an essentially political institution, acting to effect a radical reordering of American society. Proceeding without constitutional authority, the Court has struck at the family, the churches, the schools, established systems of political representation, effective treatment of criminals, and in other ways has altered or destroyed long established social, political and moral authority.

The process of destruction began with the 1954 case of Brown v. Board of Education, *which dealt once again with the aftermath of African slavery. Over the next decade-and-a-half Chief Justice Earl Warren, following the pattern of the* Brown *decision, which, however laudable its intent, had no constitutional foundation, spurred the Court to a veritable orgy of constitutional "reform," an attack which did not abate to any significant degree under Warren's successor, Chief Justice Warren Burger.*

6. Civil Rights, Judicial Wrongs

THE ISSUE BEFORE the Court in *Brown v. Board of Education of Topeka, Kansas,* decided May 17, 1954, was racial segregation in the public schools.[1] Topeka, like many other cities and school districts in the country, had provided different schools for black and white pupils, schools which were purportedly "separate but equal." The question presented in *Brown* was whether the equal protection clause of the Fourteenth Amendment prohibited the States or their political subdivisions, such as school districts, from requiring racial segregation in public facilities. Justice Felix Frankfurter instructed his law clerk, Alexander Bickel, to investigate thoroughly the history of the equal protection clause, and to determine what the framers of the Amendment had intended.

Accordingly, Bickel studied the origins of the Fourteenth Amendment in the 39th Congress, seeking through his research the climate of opinion in 1866 when the Amendment was debated, so as to understand what the framers had intended. Bickel told Frankfurter that "it is impossible to conclude that the 39th Congress intended that segregation be abolished; impossible also to conclude that they foresaw it might be, under the language they were adopting."[2] Bickel reported that the sponsors of the Fourteenth Amendment did not intend that children of all citizens be required to attend the same schools, but, rather, that it was a matter to be left to the determination of the various States. What the framers did intend to protect were such rights as the right to contract, to hold property, and to be accorded equal treatment before the criminal law.

Frankfurter had the Bickel memorandum printed and circulated to the Court. Yet, despite the then apparently indisputable knowledge of the intent of the framers on the matter of school segregation provided by the Bickel memorandum, the Supreme Court ruled exactly the opposite. It held

that the equal protection clause of the Fourteenth Amendment does prohibit segregation in the schools. How, may one ask, did such a ruling
materialize? It was a result which Justice Frankfurter attributed to divine
intervention. And he meant it! The Lord had a nice assist, however, from
Frankfurter himself.

The *Brown* case was first argued during the October term of 1952. Had
the "separate but equal" doctrine been overturned at that time, Frankfurter
listed as probable dissenters Chief Justice Vinson, and Justices Clark,
Reed, and Jackson. Because of the importance of the case, Frankfurter did
not want it decided by that narrow majority, and succeeded in having it
scheduled for reargument the following fall term, hoping for some development which would enlarge the majority vote. After reargument in the fall of
1953, but before the case could be decided, Chief Justice Vinson died.
President Dwight Eisenhower, who was later to call it the worst mistake he
ever made, appointed Earl Warren to take his place. Frankfurter, as he
dressed for the funeral of Chief Justice Vinson, was heard by his law clerk
to mutter, "An act of Providence; an act of Providence."[3]

Frankfurter spent many hours with the new Chief Justice discussing the
case. Later, in agreement with Frankfurter's view, Warren brought to bear
all the force of his own personality, and all the power of his office, to
persuade those who had been inclined to dissent to vote with the majority.
As a result, Warren not only succeeded in obtaining a unanimous Court,
but he also persuaded the other eight Justices not to write concurring
opinions which would detract from his own opinion for the Court. That
opinion bears careful examination, for it was a faithful harbinger of how far
the Court was to wander from both the letter and the intent of the Constitution in the new "Warren Era" which *Brown v. Board* inaugurated.

The Fourteenth Amendment was initiated by a two-thirds vote of both
houses of the 39th Congress in 1866, and was subsequently ratified by the
legislatures of three-fourths of the States. It was designed to prevent the
States from taking any action which would reimpose elements of slavery, or
"badges of servitude," upon the freed Negroes. Among the protections
afforded by the Fourteenth Amendment is the provision that, "No State
shall . . . deny to any person within its jurisdiction the equal protection of
the laws." This was the "equal protection clause" which Frankfurter had
directed Bickel to study.

Bickel's conclusion that the framers of that clause had not intended by its
terms that segregation be abolished was influenced by the fact that, at

approximately the same time, the 39th Congress had debated and passed the Civil Rights Act of 1866. Bickel reasoned that discussions in Congress concerning "civil rights" which occurred in relation to that Act would apply to the equal protection clause as well, and would help define the rights which the Fourteenth Amendment was designed to protect. The chairman of the House Judiciary Committee in 1866, and house manager for the Civil Rights Bill, was Rep. James F. Wilson, of Iowa. Bickel concluded that he, if anyone, could speak with authority as to the intent of the Bill. Through Bickel's research we learn that Wilson had advised the House that "civil rights . . . do not mean that all citizens shall sit on juries, or that their children shall attend the same schools. These are not civil rights."

Additional evidence as to what Congress had intended to include within the meaning of "civil rights" was to be found in the manner in which the Civil Rights Act was passed. The original Bill which resulted in the Act had contained a "no discrimination" clause. That clause was removed at the insistence of Rep. John A. Bingham, who is generally regarded as the chief architect of the Fourteenth Amendment. The clause was removed in order to make the proposed Civil Rights Act "less oppressive and therefore less objectionable." In other words, to assure its passage by the Congress. Bickel informed Frankfurter that the Civil Rights Bill of 1866 probably could not have passed with a specific "no discrimination" clause included. Bickel concluded without equivocation that "there is no evidence whatever showing that for its sponsors the civil rights formula had anything to do with unsegregated schools. Wilson, its sponsor in the House, specifically disclaimed any such notion."[4]

For those who fashioned the Fourteenth Amendment, and the Civil Rights Act of 1866, "civil rights" were matters reserved to the States. Enactments concerning such rights, therefore, were for the States to determine under the powers reserved to them by the Tenth Amendment. That Amendment is only one short sentence: "The powers not delegated to the United States by the Constitution, nor prohibited by it to the States, are reserved to the States respectively, or to the people."

In reference to the proposed "no discrimination" clause of the Civil Rights Act, Rep. Bingham, as the chief architect of the Fourteenth Amendment, protested that its inclusion would be "simply to strike down by Congressional Enactment every State's Constitution which makes a discrimination on account of race or color in any of the civil rights of the citizen." Further, Bingham specifically recognized that, at that time, nearly every State did discriminate in one manner or another. It was Bingham's intent to protect certain enumerated rights from state abuse by constitutional amendment, but not to protect the whole range of "civil rights," as then understood.[5]

In the face of the Bickel memorandum, and with no indication that the Court had any evidence to the contrary, Chief Justice Warren declared that the history surrounding the adoption of the Fourteenth Amendment was "inconclusive." He suggested that its true intent could not be ascertained because of conflicting statements of intent. He characterized the "most avid proponents" of the post-Civil War amendments as undoubtedly intending them to remove "all legal distinctions" among persons born or naturalized in the United States. He characterized their opponents as intending those amendments to have "the most limited effect." He asserted further that, "What others in Congress and the state legislatures had in mind cannot be determined with any degree of certainty."

The tactic here employed by Warren is a familiar one when the Court wants to give the Constitution new meaning. An effective first step is to declare, no matter what the evidence may be, that the clause at issue is ambiguous, its sources obscure. The way is thus prepared for a clairvoyant utterance by the Court which can dispel "uncertainty" and restore "order" to the constitutional framework.

Warren was right when he stated in *Brown v. Board* that there were in the Congress and in the state legislatures which ratified the Fourteenth Amendment those of widely differing views concerning the Amendment and its companion legislation, the 1866 Civil Rights Act. There are divergent opinions concerning almost every measure any legislature has ever passed. But that does not prevent the Court from discovering what the compromises were, how the differences were resolved, and what the final meaning and intent came to be. The intent of the framers of the Fourteenth Amendment was to exclude education and most other "civil rights" from its scope, and to leave those matters to the States. The Chief Justice, to support his "inconclusive history" theory of the Amendment's adoption, had to ignore its real history. The Court had to have known perfectly well from the Bickel memorandum that it was amending the Constitution, and that it was doing so in a manner which ignored, and therefore negated, the troublesome process for amendment provided in Article V.

Warren advanced additional reasons for the holding in *Brown* which are equally interesting. He asserted that public education had played a much smaller role a century ago than it does now, especially in the South. There education had remained largely in private hands at the end of the Civil War. Even in the North, Warren wrote, the conditions of public education did not approximate those existing today. Now, he stated, education had come to be "perhaps the most important function of state and local government." It was therefore necessary to "consider public education in the light of its full development and its present place in American life throughout the Nation."

These are very seductive thoughts, particularly when offered by the Chief Justice on behalf of a unanimous Supreme Court. Of course, the nature of public education has changed. Who can doubt that social conditions have altered? Governments at all levels carry out quite different functions today than they did a century ago. Does it not follow that the Constitution itself should mean something different now than it did then? But Warren stopped short of that last candid question. For had it been put, the Court would have been forced to the questions which inevitably follow: If the Constitution needs changing to keep up with the times, why not use the amending process provided therein? Why should there not be the same kind of give and take which led to the adoption of the Fourteenth Amendment, which the Court was "interpreting"? Why not the same political free for all which accompanied the adoption of the Constitution itself?

There is more to the Court's opinion. The Chief Justice assures us that, in any event, "we cannot turn back the clock to 1868." What, precisely, does the refusal of the Supreme Court to "turn back the clock to 1868" in a constitutional case imply in constitutional terms? What was the "clock" of 1868 to which we cannot return? The conclusion seems reasonably inescapable that the "clock" was the intent expressed by Congress and the country in adopting the Fourteenth Amendment. The Court is telling us that, in its opinion, the intent of the framers of that Amendment, the purpose of Congress in recommending it to the States, and the understanding of the legislatures of three-fourths of the States in adopting it, are all irrelevant.

The onward ticking of the Warren clock, which was set going in the *Brown* case, came to be a measure of the degeneration of our constitutional system. If an Amendment can be dealt with in this manner, what of the Constitution itself, or the Bill of Rights, when their provisions become impediments to the aims of a new Court majority? *Brown v. Board* and the decisions which followed roused many, with social views similar to those of the new Court majority, to great enthusiasm. Some even proclaimed that we were in the midst of a constitutional revolution, and proudly pointed to the Supreme Court as a "Revolutionary Committee."[6] They had solid ground for the use of that appellation.

When a new principle of law, or a new constitutional doctrine, is announced, it is always legitimate to inquire as to what the sources for such a ruling might have been. The "separate but equal" doctrine which was at issue in *Brown v. Board* had been invented by the Supreme Court nearly sixty years earlier, in *Plessy v. Ferguson*.[7] The *Brown* Court's opinion referred to its prior decision in *Plessy,* and to findings of the federal district court in the cases which led to the appeal of *Brown v. Board* to the Supreme Court. The federal district court had concluded that segregation in the schools had a detrimental effect on the "colored children" in the system. The Supreme Court, in *Brown v. Board,* agreed: "Whatever may have been the extent of psychological knowledge at the time of *Plessy v. Ferguson,*" the Court said, the finding of a detrimental effect "is amply supported by modern authority." In a footnote to that sentence, presumably to support its conclusion, the Court cited some half dozen or more sociological and psychological studies. The authors ranged from the American black sociologist, Kenneth B. Clark, to the Swedish sociologist, Gunnar Myrdal. The Court did not discuss the nature of these studies, nor did it reveal what within them it may have relied upon to come to its conclusions. "Separate educational facilities," the Court was satisfied to assert, "are inherently unequal." This determination was the principal finding of fact asserted by the Court, and represents the primary source of the constitutional ruling which the Court made in the *Brown* case.

The opinion in *Brown v. Board* makes it evident that the Court felt very strongly about its finding of fact. The Justices sincerely believed that school segregation was detrimental to black students. They were determined that such segregation should go. But the true sources in law, the legal origins of the new constitutional ruling which was to be made, were not revealed, for they did not exist. The decision had no legitimate roots in our constitutional or legal system. Something similar had occurred in *Plessy v. Ferguson*. There Justice John Marshall Harlan had registered a ringing dissent, in an opinion which reads very much like the opinion of Chief Justice Warren in *Brown v. Board*. Harlan suggested that the Louisiana statute there at issue, requiring separate railway facilities for the races, represented, for the Negro, a "badge of servitude," reminiscent of his former status as a slave. Consider this famous passage from Harlan's opinion:

> The white race deems itself to be the dominant race in this
> country . . . But in the view of the Constitution, in the eye
> of the law, there is in this country no superior, dominant,
> ruling class of citizens. There is no caste here. Our Con-
> stitution is color-blind, and neither knows nor tolerates
> classes among citizens.

What Harlan was describing, in 1896, was the way he believed things ought to have been. His opinion offers no analysis of what was intended or accepted at the time the Fourteenth Amendment was adopted. Nor does it seek to dispute what had been consistently practiced up until the time of the *Plessy* decision. By contrast, the Court's decision in *Plessy v. Ferguson*, to the extent that it recognized that segregation was a matter left by the Fourteenth Amendment to the States, was sound constitutional law. The dissent of Harlan, however admirable its sentiments, was based on morals, social ethics, and personal preference. It was not based on constitutional law as written and intended in the equal protection clause of the Fourteenth Amendment.

The two cases, *Plessy v. Ferguson* and *Brown v. Board,* serve as marvelous examples of how judicial usurpation can feed upon itself. The Court which decided *Plessy,* and was about to launch an era of judicial veto of social legislation, laid the foundation for the Warren era. The *Plessy* Court was as eager to get rid of the Negro "problem," as that Court saw it, as the Warren Court was in its effort to do what it considered "justice" to solve the problem. In avid pursuit of its cause, the *Plessy* Court reached beyond the simple and justifiable finding that such matters were properly left to the States. Instead, it fastened into the constitutional system the absurd principle that "separate" can be "equal," a doctrine which for decades undercut all political efforts to alter unequal treatment imposed by law. Revulsed, finally, at the whole repellant idea of separate "equality," the Warren Court regurgitated the *Plessy* holding, reached a series of entirely different factual and legal conclusions, and force fed its own interpretation into the constitutional system with even less ceremony than had been displayed by the *Plessy* Court half a century earlier.

Professor Archibald Cox speaks approvingly of the Court's decision in

Brown v. Board, and asserts that it "can only be described as a revolution in constitutional law."[8] Harvard's Raoul Berger agrees. He concludes that Chief Justice Warren, in *Brown,* did not only "shape" the law, "he upended it; he revised the Fourteenth Amendment to mean exactly the opposite of what its framers designed it to mean, namely, to leave suffrage and segregation beyond federal control, to leave it with the States, where control over internal domestic matters resided from the beginning."[9]

Brown v. Board has been described as a "magnetic field," which soon attracted to the Court all manner of special interest groups, most of which had lost their causes in the legislative and executive arenas. That is, they had lost out in the political processes, and now came to the Court to plead for judicial interference. Litigation after *Brown* became a candidly political weapon, with the Supreme Court lending itself willingly to use in the political arena. It is this fact which makes of the *Brown* decision, and those which followed, a radical, and in fact truly revolutionary departure in American constitutional law. The entire nature of judicial review was changed, in a massive shift by the Court from constitutional review to policy formulation.

What the Court did in *Brown,* and in subsequent cases, was to cross the constitutional boundary which sets the judicial power apart from the legislative and executive power. The Court baldly took upon itself legislative, and even executive, functions. Nothing like this had ever occurred before. Having broken the bounds in *Brown,* the Court in succeeding years felt less and less constrained by any constitutional considerations. It began to announce, in effect, in case after case, that its own current social and political views were "constitutional," and to enforce them on the country exactly as new legislation by Congress would be enforced, but without any constitutional authority to do so. Such excursions in judicial policymaking would have been incomprehensible to the framers of the Constitution.

These actions of the Supreme Court involve two fundamentally different principles for the guidance of human affairs: the principles of law and of ethics. Ethics might also be termed morals, good, or "justice." These concepts express an ideal, which may or may not be attainable, and which may or may not be agreeable to any given individual. Law expresses the result of a process for governing human affairs made legitimate, in a free society, by some form of social contract which binds members of society to adhere to the results of the process. In our society, the process to which we have bound ourselves is that set forth in the Constitution. The legal results of the constitutional process, or even the principles of the Constitution itself, may not be agreeable to everyone in all circumstances. Yet there is reason to give pause before rejecting out of hand laws or constitutional principles which may at a given time seem disagreeable. Chief Justice John Marshall uttered the memorable warning, "We must never forget that it is a *constitution* we are expounding." What he meant was that the constitutional document was designed to transcend momentary partisanship, and to lay down principles for the longer range ordering of society. Justice Oliver Wendell Holmes reminded us that, "The criterion of constitutionality is not whether we believe the law to be for the public good."[10] On another occasion Holmes put the difference even more poignantly:

> I have said to my brethren many times that I hate justice,
> which means that I know that if a man begins to talk about
> that, for one reason or another he is shirking thinking in
> legal terms.[11]

The concept of "justice" has meant many different things to the United States Supreme Court over the years. In *Dred Scott v. Sandford,* decided on the eve of the Civil War, "justice" was defined to mean the perpetuation of slavery, and the eternal subjugation of the Negro, whether slave or free.[12] At the turn of the century, in *Plessy v. Ferguson,* "justice" meant that separate was equal. To the *Brown* Court "justice" required school desegregation and repudiation of the idea that separate was equal in education.

The Supreme Court never did say, in *Brown v. Board,* just how its feelings about segregation—its ethics, its morality, its sense of outrage— had made the jump from the realm of "justice" to the realm of law. It seems fair to describe *Brown* as a kind of judicial shell game. Our attention is deftly diverted while the Court substitutes for its strong moral feelings on the subject its conclusion that the Topeka Board of Education had violated the equal protection clause of the Fourteenth Amendment. We never know exactly how the pea got from one shell to the other. And the Court did not think it necessary to tell us.

The most far-reaching questions posed by this astounding case are not those discussed in Warren's opinion, but those implicit in his discussion. To the Warren Court the Constitution was to be a document done in rubber, which the Court could stretch one way and bend another, to accommodate its own various social twists and turns. If the Constitution meant one thing when a particular social institution occupied a certain role yesterday, and means another thing, without benefit of amendment, when that institution's role changes today, what will it mean tomorrow? What are the rules by which changes in society signal to the Court that a magical metamorphosis of the Constitution is once more required? Does a written Constitution have any identifiable meaning in such circumstances? Does it even exist in any meaningful sense? Or are we back to the fumes and sputterings of Delphi, our fate hanging on the incantations of the cloistered priests?

Out of *Brown v. Board of Education* there emanated a new judicial aura. Fashioned in that decision, there began to settle upon the Court a mantle of arrogance, suspiciously purple in hue, cut of the kind of "justice" which Holmes hated, and which soon came to obscure the plain black robes of justice under law. This Imperial Judiciary is still with us.

And what of the infamous "separate but equal" doctrine which was the root evil supposedly exorcised in the Brown case? A close analysis of the Court's opinion reveals that, so careless was its reasoning, the doctrine itself was never overruled!

7. Reading, Writing, and Judicial Arithmetic

EDUCATION HAS BEEN central to the American experience. In thousands of small towns across the country the school house has been the dominant structure, and activities centering around the school often the dominant form of social life. In larger communities parents concerned with good education for their children have long bought or rented their homes according to the proximity and quality of the public schools. Parental involvement through consultations with teachers, through the PTA, through the athletic program, and through similar endeavors has been an integral part of the public school system. But clinging ominously to the public school system—whatever its virtues might have been—had been the odious shroud of segregation. In North and South—if more prevalent in the South—public authorities had seized upon the excuse of the "separate but equal" doctrine of *Plessy v. Ferguson* to establish segregated schools.

Some sixty years later a different Supreme Court decided that segregation had to go, come what may. In effecting that decision, the Court opened an era of judicial intervention in the schools the results of which—particularly the results of forced busing—have been drastically to alter the nature of the neighborhood school in particular, and of public education in general. Courts have pried into the most minute details of school administration and policy, and have required the spending of untold millions of dollars to conform to their requirements. Yet there is growing doubt as to whether the Supreme Court ever had a clear goal in mind in ordering desegregation, whether the end result has been of lasting benefit to anyone, and whether education has not suffered greater harm than improvement as a result.

When the Supreme Court addressed the problem of segregation in the schools in *Brown v. Board of Education,*[1] in 1954, it was concerned with

51

segregation created by *public* authorities through some act of law. That is, with *de jure* segregation, meaning, literally, "of the law." In the *Brown* case the Court held that segregation in public schools which resulted from any act of law, whether state or local, violated the equal protection clause of the Fourteenth Amendment. The Court directed, therefore, that schools be desegregated "with all deliberate speed." The initial result was about ten years of deliberation, and hardly any speed at all in most areas.

It was not until passage of the Civil Rights Act of 1964 that intensive efforts to desegregate schools began. And then it was the federal Department of Justice, acting under the Act—and not the courts—which accomplished the major breakthroughs towards genuine desegregation. The primary device was the threat to withhold federal funds from the schools if desegregation were not pressed, and the drive began in the urban South.

The *Brown* case had been decided on the principle—so far as there was an articulate principle—that assignment of children to schools should be made on a non-racial basis. Similarly, the Civil Rights Act of 1964 had repeatedly defined "desegregation" in schools as the assignment of pupils "without regard to their race." One might have thought that the mandate of desegregation, judicial and legislative, was therefore an incarnation of Justice Harlan's "colorblind" Constitution. But that was not to be. In a 1968 case, the Supreme Court made it clear that "color" was going back into the Constitution.

In *Green v. County School Board of New Kent County,* the Court held that, in a formerly segregated school system, if a non-racial free choice selection of schools did not result in a high degree of integration, such a system was unconstitutional.[2] This was the case which presaged such measures as busing, on the new theory that racial discrimination—that is, assigning pupils to schools on the basis of race—is justified in order to produce a higher degree of integration than would result from merely assigning pupils to schools "without regard to their race."

Chief Justice Warren had announced the *Brown* decision shortly after taking office, and that decision, taken together with the manner in which it was decided, had set the tone for the Warren era. Chief Justice Warren Earl Burger succeeded Earl Warren on June 23, 1968, and among the first decisions of his court was another case involving the schools and segregation. That case, too, was to have a profound effect upon the schools and upon the nation. Supported by congressional legislation, and spurred on by an implementing bureaucracy, Burger announced the unanimous decision in *Alexander v. Holmes,* that the "deliberate speed" concept was to be abandoned, and that every dual educational system was to be eradicated forthwith.[3]

But the Court did not say how this was to be done. Thus, it was left to federal district courts in State after State to fashion specific remedies, enforced by specific court decrees, in order to get the schools desegregated. It soon became apparent that one result would be to move the courts ever deeper into the details of school organization and administration. This new intervention by the courts often met with intransigent, and sometimes ingenious, resistance on the part of many States and school districts. But where the Warren Court had announced for the schools only the rather tentative principle of "deliberate speed," the Burger Court launched itself headlong upon a course of reform to be forced upon the schools by all the powers of the federal courts.

An early example of resistance to judicial interference in the schools arose in the Charlotte-Mecklenburg school district in North Carolina. Several stratagems had been adopted there in the hope of evading judicially enforced desegregation by obscuring the role of school district authorities in perpetuating segregation. The point was to make it appear that no *law* had been enacted, and that no action by a *public authority* had occurred, so that it could be argued that *de jure* segregation was not present. Attendance districts were drawn in such a manner that segregation resulted; student transfers were allowed which had the effect of increasing segregation; and faculties of the schools remained segregated. Charles Swann filed suit in federal district court to have these practices declared illegal. The suit, from the point of view of the plaintiff, was remarkably successful.

The District Court, acting under the broad enforcement powers implied in *Alexander v. Holmes,* declared all the contested practices to be in violation of the Supreme Court's desegregation requirements. But it did not stop there. It entered an order requiring changes to alter those practices. The District Court ordered that the faculty be desegregated, that the transfers of students contributing to segregation be restricted, that attendance districts be redrawn, and that a busing program be initiated to reduce segregation. Beyond that, the court indicated that it would apply rigorous tests by which to examine justification for the existence of any one-race school. Specifically, it would have to be shown that such a school was not the result of *de jure* segregation, either past or present, for it to be allowed to continue. The case was appealed, and made its way to the Supreme

Court. In *Swann v. Charlotte-Mecklenburg Board of Education,* decided in 1971, the Supreme Court unanimously affirmed the District Court's order.[4] The decision demonstrated that the federal district courts would, in the future, have wide discretion in ordering the affairs of school districts to effect desegregation. This applied particularly to busing, for which the case became famous—or infamous, depending upon one's point of view.

The Supreme Court did not hold that the identical measures required by the District Court in *Charlotte-Mecklenburg* would necessarily be required in other school districts. But it left no doubt as to the extent of intervention which would be allowed. It noted that, all things being equal, it might be desirable to assign students to schools nearest their homes. But the Court found that all things were not equal

> . . . in a system that has been deliberately constructed and
> maintained to enforce racial segregation. The remedy for
> such segregation may be administratively awkward, inconve-
> nient and even bizarre in some situations and may impose
> burdens on some; but all awkwardness and inconvenience
> cannot be avoided in the interim period when remedial
> adjustments are being made to eliminate the dual school
> system.

The *Charlotte-Mecklenburg* case had dealt only with *de jure* segregation. Such *de jure* acts may also be termed "state action," meaning the action of a State or one of its subdivisions, such as a school district. It is the presence of state action which activates the equal protection clause of the Fourteenth Amendment, and its requirement that, "No State shall . . . deny to any person within its jurisdiction the equal protection of the laws." It had been assumed that without *state action* in some form, the courts would have no authority to act in segregation cases since, without state action, there would be no violation of the equal protection clause of the Fourteenth Amendment. But the courts grew impatient with this restraint.

De facto segregation can easily occur without the intervention of any public act or public official. Such segregation occurs as a matter *of fact*—hence *de facto*, rather than as a matter of law—*de jure.* An example would be segregation in a school district resulting from patterns of housing, over which school officials would have no control. Even the U.S. Department of Justice, which had been diligent in enforcing desegregation in the South, had examined each case of alleged segregation within a district on a school-by-school basis, and had sought remedies only where *intentional, de jure,* segregation could be shown in a particular school. But the Supreme Court, when it determined that the time was ripe, felt no compunction about extending its edicts to cover *de facto* as well as *de jure* segregation.

In a 1973 case, *Keyes v. School District No. 1, Denver, Colorado,* the Court held that where there is convincing evidence of intentional segregation in *any* significant part of a school district, the courts must *presume* that the *entire district* has been illegally segregated.[5] The ruling, following a broad scale approach advocated by the NAACP in the case, provided that only where the district could bring to bear conclusive evidence to the contrary, would the newly imposed presumption not apply. In future, school districts were to be *presumed guilty* unless they could prove themselves innocent!

It was to be up to a school district to prove, for example, that segregation resulting from housing patterns was *de facto,* not *de jure*—and if the proof did not please the courts, such segregation would be held to be *de jure.* The result was to make *de facto* segregation virtually indistinguishable from *de jure* segregation, and to make *private action* the same as government action. Once again the Court had decided that the Constitution needed augmentation, and had moved to adjust it accordingly.

As their involvement deepened, the courts gave evidence of becoming more and more confused as to what they were doing, and how to do it. It became increasingly doubtful, as they ventured further and further from their normal judicial functions, whether they had either the facility to formulate the goals they were groping for, or the capacity to achieve them. By 1979 the unanimity which had characterized the Warren Court in handing down *Brown v. Board* had evaporated.

Cases came to the Court in that year from two Ohio cities, Dayton and Columbus, in which the District Court had issued sweeping busing orders. The Supreme Court majority upheld the lower court orders, based upon the principles announced in the *Keyes* decision. The majority added that it is the effectiveness, not the intent, of a district in remedying segregation which is the test of its compliance. Thus the majority blurred even further any remaining distinction between *de facto* and *de jure* segregation— between *private* and *governmental* acts.[6]

All of this had become rather standard in school litigation, and might have been expected. The interesting aspect of these cases was to be found in the division of the Court on the issue, and in the opinion of Justice Lewis

F. Powell, Jr. In a sharp dissent, Powell took account of a new social reality which had arisen from the Court's line of school decisions. He observed that parents are not necessarily bound by decisions which they do not like or agree with, for the reason that they may elect to withdraw their children from the public schools "in which they have lost confidence." He suggested that, "The time has come for a thoughtful re-examination of the proper limits of the role of the courts in confronting the intractable problems of public education in our complex society." Supporters of active court intervention in the schools, particularly of court ordered busing, were left uneasy by this dissent. They were not comforted by Powell's additional comment that "the type of state-enforced segregation that *Brown* properly condemned no longer exists in this country." By this, Powell was referring to *de jure* segregation in its true sense, resulting from action by a state or one of its political subdivisions.

The practical difficulties of busing and other measures ordered to establish racial balances have been graphically illustrated in a case arising in Dallas. There federal district Judge William M. Taylor, Jr. divided the 351 square mile district into sub-districts, and ordered busing to establish racial balance. However, citing problems of "time and distance," he exempted from the busing plan twenty-eight schools in East Oakcliff, one of the sub-districts, in which ninety-six percent of the 27,000 students were black. To compensate for the lack of busing, the judge ordered the district to allot extra money, staff, and equipment to the schools of that sub-district. It is possible to argue that what this order amounted to was something very much like what might be termed separate, but super equal! Its real significance is to demonstrate that the courts are sinking ever deeper into a bog of their own making in the school cases.

The Court of Appeals in 1978 ordered Judge Taylor to reopen hearings, and either to justify the large number of one race schools, or to eliminate them. The school district appealed to the Supreme Court to have the District Court order made final, and the Court agreed to hear the case.

In the meantime, in the City of Atlanta, a vast system of area wide busing had been proposed, but had been *rejected* by the federal district court. The court had held that the Constitution does not require school districts to correct school segregation resulting from "persistent social patterns," such as racial patterns in housing. In a decision handed down on May 12, 1980, the Supreme Court *refused,* by a vote of five to three, *to overturn* the lower court ruling.[7] As it had done in *Swann v. Charlotte-*

Mecklenburg, the Supreme Court merely affirmed the District Court order, without stating that such an order would necessarily apply elsewhere. However, as *Swann* had presaged intensive court intervention in the school districts, it had seemed possible that the Atlanta decision presaged the opposite. Civil liberties attorneys were quoted as viewing the latter decision as "a very discouraging, if not final, note on metropolitan desegregation."[8]

When the Supreme Court came to review the Dallas case to which we have referred, however, its action confirmed the suspicion that no clear new direction in the school cases had as yet been charted. In an unsigned opinion the Court stated that in agreeing to hear the case it had acted improvidently.[9] The matter was therefore returned to the Circuit Court of Appeals, which in turn had already ordered the District Court to justify its actions, and had imposed more strict busing requirements than had the District Court. The most significant aspect of the decision was that the former unanimity on the Court was further shattered in a dissent signed by Justices Powell, Stewart, and Rehnquist.

A principal argument of the dissent was that the Circuit Court of Appeals should have shown more deference to the findings of the District Court in its original review of the case. Normally, as we have seen, appellate courts are reluctant to disturb the findings of fact of trial courts, the courts of original jurisdiction. The dissent offered interesting figures concerning the effects of the busing and other school orders in Dallas, which had commenced in 1971. Enrollment in the district had dropped from 163,000 to 133,000, while that of Anglo students had fallen from 112,000 to fewer than 45,000. In proportion to total enrollment Anglo student population had fallen from sixty-nine percent to thirty-three percent. The dissent questioned whether the court ordered program, busing in particular, had been effective. It concluded that it emphatically had not been, and that the courts had failed to identify any link between the supposed constitutional violation and the desegregation remedy. Absent consideration of these questions, the dissent feared that court enforced orders in the schools can, "like a loose cannon, inflict indiscriminate damage" on the schools and their communities.

The school cases lead to the disheartening conclusion that busing has, for the courts, become a crusade. It seems to have been prescribed without thought or examination as to its effectiveness, or as to its acceptability in the communities upon which it has been forced. Yet there are some signs in the recent cases that judicial aggrandizement does not necessarily run in a straight line progression from usurpation to disaster. There may be stirring in the Court—prodded by recent dissents—a realization that the whole matter needs radical reconsideration.

Public reaction is an important ingredient—and in the end the determining factor—in assessing the authority of the Court to achieve compliance with its decisions. Public reaction to court imposed desegregation, and particularly to busing, for some time was difficult to assess accurately. At first it was predominantly negative, and even hostile. Subsequently, studies and impressions as the courts pressed onward with these programs did not initially reveal clearly whether opposition had truly declined, whether people were simply getting used to busing, or whether there remained a latent antipathy which was still capable of eruption. As busing continued, however, the evidence began to indicate deep seated opposition.

A view from one perspective emerges from a report of the United States Commission on Civil Rights concerning the effects of the pivotal *Swann v. Charlotte-Mecklenburg* decision of 1971. A major racial clash, involving some one hundred to two hundred black and white students, broke out at the East Mecklenburg High School in 1972. In March of 1973 clashes broke out at West and South Mecklenburg High Schools, and at several junior high schools. These required that police be called to quell the fighting, and resulted in a dozen arrests and over two dozen suspensions. In all, there were some 6500 student suspensions in 1970–71 and over 6000 in 1971–72, a majority of them black, in the Charlotte-Mecklenburg District.

According to the Commission, school authorities felt there had been a "backlash" among white parents bitter over "social advances and complaints of blacks." Such attitudes seemed to have been transmitted to children, resulting in "an apparent hardening of white racial attitudes in the face of continuing efforts at all levels to eliminate racial injustice." One official reported that continuing national controversy over busing had hurt Charlotte "terribly" by raising "false hopes" that the local busing order might be overturned. The Commission found a "continuing lack of strong public support for the efforts of the professional staff." It reported that the staff was often referred to as "egg heads and social changers" in their efforts to carry out court orders.[10]

Reaction to forced busing has been the subject of numerous other reports, many of which are inconclusive. There would appear to be a wide range of feeling among both blacks and whites, raising legitimate doubts as to whether there was ever any national consensus in support of busing. By 1976 Thomas Sowell, then a fellow at the Center for Advanced Study in the Behavioral Sciences at Stanford University, and a black, concluded that most black people had come to oppose busing. Sowell found that it is the "media-created black 'spokesman'," who, as he put it, "usually shares media-created values," who is portrayed as favoring busing. He described this "spokesman" as likely to be a middle-class black who has left the ghetto, and cannot therefore speak for the black masses. It was Sowell's opinion that busing has been of little or no help to the black student. He suggested that the true opposition is to "government heavy handedness" in carrying out the programs, and that there are signs that this resentment becomes misplaced as hostility to the "supposed beneficiaries" of the programs. According to Sowell, "the fact that there is really very little benefit to any group only completes this tragic farce."[11]

Reaction against busing was sufficient, by 1979, to initiate a constitutional amendment which would have provided that no student could be compelled to attend a school other than that nearest his home. Though this effort was defeated in the House of Representatives, late in the 1980 session Congress added to an appropriations bill an amendment which would deny the Justice Department any funds to initiate, or in any way take part in, desegregation suits that would require the busing of children to any schools other than the ones nearest their homes. The anti-busing rider passed the Senate by a vote of 42 to 38, and the House by a vote of 240 to 59.[12] Such a result would appear to have been in keeping with a *Los Angeles Times* poll reported in October of 1980. That poll showed that busing children to achieve racial integration was opposed by a six-to-one ratio of California voters. There were thirteen percent for, eighty percent against, and seven percent undecided.[13]

Results of court-ordered busing and other desegregation measures are, if anything, even more difficult to measure than public reaction. A Rand Corporation report released in 1979 stated that in a review of seventy-three studies of desegregation, forty showed positive results, twelve negative results, and twenty-one no effect on black achievement scores. Curiously, the report showed consistently better results in the South than in the North, and better results under mandatory than under voluntary integration programs. However, using much of the same data, Lawrence A. and Gifford W. Bradley found a "dearth of strong experimental evidence" to support the assumption that blacks moved to white schools would adopt achievement-related values of white students. The Bradleys concluded that "massive transfers of students in our school system may not be the best means for improving black student achievement."[14] The likelihood is that quite the contrary has resulted.

Thomas Sowell concluded that "hard evidence" does not support any of the assumptions that busing and desegregation would bring educational benefits to blacks, and presumably to whites as well. Rather, the evidence indicates lower self-esteem among black children, and greater racial antagonism on both sides, as a result of busing. Sowell offered this interesting analysis:

> Busing is not a policy but a crusade. For a policy, one can ask, "Does it work?" "At what cost?" "What is the human impact?" For a crusade, the relevant questions are: "Whose side are you on?" "Is your courage failing?" "Can we dishonor the sacrifices of those who went before by turning back now?" The last thing a crusader wants to hear is a cost-benefit analysis. And if the crusader is a white liberal whose own children are in private schools, his courage knows no bounds.[15]

Author Fred Reed has offered a scathing commentary on racial policy in the schools. Reed makes the "obvious observation, which hardly anyone seems to make," that blacks "suffer less from racism than from poor education." He suggests that anyone commenting sensibly on racial policy in the schools "would have to say that when it is not merely futile it often injures the people it is supposed to help; that it succeeds in antagonizing whites without benefiting blacks; that it has become more of an ideological battleground than a practical program; and, finally, that it is a fraud, intended principally to benefit groups that grow fat from racial programs." The most arresting charge to appear in his article is the contention that those administrating racial policy base their approach upon the paternalistic notion that blacks are incapable of competing with whites, and so need special consideration. "Racial functionaries will deny this with fervor," says Reed, "yet if they believed blacks could compete, they would advocate preparing them for competition. Instead the emphasis is on protecting them from it." Reed concludes that such "unrelenting condescension supports blacks' view of themselves as worthless." He points out that, "People who think they cannot succeed do not try."[16]

Black columnist William Raspberry, writing on June 26, 1981, offered this assessment of court-ordered busing:

> Busing for desegregation nearly always has cost more in
> political, financial and emotional capital than it was worth
> in educational gains for black children. It is an issue that has
> unified much of white America and justified some of its
> baser instincts without similarly uniting black America,
> which never really was hot for busing. It has torn commu-
> nities apart for precious little educational gain, and it has
> nearly bankrupted the National Association for the Advance-
> ment of Colored People.

And, in the end, Raspberry would appear to agree with Thomas Sowell as to the source of school busing:

> Most of the impetus for busing has come from white politi-
> cal activists and the civil-rights establishment, most notably
> the NAACP and the NAACP Legal Defense Fund . . . What
> black children have needed all along is quality education,
> and that . . . can be had in black schools as well as in inte-
> grated ones.[17]

Still, what author Richard E. Morgan felicitously terms the "rights industry" of our time has not given up its crusade, despite the evidence of its failure. Morgan finds that "the contribution of the rights industry, operating through the potent technical language of the 'law' and the 'constitution'," including a "wrong headed and sometimes vindictive pursuit of racial balance," has significantly affected declining educational standards.[18] As though to illustrate Morgan's point, one member of the "rights industry" has advanced the proposition that "citizens' preferences for incremental changes . . . must be ignored if desegregation is to succeed." Riding boldly on, the same crusader raises high the banner of her true spirit: "Judges and bureaucrats," who would be charged with imposing her Procrustean style, "may," she says, "be the least desirable agents for effecting desegregation success, except for legislators, mayors, presidents, and the general citizenry."[19]

However the crusade may go, and whatever its practical results may be, the final requirement is that the Supreme Court justify what it is doing in *constitutional* terms. Following the lead of federal district courts in formulating remedies for the mandate it laid down in *Alexander v. Holmes*—that the dual education system be eradicated forthwith—the Supreme Court has come perilously close to adopting the busing remedy as a constitutional requirement. The result is quite different than it would be if Congress had adopted busing through *legislation,* or if the executive branch had adopted it through a properly authorized *executive decree.*

Either of these political branches of government could treat such an experiment as busing as just that—an *experiment.* It could be tried and tested, evaluated and assessed, then continued or rejected depending upon the evidence, or upon changed or unforeseen conditions. The Court is not equipped to approach these questions in that manner, despite its political pretensions. When the Court gets into such a matter as busing, it is not free to experiment, test, evaluate, and change according to an ongoing assessment of the situation. Rather, the Court is forced to explain the results of its racial politics in terms of constitutional principles, and it is in so doing that the Court forces itself into the role of a crusader.

The test of ideology is adherence to "principles," whether the principles continue to apply to circumstances or not. So it is when the "principles" which the Court manufactures for itself are cast in constitutional concrete. When busing is blessed as flowing from a "constitutional" *principle,* and then does not work in *practice,* the Court is left in the awkward predicament of adopting a dogmatic defense of its announced principle, or of beating an ignominious constitutional retreat. Should it finally appear to the Court—as it has to a majority of the Congress, and to many others— that busing does not produce positive results, or that it does not continue to attract enough support to remain viable, what then? Does the Court say one fine morning that it has taken another look at the Constitution and found, lo and behold, that it does *not* require busing after all? That it was all a mistake? That the Justices are very sorry for any inconvenience they may have caused? That they will try to read the Constitution more carefully in the future?

Something like this may be happening. In the summer of 1982 the Court had before it two cases in which the people of the States involved had approved measures designed to limit school busing. An amendment to the State constitution in California forbade that State's Supreme Court from imposing, as it had attempted to do, more stringent busing requirements than those imposed by the U.S. Supreme Court. The result was to end busing in Los Angeles. By an eight-to-one vote the California amendment passed constitutional muster.[20]

Not so fortunate were the somewhat bewildered citizens of the State of Washington. There the voters had passed a statewide initiative prohibiting mandatory busing outside the neighborhood if ordered by a local school board, but not if court ordered. There were exceptions for students requiring special educational programs, where the local school was overcrowded or unsafe, or where it lacked necessary physical facilities. By a majority of five to four, the Court held that the State of Washington had sought to allow busing for non-racial reasons while prohibiting it for racial reasons, and that this was in violation of the equal protection clause of the Fourteenth Amendment.[21]

In both States the purpose had been clear enough, and that was to stop racially motivated busing. To the editors of the *Wall Street Journal* the contradictory results in these cases were part of "an elaborate vocabulary" of words and arguments, "full of hypocrisies large and small," which have developed out of the busing issue. The editorial suggested, however, that "that is what you must expect when a country is finding its way back off a dangerous policy limb."[22]

But that policy limb is a long one, and if the Supreme Court is having difficulty climbing off it, the federal district courts would appear to be struggling even more desperately for direction. In April 1987, the District Court in Topeka, Kansas reopened the case of *Brown v. Board of Education,* and considered a request by the ACLU to effect numerical balance in the schools. Judge Richard D. Rogers held that there is a difference between good faith programs to integrate the schools and numerically balanced integration. Finding that Topeka had made a good faith effort to integrate, the court refused to outlaw the district's neighborhood school system, or to impose such remedies as busing to balance the school system racially.[23]

Less successful were the taxpayers and parents of the Kansas City, Missouri school system when the federal district court in Kansas City addressed the segregation issue in September, 1987. The District Court rejected one plan for upgrading the schools, and achieving "suburban comparability," as well as "visual attractiveness," because the plan would result in "floor coverings with unsightly sections of mismatched carpeting

and tile, and individual walls possessing different shades of paint."
Instead, the court imposed a plan requiring numerous indoor Olympic-
sized swimming pools, a log cabin, a farm, greenhouses, a model United
Nations, and an amphitheater. To pay for these and other items, the court
ordered an increase in the state income tax through a 1.5 percent sur-
charge, to be paid not only by residents of the school district, but by anyone
earning compensation within the district which was subject to the Missouri
income tax.[24]

The school desegregation issue is a prime example of the limits and
embarrassments of judicial legislation. Busing, in particular, has proved ill
advised, ill conceived, and ineffectual—quite apart from the fact that it
was, from its inception, without constitutional justification. In running the
buses, adjusting numerical ratios, and dictating even the most minute
details of school district administration, the courts have engaged in a
meticulous counting of blacks, whites, hispanics, and other ethnic groups,
moving some here, balancing some there, and leaving some alone. The
question remains, and becomes more insistent—What does all this judicial
arithmetic add up to?

8. Judicial Gerrymander

ELBRIDGE GERRY WAS a leading political figure from the State of Massachusetts, and a member of the constitutional convention. At the time of the convention Massachusetts, as did other states, enjoyed an elected representative form of government. In Massachusetts, as in other states, those with the power to do so tended to draw electoral districts so as to concentrate the opposition into as few districts as possible, and to spread their own constituent majorities across as many districts as possible. This often led to some very odd-shaped districts. It appears that one such district in Massachusetts was so odd-shaped someone suggested that it looked like a salamander. Someone else, in tribute to the creative political tutelage of Mr. Gerry, suggested that it looked more like a Gerrymander. The name stuck, and the practice persisted.

Since the founding days, electoral districts at all levels of government, from congressional seats, to state legislative districts, to the local school board, have displayed characteristics of Elbridge Gerry's handiwork. Not only that, but populations within their sometimes bizarre configurations, although electing members to the same legislative body, have varied widely. In some instances the numerical inequities were unintended, simply the result of population shifts which had not yet been accounted for by redistricting. Other districts were consciously drawn to protect the seats of experienced, favored, or powerful legislators. Yet others may have been drawn with the aim of unseating an incumbent. The resulting numerical and geographical anomalies were, by and large, part of a vigorous political process.

However, there was also a more somber dislocation in the history of voting rights, one which ran without redress, political or judicial, for some decades. This was the methodical disenfranchisement of the Negro voter, particularly in the South, despite the guarantees of the Fifteenth Amendment. The recently freed slaves were first given the right to vote by an Act of Congress of March 2, 1867. Three years later the Fifteenth Amendment was ratified. That amendment makes the simple provision that, "The right of the citizens of the United States to vote shall not be denied or abridged by the United States or by any State on account of race, color, or previous condition of servitude." The Supreme Court's handling of *voting rights,* compared to its *electoral district* decisions, represents the difference between authorized and illicit judicial action.

We tend to forget that the Fourteenth Amendment, adopted in 1868, also made certain provision regarding the enfranchisement, or disenfranchisement, of the Negro. In brief, the provision is that in any State which denies any male citizen over the age of twenty-one the right to vote, the basis for representation in Congress shall be reduced proportionately. The debate surrounding the adoption of these Amendments was demonstrably conclusive as to what was intended at the time by the Reconstruction Congress which initiated the Amendments. There can be no doubt at all but that the Negro was to have the same right to vote as anyone else. But the Reconstruction Congress was hardly dominated by southerners, and the work of that Congress in dealing with the newly freed Negro population was nothing that the South had any intent to comply with. For some years after the passage of the Fifteenth Amendment, the Negro was prevented from exercising the franchise granted to him by intimidation, fraud, and violence. There were, however, practical limits to these methods. More subtle and acceptable standards were required. A patina of legality was sought to hide the ugly sores of second-class citizenship.

Two of the most effective methods were the poll tax, which most blacks could not afford, and the literacy test. The literacy test, of course, was administered in such a manner as to assure that most whites would pass, and most blacks would fail. A white might be asked to read a street sign or the inscription on the courthouse door. Perhaps all it said was "In" and "Out." For the black it was a different matter. There is at least one case on record where a Negro was asked to read and explain a complex passage from a decision of the United States Supreme Court—the sort of thing that law reviews argue about endlessly. The man is reported to have explained the passage incorrectly. Yet the literacy test was declared to be constitutional in a case decided by the Supreme Court in 1898.[1] The Court held that on their face such statutes did not deny anyone the right to vote on account of race or color, hence there was no constitutional violation. Still, literacy tests did on occasion exclude whites. To prevent that from happening another, more ingenious, device was conceived, the "grandfather clause."

The grandfather clause contained two interrelated provisions. The first established rigorous educational or property qualifications in order to vote, so rigorous that hardly anyone, black or white, could qualify. The second provision excused anyone from compliance with the first provision who had been a legal voter in 1866—the year prior to the Act of Congress first enfranchising the Negro—or who was a lineal descendant of such a voter. That is, whose "grandfather" could vote in 1866. In approaching this strategy, the United States Supreme Court displayed a greater willingness to inspect its operational reality than it had in examining the operation of the literacy test in 1898. The Court, in 1915, found that, while the grandfather clause did not, on its face, deny anyone the right to vote because of race, creed, or color, it was aimed quite obviously at the Negro since there would have been no other reason to pick out the date 1866 as the "grandfather date."[2]

As a result of this decision the State of Oklahoma, in 1916, passed a new law to replace its old grandfather law, which had been held unconstitutional. That law provided that anyone registered and qualified to vote in 1914 under the old grandfather law remained qualified. Everyone else had to register within a twelve-day period or forever lose his voting privilege. It was not until 1939 that a case reached the Supreme Court dealing with that law. When it did, the Court had little difficulty in finding, in reference to the Fifteenth Amendment, that, "The Amendment nullifies sophisticated as well as simple minded modes of discrimination."[3]

Similar ingenuity was exercised in the State of Texas in regard to a different stratagem by which to prohibit blacks from voting. That was the white primary, so called for the reason that, by state statute, Texas prohibited any Negro from participation in the Democratic primary. Not content with a mere prohibition, the Texas statute also provided that "should a Negro vote in a Democratic primary election, such ballot shall be void and election officials are herein directed to throw out such ballot, and not count the same." When this device was brought to the attention of the Supreme Court, in 1927, the decision rested, not upon the voting rights of the Fifteenth Amendment, but upon the equal protection clause of the Fourteenth Amendment. Finding that the Texas statute had denied blacks equal protection of the law, the Court observed that "it seems to us hard to imagine a more direct and obvious infringement" of that clause.[4] The discriminatory practice ordered by the statute was, quite obviously, *state action*, of the sort which is required in order for the Fourteenth Amendment to apply.

That statute was duly repealed, and the State of Texas authorized, by a new statute, that the state executive committees of the political parties might decide who could vote in their respective primaries. This statute was struck down in a subsequent case, the Court holding once again that the authorization provided by statute to the parties constituted state action, so that what followed was equally objectionable on constitutional grounds. The Texas legislature then repealed all statutes having to do with party primaries. The State Democratic convention thereafter adopted a resolution that "all white citizens" of the State might be eligible for membership in the party. In 1935 the Supreme Court held that this was not a denial of constitutional rights under the Fourteenth Amendment, for the reason that the exclusion of blacks which was effected was not the result of any *state* law or any state act. The Court held that a political party was a *private*, not a governmental body. Private persons, at least in 1935, could not violate the Fourteenth Amendment.

By 1941 the Court had changed its mind as to the nature of political parties, and held that a primary was a vital part of the election machinery of a State. But at that time the Court did not directly refer to the prior Texas cases or to the matters with which they had dealt. However, the issue had been joined, and it was decided in the 1944 case, *Smith v. Allwright*.[5]

In that case the Court agreed that it had to reexamine its prior decisions, and did so. Upon evaluating the various functions of primary elections, and of the part of the political party plays in these elections, the Court concluded that the party takes on the character of a state agency as a result of the duties imposed upon it by state statutes. It therefore overruled its 1935 decision, and held that the political party, being an instrument of the State, could not exclude blacks under the provisions of the Fifteenth Amendment. The Court was forthright in its decision, and squarely overruled prior decisions to the contrary.

This action by the Court led to a comment by Justice Roberts which, while applying in particular to the voting rights cases, also proved to be a remarkable prophecy of things to come in other areas. Roberts complained that in overruling its prior decisions the Court showed an intolerance for what it had done in the past, and indulged "an assumption that knowledge and wisdom resides in us which was denied to our predecessors." His prophecy was that "the instant decision . . . tends to bring adjudications of this tribunal into the same class as a restricted railway ticket, good for this day and train only." However that might have been, it would have seemed that electoral discrimination on the basis of race was, by 1944, as World War II was drawing to a close, at an end.

Then a most amazing event occurred in the political history of Texas. The Democratic party disappeared. At the same time, remarkably enough, there arose a new organization known as the Jaybird Democratic Association. The Jaybirds described themselves as an informal group of people interested in the public welfare. This group did not actually nominate anyone for office, of course, although it was good enough to suggest names of those who in its opinion might be qualified. Those suggested were all Jaybirds, and though they may have been blue, none were black. It was thought by some that the newly elected Jaybird officers bore resemblance to the Democrats who had formerly held their offices. In 1953 these remarkable events were called to the attention of the United States Supreme Court. The Court, as we have seen, is no stranger to politics, and in this case it could smell a Democrat inside a Jaybird at forty paces. Quickly plucked of its false plumage, the Jaybird was, sure enough, the same old Democrat. The Fifteenth Amendment triumphed at last over the best stratagems Texas could manage, and blacks had to be included in political party membership.[6]

These cases all affected the *right to vote*. The simple right to register, to go to the polling place on election day, to mark a ballot, to deposit it in the box, and to have it counted. The cases all fall squarely within the duty of the Supreme Court to enforce the Constitution. It would be hard to argue that the final result reflected other than the clear meaning, or the known intent, of the framers of the Fourteenth or Fifteenth Amendments. By contrast, the *apportionment* of electoral *districts* is quite a different matter, and does not necessarily have any connection with the Fourteenth or Fifteenth Amendments' right to vote. When the Court was asked to extend its interest in the electoral process to reapportionment in 1946, and again in 1950, it flatly refused.

The State of Illinois had for many years failed to reapportion the districts from which its state senators and representatives were elected. As a consequence there had also been no reapportionment of congressional districts either. In the meantime, Cook County had come to contain half the population in the State. In one congressional district in Chicago there were over 900,000 residents, while in the smallest congressional district in downstate Illinois there were only some 112,000. A suit was brought by individuals who were voters in large districts, claiming that the system of unequal apportionment deprived them of the equal protection of the laws of Illinois, in violation of the equal protection clause of the Fourteenth Amendment. What they sought was to restrain elections under the existing system, and to force all congressmen from Illinois to run at large, which would have led to an election in which very little would have been known about most candidates by most voters.

Writing for the majority of a divided Court in 1946, Justice Felix Frankfurter held that, "It is hostile to a democratic system to involve the judiciary in the politics of the people." He pointed out that the Constitution leaves it up to the States to apportion congressional districts, and to the House of Representatives itself to determine the qualifications to its members. He said that if Congress fails in exercising its powers, the remedy ultimately lies with the people, not with the courts. "Courts," said Frankfurter, "ought not to enter this political thicket."[7] The Supreme Court reiterated the same position in a similar case from Georgia, in 1950. There the Court said that, "Federal Courts consistently refuse to exercise their equity powers in cases posing political issues from a state's geographical distribution of electoral strength among its political subdivisions."[8]

Twelve years later, following a substantial change in personnel, the Court changed its mind as well. The case was *Baker v. Carr*,[9] and came from the State of Tennessee, where it was alleged that failure to reapportion districts which elected members to the state General Assembly violated the equal protection clause of the Fourteenth Amendment. This was essentially the same argument which had been dealt with by the Court in the Illinois case of 1946. In *Baker v. Carr*, however, the Court held that federal courts *do* have jurisdiction to hear such cases. It ruled that the voters who originally sued in federal district court in Tennessee had a right to bring such a cause of action, and that the federal courts were authorized, upon proper showing, to grant relief.

The District Court which had originally heard the case in Tennessee, relying on prior Supreme Court decisions, had stated that it had "no doubt" but that the federal courts lacked the authority to intervene to compel legislative reapportionment in the states. That, the Supreme Court now said, was to "misconceive the holding" of prior cases. This meant that, while the Court had changed its mind once again, this time, for whatever reason, it did not want to admit it. The Court observed that malapportionment had existed in the State of Tennessee for some decades, and that the courts of the State had refused to intervene to change the situation. The Supreme Court concluded, therefore, that if it did not take on the case itself, there would be no reapportionment. The case was decided by a six to two vote. The dissent argued that the matter was a political question, as it always had been, and that the courts had no constitutional authority to intervene.

Baker v. Carr opened the door to a long series of cases, still continuing, which has led to the reapportionment of nearly *every district* in the country used as a basis for electing any representative to *any legislative body*, with the exception of the United States Senate. School districts, county boards of supervisors, city councils, and state legislatures have all been affected. The only reason the Court has shied away from reapportionment of the United States Senate, it would appear, is that its composition is specifically provided for in the constitution. Each State, regardless of size, gets two Senators.

In *Baker v. Carr*, the Court had barely stuck its foot in the water. It was in the case of *Gray v. Sanders*,[10] decided in 1963, a year later, that it opened the floodgates to drastic reordering of the American electoral system. The case once again involved the Georgia county unit system, as had the 1950 case in which the Court had held that such matters were none of its judicial business. The unit system consolidated votes in primary elections in such a way as to have the undoubted effect of multiplying the value of votes in some counties, and similarly diminishing the value of votes in others. These facts being undisputed, the question was whether the Court was constitutionally authorized to deal with them. In the 1950 case a dissent had been registered by Justices Hugo Black and William O. Douglas, claiming that the Court did have the authority to act. In *Gray v. Sanders* the majority opinion was written by Justice Douglas, and the dissenting view of 1950 became the law of the land in 1963. The holding of the case was that, once a geographical unit for which a representative is to be chosen is designated, all who vote must have an equal vote.

The question remained as to whether the same rule would also apply in regard to apportionment of congressional districts for the purpose of electing members to Congress. In another Georgia case, *Wesberry v. Sanders*, the Court held that the new rights did also apply to congressional elections.[11] In that case voters of Fulton County, which includes Atlanta, claimed that their congressional district contained two to three times as many people as other districts in the State, and that this was an unconstitutional denial of their right to an equal vote. This was the same question, of course, that had been raised with regard to Illinois congressional districts in the 1946 case. There the Court had held the matter to be a "political thicket" into which the judicial system ought not enter.

The constitutional question raised in *Wesberry* had not been resolved by the *Baker* and *Gray* cases. Those cases had been decided under the equal protection clause of the Fourteenth Amendment, which applies only against *state* action. There is no equal protection clause in the Constitution, or in any of its Amendments, which applies against the *federal* government. Therefore, the basis upon which *Baker* and *Gray* had been decided was not available to the Court for the decision in the *Wesberry* case. This proved to be no obstacle to the Court. Justice Black, the other principal dissenter in the earlier voting cases, wrote the opinion. Article I, Section 2, of the Constitution provides that members of the House of Representatives shall be chosen "by the People of the several States." Justice Black found this to mean, in its "historical" context, that, "as nearly as is practicable one man's vote in a congressional election is to be worth as much as another's."

Justice Black pointed out that the question of the composition of the national legislature was perhaps the most bitter controversy at the constitutional convention. He quoted James Madison as having urged that power in the legislature should be "immediately derived from the people, in proportion to their numbers." James Wilson of Pennsylvania had stated that equal numbers of people ought to have an equal number of representatives, and that the representatives of different districts ought to hold the same proportion to each other as their respective constituents held to each other. From these and similar observations Black drew the conclusion that the principle "solemnly embodied in the Great Compromise" was that there should be "equal representation in the House of equal numbers of people."

Examining the same history in his dissenting opinion, Justice Harlan characterized the "historical context" of Justice Black as one "which bears little resemblance to the evidence found in the pages of history." As to the expressions of the constitutional convention which the Court cited, Harlan offered the observation that there were also many statements favoring limited monarchy, property qualifications for suffrage, and disapproval of unrestricted democracy. To Harlan, "the Constitutional right which the Court creates is manufactured out of the whole cloth."

Whatever they were made of, the Court's opinions in these cases have permeated and revolutionized the apportionment of electoral districts throughout the country, and at every level of government. Like some other newly invented "constitutional" doctrines, the "one man-one vote" rule appears to raise more questions in its application than it resolves. The Warren Court interpreted the rule with an almost humorous rigidity. It disallowed congressional districting in which the largest and the smallest districts differed from one another in population by only six percent. In rejecting that deviation, the Court stated that its one man–one vote principle required a good faith effort to achieve "precise mathematical equality," and that it required justification of any variance "no matter how small."[12] In Colorado, the Court struck down a reapportionment plan for the State which had been approved by a two to one majority of all voters in the State, and which had carried every county in the State, apparently because of its mathematical imprecision.[13]

The Burger Court has allowed a twelve percent variation in district apportionment for the board of supervisors in Rockland County, New York, while a population deviation in districting for the Virginia House of Delegates of 16.4 percent was allowed by the Court in 1975. Yet in a case decided during the same term, the Court struck down a districting formula for the election of congressmen where the maximum variation in population was only 4.1 percent. Similar inconsistencies in later cases appear to suggest that the Burger Court had become disenchanted with the "mathematical exactness" instituted by its predecessor, but had not discovered any more workable alternative.

Former United States Solicitor General, and later Court of Appeals Judge, Robert Bork, has pointed out that no clear rationale for the "one man-one vote" rule has ever been forthcoming from the Court. Bork comments, somewhat acidly, that "the Reapportionment cases are wrong. They are not merely wrong, but simplistically wrong in the absolute sense that there is nothing in the Constitution, in its history, or in American political theory or usage that can conceivably support these decisions."[14] Justice Harlan, dissenting in *Baker v. Carr*, had been disturbed, if not somber: "Those who consider that continuing national respect for the Court's authority depends in large measure upon its wise exercise of self-restraint and discipline in constitutional adjudication, will view this decision with deep concern." But the majority, exhibiting no concern at all, soon became mesmerized by its incantation of the slogan, "one man–one vote," and displayed no capacity to think about what representative government might mean apart from "mathematical exactitude."

The Court has yet to demonstrate that entrancement with deviations of two percent, six percent, twenty percent—or even a hundred and twenty percent, for that matter—have anything to do with the quality of government produced by elected representatives, or with how well those who are elected represent their constituents. The idea of pure quantitative equality has woven a spell over Court and country alike. It has exercised what Michael M. Uhlmann has termed a "debilitating charm over the minds of those who are supposed to think about such matters as the nature and meaning of representation."[15] The Court has seemed to say that its principal concern has been that all shall have an opportunity to participate in the political process, and that none shall be relegated to the status of a permanent minority. Yet there is very little evidence to show that, as a result of the Court's arithmetic, minorities participate more effectively, or that the legislative process has improved—much less that the Gerrymander, that endemic symptom of alleged representational problems, has become extinct.

Even the high water mark of the Warren era produced a rather amusing rebuttal to any such presumption. St. Louis County, Missouri, following the arithmetical dictates of the high Court, had divided itself into nearly perfect mathematical proportions—five districts of almost exactly equal population. The districts were, however, observed to be of rather peculiar shapes. One was compared to a "flying turtle," another to a "moose with antlers." When this redistricting system was before the Supreme Court, Chief Justice Warren commented that the moose shape was "most unusual," and asked why it had been necessary to go about the matter in such a "circuitous way." Nevertheless, whatever misgivings the Court might have had, the mathematics were perfect. Both the moose and the flying turtle were fit squarely within the four corners of the Constitution.[16] The spirit of Elbridge Gerry must have kicked up its ghostly heels, and cracked an indulgent smile at the durability of his work.

At no time, in any of its long series of reapportionment cases, has the Court majority demonstrated a degree of thoughtfulness remotely approaching the fundamental debates which are reported from the constitutional convention, in the *Federalist Papers,* or in the ratifying conventions of the various States. There is nothing resembling the deliberations surrounding the adoption of the Fourteenth and Fifteenth Amendments in the post-Civil War period. Those were periods of crisis and creativity, periods when the nation was formed and tested, periods when those who participated knew that they were involved in life or death matters. The participants in those periods debated vigorously, listened carefully, and thought about what they were doing. They knew the people they represented, they knew the manner in which elections were carried off, and they knew that districts were different sizes and different shapes. They knew at Philadelphia that if they did not succeed there would be anarchy, and they knew in the reconstruction Congress that the nation had very nearly perished. They all knew that government "of the people, by the people, and for the people" is no easy or simplistic matter.

As a result, what was agreed to—both in Philadelphia and in the 39th Congress following the Civil War—was that suffrage was to be left to the States. Commentator Raoul Berger has convincingly demonstrated that no conclusion to the contrary can be drawn from anything that the Court majority has cited in any of its reapportionment decisions.[17] Worse than not having thought very clearly about what it has been doing, the Court has done it in the face of flatly contradictory provisions and intent.

A curious omission on the part of the Court has been its refusal to make an analogy between the representational system provided for Congress in the Constitution, and similar systems which it has rejected for use by the States. If the United States Senate can be composed on the basis of geographical units—two Senators for each state, no matter what the population—and the House of Representatives on the basis of population, why is that not a sufficient precedent for States which may want to allow for a similar arrangement in their bicameral legislatures? A common state provision had been for members of the upper house of the legislature to be elected from counties, and those of the lower house from more or less similarly sized districts based on population. Such arrangements—now prohibited by the Court's mesmerizing invocation of its dogma that "one man" shall have "one vote" in a "mathematically precise" district—were often based upon complexities of political life quite similar to those which led the founding fathers to compose the Congress as they did.

On the other hand, it may be too soon to assume that the Court is happy with what the Constitution provides for the U.S. Senate. Given the Court's creative proclivities in other areas, perhaps the Senate should not rest too easily.

Justice Frankfurter, although he let slip on occasion, had an abiding love for the Constitution, and an abiding passion to interpret it scrupulously. His dissent in the first of the reapportionment cases, *Baker v. Carr*, has been truly described as his farewell address to the Court and to the country. He retired shortly after the case was decided, and died three years later.

In Frankfurter's view, the Court in *Baker v. Carr* was asked to choose among competing theories of political philosophy. Not only would the case establish an appropriate framework of government for the State of Tennessee, but the Court's decision would also mean that the same standard would be applied to all States of the union. Frankfurter attempted to articulate the theory upon which the majority had apparently rested its decision. That theory seemed to be that representation proportioned to the geographic spread of population was so universally accepted as a necessary element of equality between man and man that it must be taken to be the standard of political equality preserved by the Fourteenth Amendment. Such a theory was, in Frankfurter's words, "to put it bluntly, not true."

The truth of the matter was not hard to find. The truth was that the theory of the Court had *never* been practiced—not at the time the Constitution was drawn, at the time the Fourteenth Amendment was drawn, or at the time the Court decided *Baker v. Carr*. Frankfurter went on to state the obvious, which was that if there had been any generally prevailing feature of American politics, that feature was population inequality in relation to the geographic standard. The "history" which the majority attempted to rely upon in *Baker v. Carr*, and in succeeding cases, was fabricated history.

After citing numerous examples in his dissenting opinion, Justice Frankfurter presented an insightful summary of what the realities were:

> Apportionment, by its character, is a subject of extraordinary complexity, involving—even after the fundamental theoretical issues concerning what is to be represented in a representative legislature have been fought out or compromised—considerations of geography, demography, electoral convenience, economic and social cohesions or divergencies among particular local groups, communications, the practical effects of political institutions like the lobby and the city machine, ancient traditions and ties, settled usage, respect for proven incumbents of long experience and senior status, mathematical mechanics, censuses compiling relevant data, and a host of others.[18]

Frankfurter was not noted for short sentences—he had, after all, once been a professor. But his style did not impede his insight, and he knew that apportionment was but one result of an intricate web of values operating amongst the contending forces of partisan politics. He knew that apportionment battles "are overwhelmingly party or intra-party contests." That is why he admonished the Court to stay out of the "political thicket."

What the Court did in these cases could not have been more appropriately characterized than by an admiring devotee of the results, A. A. Berle. It was Berle's opinion that the reapportionment decisions were proof that "ultimate legislative power in the United States has come to rest in the Supreme Court."[19] Berle's observation is amply supported in the opinions of Justice Douglas and Chief Justice Warren. Douglas, writing for the majority in *Gray v. Sanders,* informs us that "the conception of political equality from the Declaration of Independence to Lincoln's Gettysburg Address, to the Fifteenth, Seventeenth, and Nineteenth Amendments can mean only one thing—one person, one vote."[20] This passage is quoted with approval by Chief Justice Warren, writing for the Court in *Reynolds v. Sims.*[21]

One inclined to skepticism about such assertions may want to examine the Declaration of Independence or the Gettysburg Address. Yet no amount of patient analysis will reveal in those documents any reference to the "one person–one vote" incantation advanced by the Court in these cases. Nor does any such reference appear in any of the Amendments cited by the Court. In regard to the Amendments cited, it is well to recall that the reforms to which they were addressed—the right of Negroes to vote, direct election of Senators, and the enfranchisement of women—had been effected as provided for in the Constitution: by *amendment.*

It has been the style of the Court in the reapportionment cases, by contrast, to confirm Professor Berle's dictum; but the Court has done more than merely act as the "ultimate legislative power in the United States." Another admirer of this approach, Professor Andrew Hacker, has offered the opinion that, "Citizens should be given the blessings of equality whether they want them or not."[22] As though following Professor Hacker's advice, and whether the American people want it or not, the Court has transformed their constitutional provisions concerning representative government—and the complex political institutions which have grown out of those provisions—into a single slogan of mind-shattering simplicity.

Is it really plausible that all of the complexities of democratic representative government can be comprehended in the rhythmic chant, "one man-one vote"? A chant conceived in the secluded secrecy and mysterious isolation of the Oracle of Washington? Professor Wallace Mendelson has suggested that the slogan, though seemingly irresistible, "promises much more than it delivers," and that its application may well produce a "credibility gap" that "activist judges perhaps can endure even less than can acknowledged politicians."[23]

Yet one still hears it devoutly urged—by both radical and conservative commentators—that reapportionment truly is the one area where only a judicial solution could have been effected. That, by its very nature, a representative body based on unequal districts would remain that way because its members depend for their political existence upon a continuation of the status quo. But even this argument implies that something significant has changed; that an identified evil has been expunged; that representative democracy now works better, thanks to the Court's radical surgery. These assumptions seem doubtful at best.

A *Michigan Law Review* assessment written in 1968 was rather inclined to see great change in such state policies as increased aid for schools, greater home rule, increased consumer protection, stronger civil rights legislation, curbs on air and water pollution, and reform in the criminal justice system—all as a result of reapportionment.[24] An appraisal by Professor Nathan Glazer some seven years later may be closer to the mark.

Glazer refuted an original, and widely held, assumption that reapportionment would shift power to the liberal cities, or to the minorities who lived in them, and concluded that, *at most,* it had helped the conservative suburbs. But in the end Glazer found that reapportionment had turned out to have "almost no consequence at all." He characterized it as, "An ideological exercise . . . carried out by those who thought they knew better," which had the effect, unfortunately, of "stripping away the last shred of pretense that states had some degree of sovereignty," and in the process of "losing great stores of respect for the neutrality and objectivity of the courts."[25]

In his book on the subject, Professor Timothy O'Rourke reports the results of an examination of reapportionment in six States—Kansas, South Dakota, Tennessee, New Jersey, Oregon, and Delaware. He concludes that, "In no state examined did redistricting yield political changes of the sort that would justify the characterization of 'reapportionment revolution.' " O'Rourke asserts, on the contrary, that "the overall influence of reapportionment on policy has been rather limited and immeasurable."[26]

The Court as yet shows no tendency to extricate itself from the mathematical madness of its reapportionment decisions. As recently as 1983, in the case of *Karcher v. Daggett,* the Court refused to validate congressional districting in New Jersey where the maximum population deviation in districts of some half million persons was set at less than one percent.[27] While the majority of the Court declined to consider any criteria of fairness or equality beyond its hallowed sums, Justice Stevens suggested that the equal protection clause of the Fourteenth Amendment comprehends much more. He would have required analysis of the degree of irregularity in the shape of district boundaries, of the relative compactness of districts, of the degree of deviation from existing political subdivision boundaries, and of the relative neutrality and openness of the decision making process leading to the adoption of the challenged plan.

The pressure to move on to such an analysis was illustrated by results of the 1984 congressional elections. Thanks in large part to traditional gerrymandering (with careful attention to equality of population, of course), Republicans, while polling just under one-half the votes for congressional seats nationwide, won only 182 seats in the House of Representatives compared to the Democrats' 253. In California, where the GOP outpolled the Democrats by 100,000 votes, Republicans won but eighteen House seats to twenty-seven for the Democrats.[28] As one commentator put it, gerrymandering is "a lot like pornography. You know it when you see it, but it's awfully hard to define."[29] That commentator underestimated the Supreme Court's confidence in its powers of definition.

In an opinion handed down June 30, 1986, *Davis v. Bandemer,* the Court held that there are "judicially discernible and manageable standards" by which to determine when unconstitutional gerrymandering has occurred.[30] Having plunged into Justice Frankfurter's "political thicket" when it decided in *Baker v. Carr* that questions of apportionment are justiciable, the Court has now been moved by the implacable dynamics of that venture to grope yet further into a darkening labyrinth of unknown political consequences. Writing for the Court majority, Justice White opined that "unconstitutional discrimination occurs only when the electoral system is arranged in a manner that will consistently degrade a voter's or a group of voters' influence on the political process as a whole." However, "a mere lack of proportionate results in one election cannot suffice in this regard." Hence, while Democrats won only forty-three of one hundred seats in the Indiana House of Delegates in 1982, even though they received 51.9 percent of the votes, no unconstitutional result could be discerned in the *Davis* case.

Justice White's opinion was joined by Justices Brennan, Marshall and Blackmun. Justices Powell and Stevens joined only in holding that federal courts may rule in cases of political gerrymandering. They also joined in a separate opinion which would have struck down the Indiana plan on a showing of "uncontradicted proof that certain key districts were grossly gerrymandered to enhance the election prospects of Republican candidates." The constitutional "standards" which the Court has been willing to infer would appear to lurk well beyond the confines of the constitutional document.

Chief Justice Burger and Justice Rehnquist joined in a dissenting opinion by Justice O'Connor which would have held that the entire question was "a nonjusticiable political question that the judiciary should leave to the legislative branch as the Framers of the Constitution unquestionably intended." The dissent feared that the ruling in the case would inevitably move the Court "toward some form of rough proportional representation for all political groups," and that the "consequences of this shift will be as immense as they are unfortunate." It may well be that the worst fears of the dissent will not be realized, as the worst fears of Justice Frankfurter were not realized in the aftermath of *Baker v. Carr.* The point is that no one knows what the case will lead to. The decision illustrates once again how difficult it is to arrest a judicial juggernaut once set on a course of political policy making outside the restraints of the Constitution. If there is some evidence that Chief Justice Burger had, at last, some second thoughts, the *Davis* case also demonstrates that there was nothing of significance to distinguish the Burger Court's propensity for constitutional interloping from that of its predecessor, the Warren Court.

What the Court has done in reapportionment cases stands in vivid and revealing contrast to its actions in the voting rights cases, which were considered at the beginning of this chapter. Voting rights were provided in the Fourteenth and Fifteenth Amendments for all individuals—black or white. After a rather sorry beginning, the Court finally came to see its constitutional duty to enforce those rights as written and intended. In that pursuit it was performing its highest constitutional function. An individual right, provided for in the Constitution, was vindicated and enforced.

In reapportionment, by contrast, the Court has no constitutional mandate. The negative results of its actions include the infliction of great damage to the constitutional role of the States in the federal system, while the positive results—if any—remain tenuous and elusive. The necessity for its taking any such action at all remains unconvincing, and what the Court itself hopes, has in mind, or aims for has never been articulated.

In the reapportionment cases the Court has again indulged an urge—supreme and overpowering—to upset yet another element of the constitutional scheme in pursuit of an amorphous social "good." Is such an impulse—so lamentably unsupported by reason, necessity, or even results—really much different from the "reasons of state" by which tyrants throughout the ages have sought to justify tampering with the foundations of individual rights or representative government?

9. To Be or Not to Be

IN SHAKESPEARE'S PLAY, Hamlet considered the "whips and scorns of time/The oppressor's wrong;" he weighed the "thousand natural shocks/That flesh is heir to;" and he feared "what dreams may come/When we have shuffled off this mortal coil." Finally, this young man whose incapacity to act continues to fascinate and inform us, decided that making any decision at all was just too complicated.[1] For Hamlet, only one being was at stake—the questions he put related only to his own existence. The answer was in his own hands. When we consider the question of abortion, uncounted millions of lives are at stake, and the decision is not in the hands of the lives which are to be—or not to be.

Abortion, involving as it does strongly held religious, ethical, personal, and moral beliefs, is an area which law and government have approached in widely divergent ways from one era to another. Nothing at all is said about abortion—or about anything remotely relating to abortion—in the U.S. Constitution. Yet, in 1973, in the case of *Roe v. Wade*, the Supreme Court held that every woman has a right to an abortion.[2] That decision is one of the most extraordinary of all the Court's constitutional transgressions.

Ms. Roe was a single woman, she was pregnant, and she wanted to have an abortion. But she lived in Texas, which, by statute, had made it a crime either to procure or to attempt an abortion, except for the purpose of saving the life of the mother. So she brought suit challenging the constitutionality of the Texas statute. Roe argued ardently that the *quality* of her life would be drastically affected were the unwanted pregnancy to go to term. But she could *not* argue successfully that her *life itself* would be threatened, and therefore she could not legally procure an abortion under the one exception allowed by Texas law. We know nothing more of Ms. Roe herself for the reason that she sued under the assumed name of Roe, knowing that the suit would attract wide publicity, and wishing not to be identified.

A three-judge federal district court found that the Texas statute was overly broad and vague, and that it was therefore in violation of certain constitutional rights. Just which rights had been violated raised questions at least as broad and vague as the Texas statute allegedly had been. In order to appreciate fully the Supreme Court's opinion in *Roe v. Wade,* it would be well to review briefly some of the moral, ethical, personal, historical, medical, and legal considerations necessarily involved in the question of abortion.

Historically, under the common law, the question of whether there had been any criminal act in performing an abortion involved the "quickening" of the fetus. Quickening referred to the first recognizable movement of the fetus, believed to occur between the sixteenth and eighteenth week of pregnancy. Abortion performed before this time was not an indictable offense at common law. This view appears to have been related to the theological determination of when a fetus became infused with a "soul," and thus became "animated."

Christian theology and canon law had come to fix the point of animation at forty days for a male and eighty days for a female. We shall not pause over this curious distinction, which would surely be viewed as "sexist" in today's society. There is also a distressing lack of evidence as to how maleness and femaleness of the fetus was determined by the Christian fathers. In any event, it was agreed that prior to the point of quickening, or animation, the fetus was regarded as a part of the mother. Its destruction, therefore, could not be considered homicide, since that crime necessarily involves taking the life of an individual human being.

The next question, of course, concerned the "quick" or animated fetus. There appears to have been a generally accepted rule of common law holding it to be a crime, either a felony or of a lesser degree, to abort a quick fetus.

Turning to the ancient societies which are the foundations of western civilization, Greece and Rome, abortion appears to have been rather freely practiced, although not everyone agreed that it should have been. Greek and Roman law afforded little protection to the unborn. In Athens even infanticide was practiced when unwanted children, particularly females, were born. The religions of the times did not prohibit abortion.

Despite this history, the oath of Hippocrates, dating from the fourth century, B.C.—which still serves as the basis for the ethical responsibility of the medical profession—required a pledge not to give a woman an abortive remedy. But even the prestige of Hippocrates, and the general recognition that he was the "wisest and greatest practitioner of his art," was not conclusive. Other equally influential Greeks of the same period approved of abortion, including Plato and Aristotle.

In the United States, following the English common law, abortion was not generally dealt with as a statutory crime in most States until the nineteenth century. Connecticut, in 1821, was the first State to enact legislation outlawing abortion. In 1828 an act of New York prohibited destruction both of the unquickened and the quickened fetus, but made the former act a misdemeanor, while prescribing that the latter should constitute second degree manslaughter. The New York law also incorporated what came to be a commonly recognized exception—the exception included in the Texas statute—abortion necessary to preserve the life of the mother. Similar anti-abortion statutes of other States date from the latter part of the nineteenth century.

In considering whether or not Ms. Roe should have won her case against the State of Texas, the underlying quandary is the difficulty in defining whose rights, or what rights, are critical to the case. The abortion issue, unfortunately, tends to be characterized by attitudes of righteousness, and by emotional fervor. Both those who favor abortion and those who oppose it often believe their respective positions to be morally self-evident. It is undeniable that an unwanted child can have a detrimental, even a catastrophic, effect on the life of the mother who does not want it. The effect can be compounded where the child is the result of rape or incest. Yet there is at stake another life as well. One side argues for the rights of the fetus, the other for the rights of the woman who does not want it. Others suggest that the rights of the woman be balanced, somehow, against the rights of the fetus. There are some who hold that the child to be has a right to be wanted, and that if it is not wanted, abortion is permissible. What the resulting "rights" of the mother, and those of the fetus, may be must be considered before those rights can be put in legal or constitutional terms.

Is the fetus a person? Is it possessed of normally recognized qualities of personhood? Does it possess such qualities of humanity as consciousness, self-awareness, self-motivated activity, communication, or reasoning? Looking at the abortion issue from the perspective of the law, abortion, like many other issues, may involve a balancing of rights against duties or obligations. For example, the rights set forth in the Constitution, and by law, are contingent upon obedience to duly enacted law. If one disobeys the law, sanctions up to and including death may be imposed. Can the state of incipient life in a fetus be described as having any true relationship to the complexities of such arrangements? In other words, can it be said to have either moral rights or moral responsibilities? Should the rights of an actual person outweigh those of a potential person? If a fetus has a right to life, does the woman who carries it always have an obligation not to terminate an unwanted life?[3]

One might suppose that the Supreme Court, in its effort to answer some of these questions, and to define the right or rights with which it was about to deal in the case of Ms. Roe, could look to medical opinion for expert guidance. But the actions of the American Medical Association on the issue of abortion over the past century indicate that its dealings with the matter have been no more grounded in exact science than were the views of Greece, Rome, or medieval theology.

As early as 1857 the American Medical Association, through its Committee on Criminal Abortion, noted a widespread practice of abortion which it characterized as a "general demoralization." The same committee, in 1871, adopted resolutions condemning the practice and seeking to limit its scope. The committee also attempted to call "the attention of the clergy of all denominations to the perverted views of morality entertained by a large class of females—aye, and men also, on this important question."[4] The AMA appears to have adhered to this position for over a century, its House of Delegates having indicated continuing opposition to abortion in a resolution adopted as recently as 1967.

Yet, by 1970 the Association was forced to note a "polarization of the medical profession on this controversial issue." As a result, resolutions were adopted noting changes in state laws, and changes induced by judicial decisions, which led the AMA to emphasize "the best interests of the patient," "sound clinical judgment," and "informed patient consent"— the latter in contrast to "mere acquiescence to the patient's demand."[5] Where abortion was decided upon, the Association asked that the procedure should not require any party to violate personally held moral principles. In the same year the American Public Health Association took an even more unequivocal position, advocating that abortion be widely available under hospital conditions.

In 1972 the American Bar Association entered the picture, adopting a

Uniform Abortion Act which countenanced abortion within the first twenty weeks after commencement of the pregnancy. After twenty weeks abortion would be allowed only if the life or health of the mother were believed to be greatly endangered, if it appeared that there would be a grave physical or mental defect in the child, or if the pregnancy resulted from rape or incest.

It is evident enough that the subject of abortion is difficult to manage on objective terms. Actions such as those of the American Medical Association or the American Bar Association do not reflect either convincing scientific data, or a basis for clear legal distinctions upon which the courts might rely. And such opinions do not begin to touch—much less determine—moral and religious views on the subject. In approaching *Roe v. Wade,* the Supreme Court had, in fact, very little in the way of objective criteria to inform its deliberations. What it did have was a rather novel creation of its own called the "right of privacy."

The "right of privacy" had been discovered by the Court in a 1964 case, *Griswold v. Connecticut,* as a sort of miracle, spontaneously manifesting itself from an ethereal nowhere.[6] The Planned Parenthood League of Connecticut had opened a center in New Haven on November 1, 1961 for the purpose of instructing married persons who did not want children—or who did not want them at a particular time—as to the means of preventing conception. The center would examine the wife, and would prescribe a contraceptive device or material for her to use. On November 10, 1961 executive director Griswold, together with the medical director of the center, was arrested for violation of certain provisions of the General Statutes of Connecticut. One provision of the statutes was that any person who uses any drug, medicinal article, or instrument for the purpose of preventing conception should be fined not less than fifty dollars, or imprisoned not less than sixty days nor more than one year, or be both fined and imprisoned. That statute defined the principal offense.

As is often the case, another provision of state law made it a crime—to be punished as *if* it were the principal offense—to assist, abet, counsel, cause, hire, or command any other person to commit any offense elsewhere stated. Griswold and his medical director were found guilty as accessories under the latter statutory provision, and were fined one hundred dollars each. The conviction was upheld through the appellate process in Connecticut, and was appealed to the U.S. Supreme Court.

The opinion of the Court in *Griswold v. Connecticut* had included in its opening pages the following statement: "We do not sit as a super-legislature to determine the wisdom, need, and propriety of laws that touch economic problems, business affairs, or social conditions." Anyone familiar with the operation of the Supreme Court in recent years is put on notice immediately by such a disclaimer that the Court is about to do *exactly* what it *says* it is *not* going to do—it is going to "super-legislate." The best that can be said for the disclaimer is that it furnishes evidence that the Court does admit, at least implicitly, somewhere in its inner workings, that it is not *supposed* to super-legislate, or even legislate, and that to do so is in violation of its constitutional powers.

In the *Griswold* case Justice William O. Douglas, writing for the Court, conceded that the right of privacy is nowhere mentioned in the Constitution or its Amendments. So what the Court did was to quote *itself* in previous cases (but *not* the Constitution) in order to *invent* its right of privacy. Douglas referred to the "sanctity of a man's home and the privacies of life;" to a "right of privacy, no less important than any other right carefully and particularly reserved to the people;" and to "various guarantees" which create "zones of privacy." These prior expressions of judicial opinion, Douglas asserted, "suggest that specific guarantees in the Bill of Rights have penumbras, formed by emanations from those guarantees that helped give them life and substance."[7]

A penumbra is a partly lighted area surrounding the complete shadow of a body, such as the moon, in full eclipse—hardly a concept of constitutional precision. But, perhaps the Court was candid, after all, in characterizing its new-found "right of privacy" as an "emanation" from such a "penumbra," for it had offered nothing less gossamer upon which to rest its finding. Pleased at the discovery of this redeeming astronomical metaphor, the Court applied the new emanational and penumbral theory to the statute at issue in the *Griswold* case.

The statute was found to be faulty in forbidding the *use* of contraceptives, rather than merely regulating their manufacture or sale. This, the Court concluded, was a method of seeking to achieve the goals of the statute "by means having a maximum destructive impact" upon the marriage relationship. The Court envisioned police searches of the "sacred precincts of marital bedrooms" for "tell-tale signs of the use of contraceptives." Responding to its self-induced horror at the suggestion of such procedures—there had been no suggestion of any such searches in the case—the Court characterized them as "repulsive to the notions of privacy surrounding the marriage relationship." The Court pondered further that in the marriage relationship, "We deal with a right of privacy older than the Bill of Rights—older than our political parties, older than our school system. Marriage is a coming together for better or for worse, hopefully enduring, and intimate to the degree of being sacred. It is an association that promotes a way of life, not causes; a harmony in living, not political faiths; a bilateral loyalty, not commercial or social projects. Yet it is an association for as noble a purpose as any involved in our prior decisions."

This passage might conceivably be considered an elevating paean to the institution of marriage, and a touching tribute to the sentiments of the Court on the subject. What it lacks is any connection between what the Court was doing and any right or principle set forth in the Constitution. The passage is but an exercise of the Court's judicial magicianship, by use of which it was evidently hoped that our attention would be diverted from any embarrassing question as to the Court's authority for the decision it was about to render. The decision was that the Connecticut statute at issue was unconstitutional because it violated the Court's new "right of privacy," whatever the source of that right might have been.

Dean Griswold of Harvard Law School—who apparently was no relation to the plaintiff in the case—commented on the "penumbras" to which the Court referred in *Griswold v. Connecticut*. He did "not know where these penumbras come from, nor do I know their extent or limitation." Griswold suspected "that the true meaning of penumbra . . . is that the Constitution does not cover the subject but ought to because it does so much else that is desirable."[8]

Thus, as it came to decide the case of the anonymous Ms. Roe, and whether the Texas statute making abortion a criminal offense was constitutional, the Supreme Court had as a backdrop a myriad of moral, ethical, historical, and legal opinions on the question of abortion. And it had its own bright new discovery, the right of privacy, upon which the decision in *Roe v. Wade* was ultimately to be grounded. Or did it? As it commenced its final disquisition in the case, the Court admitted that, "The Constitution does not explicitly mention any right of privacy." And so, just to be sure, the Court invented it all over again. We were assured that, "In varying contexts, the Court or individual Justices have, indeed, found at least the roots of that right in the First Amendment," or in the Fourth and Fifth Amendments, or if not there, in the "penumbras of the Bill of Rights." In the event that the reader were not yet convinced, reference was made to the Ninth Amendment, which provides that, "The enumeration in the Constitution of certain rights shall not be construed to deny or disparage others retained by the people." The Court did not say just how this provision applied to the case. Finally, the Court invoked "the concept of liberty guaranteed by the first section of the Fourteenth Amendment."

Apparently feeling secure at last that this barrage of constitutional invocations had pulverized any remaining opposition, the Court charged triumphantly onward to proclaim hegemony for the "right of privacy," and to assert that that right "is broad enough to encompass a woman's decision whether or not to terminate her pregnancy." One gasps to keep pace. But there was yet more. Its newly coined right to abortion, the Court conceded, "is not unqualified and must be considered against important State interests in regulation."

This meant that, in some situations, the Court was going to allow States to prohibit abortions, and to punish with criminal sanctions anyone who violated certain prohibitions. The Court recognized that the States still have some interest in both the mother and the fetus. These interests, the Court announced, mature with the fetus, and change over time. What a State might be allowed to regulate at one stage in pregnancy, it might not be allowed to regulate at another stage.

During the first trimester of pregnancy, the Court held, the State has no interest in either the fetus or the mother compelling enough to allow state regulation. A pregnant woman, therefore, has the constitutional right to an abortion during the first trimester, regardless of any state legislation to the contrary—including legislation designed to regulate the conditions under which an abortion is performed.

During the second trimester, the interest in protecting the fetus is still not compelling, but the interest in maternal health may be. Therefore, in the second trimester, States may regulate the conditions under which an abortion is obtained, but only with the interest in mind of protecting maternal health, since risks to health in an abortion during this period may exceed those of childbirth.

Departing from the more ancient concepts as to when a fetus "quickens," the Court in *Roe v. Wade* determined that it becomes "viable" somewhere between the twenty-fourth and twenty-eighth week of pregnancy. At that point, the interest of the State in protecting the fetus becomes compelling. Therefore, from that point on the State can prohibit abortions except where they are necessary to protect maternal life or health.

This wonderful new discovery in secular trinitarianism, it must be borne in mind, was announced by the Supreme Court as a command of the United States Constitution. It was solemnly handed down as a principle embodied in that document—quickening fetuses, trimesters, differentially developing state interests, maternal health, and all.

Shortly after the decision was announced in *Roe v. Wade,* Professor John Hart Ely, then of Yale Law School, offered a thoughtful commentary on the case. Sympathizing with the Court's observations concerning the serious, life-shaping costs of having a child, Ely observed that "even though a human life, or a potential human life, hangs in the balance, the moral dilemma abortion poses is so difficult as to be heartbreaking." But the problem becomes one, not of sentiment, but of *constitutional law* once the Court takes the matter upon itself. In that respect, Ely laments that the Justices "fail to . . . even begin to resolve" the moral dilemma abortion poses "so far as our governmental system is concerned by associating either side of the balance with a value inferable from the Constitution." Ely concluded that *Roe v. Wade* was "a very bad decision." To Ely, "It is bad because it is bad constitutional law, or rather because it is *not* constitutional law and gives almost no sense of an obligation to try to be."[9]

To a certain extent the furor created by *Roe v. Wade* can be compared to the national uproar engendered by adoption of the Eighteenth Amendment in 1919, prohibiting the manufacture, sale, or transportation of intoxicating liquors within the United States. Each represents a social issue of immense volatility and delicacy. National regulation of prohibition proved unworkable, and the matter was turned back to the States by the Twenty-First Amendment, ratified in 1933. Abortion, too, had been left to the "laboratories of the States"—as the federal system is sometimes termed—until it was hijacked into the Constitution in *Roe v. Wade*. Prohibition, at all events—both in its imposition and its repeal—conformed to the constitutional provisions for changing that document which are set forth therein. The same can hardly be said in the case of abortion.

Making a national—and a constitutional—issue of a subject so inflamed as that of abortion may well prove as divisive to the nation, and as threatening to the processes of law and justice, as were the "speakeasy" days of prohibition. Once again the Court seems to have been impelled blindly onward by its own prejudices and predilections, with little thought given either to the justification or to the probable consequences of its action.

Congressional counterattack against the "right to abortion" soon produced a divisive and impassioned result, and one which may presage future relations between Congress and the Supreme Court. In 1976 Congress, in appropriating money for the Medicaid program, provided, at the instigation of Rep. Henry J. Hyde, that no money be appropriated to pay for abortions. This provision, which came to be popularly known as the Hyde amendment, was later declared unconstitutional in federal district court. The case became a *cause celebre*, and was appealed to the Supreme Court. As the appeal was set for hearing a "friend of the Court" brief was filed by no fewer than two hundred forty-seven members of the House of Representatives and the United States Senate. The brief argued that the ruling of the District Court subverted the Constitution in a most fundamental way, by making meaningless the reservation to Congress of the right to determine when money shall be drawn from the treasury. The issue raised was not abortion, as such, but concerned the fundamental distribution of power in our constitutional system.

The Constitution provides, in Article I, Section 9, in no uncertain terms, that, "No money shall be drawn from the Treasury, but in Consequence of Appropriations made by Law . . ." The very first provision of Article I of the Constitution is that, "All legislative powers herein granted shall be vested in a Congress of the United States . . ." The Hyde amendment decision was handed down by the Supreme Court on June 30, 1980.[10] The decision upheld the authority of Congress to refuse to pay for abortions, even when they are found to be needed to preserve the health of indigent women. The majority held that, despite the fact that the Court had previously found that a woman is guaranteed the right to decide during the early months of pregnancy whether to have an abortion, it does not necessarily follow that the freedom of choice thus guaranteed carries with it a constitutional entitlement to the financial resources by which to avail herself of the full range of protected choices.

There was a vociferous outcry against this decision on the grounds of the policy which it enunciated. The protestors urged, with every evidence of being correct, that the result would be to leave the rich unaffected, while the poor would be left to bear their unwanted children, or to seek unsafe, unsanitary, and often exceedingly dangerous methods of abortion. One columnist put the matter with particular poignancy, first quoting the dissent of Justice William J. Brennan, Jr., who had protested, *inter alia*, that, "Antipathy to abortion, in short, has been permitted to ride roughshod over a woman's constitutional right." The columnist added his own lament, suggesting that, "What a majority of the Court said is that the Constitution is for sale. Abortion is a right, but only if you've got the money to pay for it. Those with money can have abortions for whatever reason they want. Those without money cannot. In America, the court ruled, you can have all the justice that money can buy."[11]

These cries of outrage, it should be noted, were raised against what was in fact merely a newly modified *social policy* of the Court. Having indulged the winds of pro-abortionist sentiment in deciding *Roe v. Wade*, the Court was required to weather the whirlwind of anti-abortionist public reaction to the result. The Court backed down, partly at least because of a change in membership, and agreed to allow the anti-abortionist sentiment represented in Congress to prevail. It experienced a retribution to which it had exposed itself when it created the "constitutional" right to an abortion in the first place.

Emanations from *Roe v. Wade* have been haunting the Supreme Court ever since its decision in that case. These instances include a decision handed down June 15, 1983, *City of Akron v. Akron Center for Reproductive Health*, together with two companion cases.[12] The *Akron* case involved the validity of an abortion ordinance of the City of Akron. The ordinance was complex, and so was the holding of the Court. Among the Court's holdings were the following: while the State may encourage parental involvement in the decision of a minor to have an abortion, it may not interfere with the constitutional right of a "mature minor," or of an immature minor whose "best interests" are contrary to parental involvement, to have an abortion (the ordinance dealt with unmarried minors under the age of fifteen); it is an unreasonable infringement on a woman's right to an abortion to require that all second trimester abortions be performed in a hospital, based on "present medical knowledge" and high cost, among other reasons; a State may require that a physician verify that the woman has been provided adequate counseling, and that her consent to an abortion is "informed," but may not require explanations by the physician which the Court finds are "designed not to inform the woman's consent, but rather to persuade her to withhold it altogether;" and that the State may not require a 24-hour waiting period between consent and performance of the abortion.

From our present point of view, the most interesting aspect of the *Akron* case is the dissent of Justice Sandra O'Connor, joined by Justices White and Rehnquist. Justice O'Connor concluded that the entire framework of *Roe v. Wade*, based on the trimester analysis, "is clearly on a collision course with itself." She rejected an analytical framework which "varies according to 'stages' of pregnancy," and where standards of review differ "according to the level of medical technology available when a particular challenge to state regulation occurs." She observed that the Court had decided in *Akron* that "the state's compelling interest in maternal health changes as medical technology changes," while requiring that health regulations must not "depart from accepted medical practice." Such standards, the dissent argues, mean that, "As medical science becomes better able to provide for the separate existence of the fetus, the point of viability (where the Court says the state's interest becomes paramount) is moved further back toward conception." To the dissent, the entire trimester analysis fails to provide the essential definite and neutral principles upon which judicial decision-making should be based.

The dissent rejected the trimester framework adopted in *Roe,* "Even assuming that there is a fundamental right to terminate pregnancy in some situations. . . ." Although the dissenting Justices did not directly attack the constitutionality of the *Roe* decision as such, this remark seems to indicate that they might be inclined to do so on an appropriate occasion.

The *Akron* dissent, the Hyde amendment, the growing anti-abortion movement, the efforts of States and municipalities to regulate abortion, and other evidence of dissatisfaction with the Court's abortion stance, all point in the same direction. It may be that we are witnessing the beginning of a complex and emotional reaction by a large segment of the American people against having *social values* imposed upon them, in the guise of constitutional mandates, with which they deeply—and in many cases reverently—disagree.

Professor John T. Noonan, Jr., now a Judge on the Ninth Circuit Court of Appeals, observed that for a decade "critics of all persuasions on abortion had been unable to discover a rational basis" for the *Roe* decision. In view of that fact, Noonan inquires whether, in addressing abortion once more in *Akron,* a "minimal respect for the rule of law and the decent opinion of mankind" might not have called for the Court "to assert a basis other than arbitrary power" for its renewed adherence to the *Roe* decision. The Court, of course, did not do so. Terming the *Akron* decision "unworkmanlike," "undemocratic," and "insensitive," Noonan predicts that, "Prayer and love, work and education, action by the Congress, leadership by the

President, constitutional response by the people—these must, and some-day will, right the wrong now written into law."[13]

Unfortunately, such noble sentiments have not as yet worked their way into the conscience of the Supreme Court. Quite the contrary. In the recent abortion decision, *Thornburgh v. American College of Obstetricians and Gynecologists,* decided June 11, 1986,[14] the Court reaffirmed *Roe v. Wade,* and prohibited state action which would require a sensible discussion of the matter between a woman contemplating abortion and her doctors or other counsellors prior to the event. The Pennsylvania law at issue included the requirement that doctors give a woman a variety of information before performing an abortion. This would include details of the "probable . . . characteristics" of the fetus at her stage of pregnancy, a list of social service agencies which would help if she had the baby, the fact that the father would have to furnish financial support for the baby, and warnings about the possible medical and psychological effects of abortion.

The opinion of the Court in *Thornburgh* was written by Justice Harry Blackmun, who also wrote the decision in *Roe v. Wade,* and who defended his progeny in terms bordering on hysteria. Said Justice Blackmun, "All this is, or comes close to being, state medicine imposed upon the woman, not the professional medical guidance she seeks." The Justice observed that, "Few decisions are more personal and intimate, more properly pri-vate, or more basic to individual dignity and autonomy, than a woman's decision . . . whether to end her pregnancy." Presumably a woman's dig-nity, privacy, and autonomy are to be enhanced in a state of ignorance. In any event, "The states are not free, under the guise of protecting maternal health or potential life," we are told, "to intimidate women into continuing pregnancies."

The *Thornburgh* vote was five to four, with Chief Justice Burger voting to uphold the Pennsylvania requirements, and suggesting that it may be time to "reexamine *Roe.*" Justice White and Justice Rehnquist had previ-ously urged that *Roe* be overturned, while Justice O'Connor had voiced strong doubts about its validity. In *Thornburgh,* nevertheless, an adamant five vote majority rejected even the "informed consent" concept embodied in the invalidated Pennsylvania legislation.

The entire "right" to abortion, the Court would have us believe, sprang full blown from the brows of Thomas Jefferson and Alexander Hamilton. It is a right which supposedly was—and always had been—embodied in the Constitution. But as the heat begins to build against what is patently a social policy instead, the Court hardly knows what to do. It is brought closer to the point of having to admit that what it has said is a right, and always has been, really is not, and never was. But the Court still has on its hands *Roe v. Wade*, reaffirmed in *Thornburgh*, and in other issue of that case. The offspring are of questionable parentage, and, in the opinion of many, of poor character. The abortion issue may yet, with poetic justice, prove to be a crucial factor in aborting the Court's own grasp for illegitimate power.

In Federalist Paper Number 81, Alexander Hamilton addressed those who feared that the proposed Supreme Court would, by construing the law according to the "spirit" of the Constitution—rather than by its wording and stated intent—mold the laws into whatever shape it might think proper. To Hamilton, there was "not a syllable" in the proposed constitutional plan which "empowers the national courts to construe the laws according to the spirit of the Constitution." If nothing so vague and elusive as Court interpretation of the Constitution according to its "spirit" was contemplated, one wonders what Hamilton's thoughts might have been regarding "penumbras" and "emanations." Charles Dickens' character, Mr. Bumble, asserted that "the law is a ass, a idiot."[15] In the contraceptive and abortion cases the Supreme Court has taken no pains to disprove Bumble's assessment.

Among the other "slings and arrows of outrageous fortune" which undid Hamlet's "native hue of resolution" was "the insolence of office." Which is but another description of the symptoms of power, and its tendency to corrupt. To be, or not to be—that is a question which should have been left to poets, priests, or legislators. It is a question whose spirit should never have troubled the Court or clouded the Constitution.

10.   Beat the Rap

POLICE RADIOS CRACKLED, gears shifted, engines raced, and squad cars converged on the Cleveland house of Dolly Mapp, who was reported to be harboring a "wanted" person. Startled by a thunderous pounding at her door, Ms. Mapp thrust her head out of an upstairs window to inquire what the matter was. She was wanted for questioning, the police responded. Did they have a warrant? Ms. Mapp inquired. The police were not clear about that, so she called her attorney, who informed her that police had no right either to question her or to enter her house without a warrant. Dolly Mapp shouted this information down to the officers gathered at the door below. Radios crackled once again, more machines sped through the city, reinforcements arrived, and the house was surrounded. Ms. Mapp's attorney also appeared at the scene. Now, the police said, they had a warrant. But instead of showing it to anyone, they kicked in the back door.

Dolly Mapp stood bravely on the stairs, demanding to see the warrant before the police went further. The officers pushed her brusquely aside, one of them waving a paper which he claimed to be the necessary document. The good woman snatched the paper and in the same sweeping movement deftly pushed it down her bosom, from which repository the officers immediately and forcefully removed it. For her impertinence Dolly was handcuffed to a burly gentleman of the force, who sat her down on a bed while his fellow officers ransacked her building from cellar to garret. The "wanted" person was nowhere to be found, but presently, in a trunk in the basement, criminal material was discovered. In due course Dolly Mapp was tried and convicted for its possession.

The conviction was appealed, and the resulting decision of the Supreme Court, *Mapp v. Ohio*,[1] became yet another landmark case in the judicial rewriting of the Constitution. And what was the crucial contraband which led to Ms. Mapp's conviction? In the words of a concurring Justice, "one must understand that this case is based on the knowing possession of four little pamphlets, a couple of photographs and a little pencil doodle—all of which are alleged to be pornographic."

Dolly Mapp was hardly the first person in history to have herself or her house searched without benefit of a warrant. Nor was she the first to have been presented, however briefly, with a fraudulent substitute for a warrant. In eighteenth century England there was, for example, wide usage of a device called a writ of assistance. The writ of assistance authorized law enforcement officers to conduct searches and seizures. However, the writ was unlimited in time, it did not require a showing of probable cause for its issuance, it did not describe the place to be searched or the materials sought, and it did not designate or limit those who might exercise the powers it conferred. A writ of assistance thus amounted to a kind of general warrant which could be used by any government official, at any time, for almost any purpose. It was characterized by James Otis, in 1761, as "the worst instrument of arbitrary power, the most destructive of English liberty, and the fundamental principles of law, that ever was found in an English law book."[2]

A similar device was employed in eighteenth Century France, the *lettre de cachet,* at first required to be countersigned by the King, but by 1770 the practice of issuing them in blank had become common. The *lettre* could be used arbitrarily to detain or imprison anyone against whom it was directed, the name to be filled in as required. A remark made by a courtier to Louis XV informed the King that "no citizen of your realm is guaranteed against having his liberty sacrificed to revenge. For no one is great enough to be beyond the hate of some minister, nor small enough to be beyond the hate of some clerk."[3]

When the First Congress considered the Bill of Rights in 1789, the framers of the Fourth Amendment were well aware of these abuses, as they were of the abuses of the agents of King George III in the colonies. The framers therefore provided in that Amendment that,

> The right of the people to be secure in their persons, houses, papers, and effects, against unreasonable searches and seizures, shall not be violated, and no Warrants shall issue, but upon probable cause, supported by Oath or affirmation, and particularly describing the place to be searched, and persons or things to be seized.

There has been a running debate as to precisely how this Fourth Amendment right of the people "to be secure . . . against unreasonable searches and seizures" is to be enforced.

The general rule is that searches and seizures should be made only as authorized by a properly issued warrant. There must be a showing of "probable cause" for the issuance of the warrant, and that showing must be made, not to the police, but to an impartial judicial officer, a magistrate or a judge. This means that the police are required, beforehand, to justify what they propose to do. There are some exceptions to this rule, such as searches incident to a lawful arrest, with which we are not here concerned. We are interested in what the Supreme Court has done over the years when the police do not get a warrant—when they go in anyway, and when they find incriminating material. The issue is whether such material can lawfully be used to convict the person of a crime, either for possessing the material itself, or for some other crime which the seized material tends to prove.

Dolly Mapp was treated roughly, and her "crime" would hardly seem heinous. With little change in script the whole episode of her apprehension, search, and conviction would serve equally well for a summer night's melodrama or a comic opera. But in many other cases the contraband uncovered in the absence of a warrant is of quite a different nature. It could be a cache of illegal drugs, the weapon used to commit a murder, the telltale shreds of clothing which identify a rapist, or an armory of guns and bombs leading to a terrorist organization. These cases are as serious as the Mapp case was absurd. What should be done if this kind of evidence is procured in an illegal search? May it be used in court to convict those whose guilt is indicated by the evidence?

The Fourth Amendment says nothing concerning the remedy to be had in the event of a breach of its guarantees against unreasonable searches and seizures. An offending officer might be sued for trespass under the common law, or he might be prosecuted for violation of the civil rights of the person searched without a warrant under existing statutory law. Conceivably Congress or a state legislature could provide penalties to be assessed against the law enforcement agency itself. For well over a century after the adoption of the Fourth Amendment the problem of enforcement received little attention, and was not squarely addressed by the Supreme Court. Then, in 1914, the Court invented a new enforcement device to deal with illegally seized evidence.

A criminal defendant had been accused of illegally using the U.S. mails for the purpose of carrying on a lottery. In a search which led to his arrest, certain papers, books, and other property had been seized without a warrant, had been presented in evidence at his subsequent trial, and had been a factor in his conviction. The conviction was appealed and made its way to the Supreme Court. In *Weeks v. United States*[4] the Court held that the illegally obtained materials should not have been admitted as evidence at the defendant's trial. His conviction was therefore reversed. What has since been termed the exclusionary rule was thus established as a remedy against the use for conviction of illegally obtained evidence. Under the exclusionary rule, evidence illegally obtained must be excluded from a subsequent criminal trial.

Weeks v. United States was a federal case, tried in United States District Court, involving a federal crime. Most crimes, such as murder, rape, larceny, and so forth are defined by, and punished under, state law. This is one aspect of the federal nature of our constitutional system. Only a relatively few crimes, such as the illegal use of the mails which was involved in the *Weeks* case, crimes involving activities which cross State borders, and other crimes delineated by Congress are punishable under federal law.

An important aspect of the *Weeks* case is the relationship of the Supreme Court to the lower federal courts as administrator of the federal court system. Under its powers to supervise that system, the Supreme Court can prescribe rules of evidence to be followed in the lower federal courts, not as a matter of constitutional law, but administratively. The question arose whether that is what the Court had done in the *Weeks* case, or whether it had said that the exclusionary rule was required as a matter of constitutional law under the Fourth Amendment. The question remained unanswered until it was presented directly to the Court in the 1949 case of *Wolf v. Colorado*.[5] There the Court held that the application of the exclusionary rule in the *Weeks* case had been merely an exercise of the Court's function in administering the lower federal court system, not a requirement of the Constitution.

The holding in *Wolf v. Colorado* did not bode well for Dolly Mapp, for what she was asking of the Supreme Court was that the booklets and the little doodle found in the trunk in her basement be thrown out as evidence in her trial, and that the exclusionary rule be applied to her case. But her case arose, not in federal court, but in the courts of the State of Ohio. If the exclusionary rule were merely an administrative requirement applied by the Supreme Court to the lower federal courts, there would be no basis for extending the rule to a state court criminal proceeding. The Supreme Court has no authority to set administrative rules for state courts, only for the federal court system.

To enforce the exclusionary rule as Ms. Mapp requested, the Court would have to reverse its holding in *Wolf v. Colorado,* and hold that the exclusionary rule was constitutionally authorized to apply against the States. But if the Court so held, there was a fundamental constitutional difficulty to be overcome.

The Fourth Amendment, along with the other of the first eight Amendments which comprise the Bill of Rights, was designed to apply only against the federal government. There was no concern about excessive power in the States in 1789—the fear was of too great a power in the newly created national government. Hence none of the Bill of Rights was directed against the exercise of state power, or state police action such as that at issue in *Mapp v. Ohio.* A second requirement, therefore, if Dolly Mapp were to prevail, would be to apply constitutional prohibitions deriving from the Fourth Amendment to the States as well as to the federal government. The purpose and intent of the Fourth Amendment would have to be altered and expanded. As it happened, the foundation had been laid for just such an expansion well before Dolly Mapp pressed her arguments before the Supreme Court in 1961.

This expansion involves the "incorporation" doctrine, by which parts of the Bill of Rights have been "incorporated" into the Fourteenth Amendment to apply against the States. The essence of that doctrine centers on the "due process" clause of the Fourteenth Amendment, and the requirement that no State shall deprive any person of "liberty" without due process of law. It came to be argued that each of the guarantees of the Bill of Rights was a "liberty," and that at least some of those liberties were included within the meaning of the term "liberty" as used in the Fourteenth Amendment. Therefore, it was contended, the liberties contained in the Bill of Rights, as applied against the federal government, were "incorporated" within the "liberty" guaranteed against state action by the Fourteenth Amendment. As we have seen in previous chapters, the framers of the Fourteenth Amendment expressed no such intent, and, if anything, a contrary intent. But that fact has not prevented the Supreme Court from entertaining the incorporation theory.

The Court began "incorporating" the Bill of Rights in *Gitlow v. New*

York,[6] decided in 1925, a case involving freedom of speech and press. Since that time none of the Justices, whether "conservative" or "liberal," has ever been quite able to resist the temptation to "incorporate." Some have held that only certain of the liberties set forth in the Bill of Rights are incorporated, others have insisted that they all are.

Once Pandora's box had been opened, pressure mounted to incorporate all of the first eight Amendments within the Fourteenth Amendment. For a time the Court resisted the pressure, and the manner in which it did so illustrates vividly that what the Court was doing was not applying the Constitution, but rewriting it. In a case decided twelve years after the *Gitlow* case, *Palko v. Connecticut,*[7] the Court enunciated the interesting doctrine of "selective incorporation." Only those elements of the first eight Amendments which were "implicit in the concept of ordered liberty," the Court told us, were to be incorporated. Others, which were on a "different plane of social and moral values," were not. The Court did not advise us in *Palko* which was which. Over the years some guarantees of the Bill of Rights were ordained for incorporation, while others were thrust to the lowest rung of "social and moral values." The question in *Mapp v. Ohio* was into which category, the blessed or the damned, the exclusionary rule would fall.

In the end, Dolly Mapp and her pornographic doodle were vindicated. The doodle, the photographs, and the pamphlets were all ruled inadmissible in the prosecution against her. Her conviction was reversed. And who would have had it otherwise in such a case? In order for this felicitous consummation to be reached, however, it was necessary for the exclusionary rule to experience a miraculous apotheosis. It went to sleep one evening a mere administrative rule of evidence applicable in federal courts, and awoke the next morning to the glorious knowledge that, through the injustice done to Dolly Mapp, it had been enshrined as constitutional doctrine. The business was a kind of constitutional passion play in two acts.

The Court first elevated the exclusionary rule from a simple rule of evidence of the federal courts—which the Court had said it was in *Wolf v. Colorado*—to a requirement of the Fourth Amendment. That amended the Fourth Amendment. End of first act. Then, as constitutional doctrine, the exclusionary rule could be sifted through the screen of the Court's "selective incorporation" test to see whether it was one of those elegant beings "implicit in the concept of ordered liberty," or merely a creature of some lower order. Happily, the rule passed the test. The Fourteenth Amendment was also amended, and the curtain rung down on the second act. It was thereafter a matter of "constitutional law" that, in both state and federal criminal prosecutions, illegally seized material could not be used as evidence to convict. The doodle, the photograph, and the pamphlets were the first to go.

At least that is what had *appeared* to have happened to the exclusionary rule upon a close reading of *Mapp v. Ohio*. The Court had clearly stated that, "We hold that all evidence obtained by searches and seizures in violation of the Constitution is, by that same authority, inadmissible in a state court." The Court added that "the exclusionary rule is an essential part of both the Fourth and Fourteenth Amendments" as resulting not only from "the logical dictate of prior cases," but because "it also makes very good sense." In his dissenting opinion, Justice Harlan observed that at the heart of the majority opinion is the assumption that the exclusionary rule is "part and parcel" of the Fourth Amendment. But, as we are discovering, when the Supreme Court begins fussing with the Constitution, the results often fall short of clarity in concept, or precision in results.

Despite the wording of the *Mapp* decision, a majority of the Court appears to have reverted to the theory that the exclusionary rule remains a judge-made rule, designed to enforce the requirements of the Fourth Amendment, but not a constitutionally hallowed doctrine in and of itself. Under this theory, it is only the Fourth Amendment itself which was held to apply to the states in *Mapp v. Ohio,* as a *constitutional* requirement, with the exclusionary rule merely tagging along as a non-constitutional enforcement device, as it had been held to be in *Wolf v. Colorado*. This is the view which the Court seems to have taken, for example, in its consideration of the matter in *Illinois v. Gates*.[8] In *Gates*, while the Court had solicited briefs on the question whether the exclusionary rule "should to any extent be modified," it declined to consider that issue on the ground that it had not been "pressed or passed upon" in the state courts below.

It is important to note, amidst the constitutional subtleties of the *Mapp* case and its aftermath, that the question of whether Dolly Mapp was guilty as charged became entirely obscured. While we may agree that in her case that did not much matter, in other cases it was to matter a great deal. In one such case a young girl, missing for eight days, had been found with her throat slit and a bullet in her head. When police contacted a woman whose car was like one seen near the scene of the crime, she willingly gave them her husband's guns. Tests proved that one of the guns had fired the fatal bullet. A warrant was issued, the suspect and his car were seized, and sweepings from the auto matched the victim's clothing. The conviction was reversed because the warrant had been issued, not by a "neutral and detached magistrate," but by the attorney general of the State.[9]

In another case two police officers patrolling a residential area observed a man driving a car in a manner which suggested to them that he was "sizing up" the area. When he was stopped and identified, it was learned that a warrant was outstanding for his arrest. A search of his car produced a loaded .38 calibre magnum and an unregistered sawed-off shotgun. His subsequent conviction for possession of illegal weapons was reversed on the ground that there had been no probable cause for the officers to stop him in the first place, so that all evidence seized thereafter was inadmissible. Once the revolver and the sawed-off shotgun were excluded as evidence, there was no ground for retrial, and the man went free.[10]

These were both federal cases. The same results obtain in state courts. The California Supreme Court has held that, in making a valid arrest, officers had the right to search the *trunk* of the car which the suspect was driving, but not the contents of a tote bag *inside* the trunk. The tote bag was found to contain clothing similar to that worn by a robbery suspect, three guns, and a roll of pennies in a wrapper from the store which had been robbed. All were excluded, and the conviction overturned.[11]

The chief objection to the exclusionary rule has been that evidence which is concededly valid, and which would tend to convict, may not be introduced because of the type of technical flaw in its acquisition illustrated by the preceding examples. Dean Wigmore, long recognized as a preeminent national authority on the law of evidence, complained about this aspect of the exclusionary rule shortly after its initial adoption in *Weeks v. United States*. Dean Wigmore explained the operation of the rule—here paraphrased only slightly—as a court might explain it to a guilty defendant, Jones, and a policeman, Smith, who had obtained the crucial evidence illegally:

> Jones, you are guilty of selling heroin to minors. Officer
> Smith, you have violated the Constitution by finding the her-
> oin in Jones' house without a search warrant. Jones ought to
> go to prison for the crime, and Smith should be fined for
> contempt. However, we are going to let you both go free. We

are not going to punish Smith directly, but shall do so by
reversing Jones' conviction. This is our way of securing
respect for the Constitution. We uphold it, not by striking at
the man who breaks it, but by letting somebody else off who
broke something else.[12]

Justice Charles G. Douglas, III, of the New Hampshire Supreme Court,
has written that, "The smothering uniformity of *Mapp's* exclusionary rule
has prevented the development of reasonable alternatives to guide police
conduct. The rule has failed because the courts' definitions of a 'reasonable' search are vague, changing and obscure. We penalize a cop for failing
to conduct a search under rules that any reader of this article himself could
not readily articulate in a squad car at 3 A.M. The failure of the strategy has
been felt nationwide because of the incorporation approach."[13] Or, as
Justice Cardoza complained as early as 1926, "The criminal is to go free
because the constable has blundered."[14]

In deciding *Mapp v. Ohio* the Court had asserted that application of the
exclusionary rule to the States was required to maintain the integrity of the
courts, and as a deterrent to police in making illegal searches and seizures.
After twenty years of application, there is considerable dispute—and forceful arguments can be made on both sides—as to whether either of these
objectives has been accomplished. It is clear that a strong motivation of the
Court in adopting and expanding the exclusionary rule has been to stand
apart from the "dirty business" of using tainted evidence. And, while
legislative action to remedy police abuses is certainly possible, the critics
are correct in pointing out that, prior to the application of the exclusionary
rule to the States, very little such legislation had been forthcoming, and no
effective means to prevent the taking of illegal evidence had been implemented. However this may be, there is strong evidence that the tide is
turning, and that the exclusionary rule is heading for rougher waters.

Commenting on criticism that no legislative remedies for improper
police searches and seizures have been forthcoming to replace the exclusionary rule, Chief Justice Warren Burger observed that, "Legislatures are
unlikely to create statutory alternatives (to the exclusionary rule), or
impose direct sanctions on errant police officers or on the public treasury
by way of court actions, so long as persons who commit serious crimes
continue to reap the enormous and undeserved benefits of the exclusionary
rule."[15] The Chief Justice expressed himself even more forcefully in

addressing the American Bar Association in February of 1981. "Our search for justice," he told the lawyers, "must not be twisted into a search for technical errors;" he insisted that "guilt is not irrelevant" in evaluating search and seizure cases. "Is society redeemed," Burger asked, "if it provides massive safeguards for accused persons and yet fails to provide elementary protection for its decent law-abiding citizens?"[16]

The exclusionary rule provides a remedy only for the guilty, but leaves the innocent unprotected. If there is an illegal search and contraband is turned up, those guilty of possessing the illicit material are protected by prohibiting its use as evidence to secure their conviction. If an illegal search is conducted and nothing is found, the innocent victim of that search has no remedy under the exclusionary rule. The rule is not concerned with the innocent victims of illegal searches, only with those who are likely to be guilty.

If the Court moves in the direction suggested by the remarks of Chief Justice Burger, then it will be forced to reconsider its ruling in *Mapp v. Ohio*. In any such reconsideration the Court will again find itself painted into a corner. Extrication will be possible, but at best difficult and not a little embarrassing.

Involved in any reconsideration is the still unresolved question as to the precise nature of the exclusionary rule. Is it a personal right of the defendant, such as the right to an attorney or the right against self-incrimination? Or is it only a judicially created remedy for violation by police of the requirements of the Fourth Amendment? What may become a majority view on the subject is stated in an opinion by Justice Powell, dissenting in a 1974 case, *United States v. Calandra*.[17] According to that view, the exclusionary rule is merely a "judicially created remedy" and not a "personal constitutional right of the party aggrieved."

This view might suggest that the Court stands ready to desanctify the exclusionary rule, to strip it of its constitutional status, and to return it to its former position as an administrative rule of law. That is fine so far as the federal court system is concerned, but what about the state courts? In order to apply against the States in the first place, the rule had to be a "liberty" capable of incorporation within the meaning of that term as used in the Fourteenth Amendment. This necessarily means that it was a "personal constitutional right," and not merely a "judicially created remedy." The problem can be solved, of course, by the Court simply overruling *Mapp v. Ohio*, announcing that the exclusionary rule is not a constitutional right under either the Fourth or the Fourteenth Amendments, and creating some other rule to take its place.

Whatever expectations as to the imminent demise of the exclusionary rule some of the Justices might have engendered, all the Court has been willing to do so far is to carve out a few exceptions. Two of these appeared in *Nix v. Williams* and *U.S. v. Leon*, decided in 1984. In *Nix v. Williams* the Court held that if evidence improperly obtained under the exclusionary rule would "inevitably" have been found anyway, its use in court would not be prohibited.[18] Thus the "inevitable discovery" exception to the rule was invented.

A "good faith" exception was created by the Court in *U.S. v. Leon*,[19] and its companion case, *Massachusetts v. Sheppard*.[20] In these cases, defective warrants were used for searches which turned up incriminating evidence, though the police officers involved believed the warrants to have been valid. Since the officers had acted in good faith, the incriminating evidence was held to be admissible. The rationale of the Court in *Leon* seemed once again to indicate that the Justices have come to consider the exclusionary rule not to be constitutionally based. But the decision barely mentions *Mapp v. Ohio*, and does not begin to address basic constitutional issues such as the Court's role in interpreting the Fourth Amendment, or how its activism in this area has affected state administration of criminal law within the federal structure.

In any event, these narrow exceptions barely scratch the surface of the procedural monster which the Supreme Court has created in the enforcement of criminal law. In his recent book, *Disabling America*, Professor Richard E. Morgan of Bowdoin College arrests our attention with the observation that,

> . . . there is a huge black hole in the conception of "justice"
> subscribed to today by many legal intellectuals and activists.
> It is thought an "injustice" if the nicest points of investiga-
> tive or trial procedure are not observed; to admit any
> evidence (no matter how useful to the truth-finding function
> of the trial) that is "illegally obtained" is unjust. But for
> morally guilty persons to walk away from their crimes in
> massive numbers or "cop out" for suspended or minor sen-
> tences is not perceived as revolting.[21]

If the intellectuals and activists are not revolted by these conditions, it is becoming clear that their victims, and potential victims, are.

Yet another basic assumption of the framers of the Constitution has been distorted, if not repudiated, in cases having to do with admission of evidence and criminal rights. That assumption was that the jury, exercising common sense, would be the guarantor of fairness and justice in criminal actions. What the exclusionary rule does is to keep essential evidence away from the jury, and to force the jury to act in ignorance of relevant facts. The founders knew that judges, as legal technicians, tend to become immersed in technical niceties, and thereby lose track of the simple and basic question of guilt or innocence. The fact is that they did not particularly trust judges, and so provided that juries, not judges, should have the last word in criminal trials as the best guarantee against abuse in the criminal justice system. [22]

Rather than leaving the jury at the center of that system, the Supreme Court, in its treatment of the exclusionary rule and in other procedural departures, has turned away from the common sense of the jury, and has enshrined technicalities which focus on the defendant and his desire to avoid punishment. The principal object of a civilized penal system, the protection of society, has been subverted by a gross distortion of values—procedural, moral, and constitutional.

11. Obscenity in Law and Fact

AT A NEW JERSEY school board meeting opinion was sharply divided. Tempers—perhaps as much through calculation as from spontaneous emotion—pushed to the boiling point among a protesting minority. As antagonist Rosenfeld jumped to his feet, shouting and gesticulating, there were in the audience a number of school children, along with their mothers and fathers. Rosenfeld punctuated his defiance by calling the teachers of the district a bunch of "mother f—ers." He screamed the same epithet separately and distinctly at the school board, the school district, the town, and the country. Subsequently he was convicted under a state statute prohibiting use of "indecent" and "offensive" language in public places. In a 1972 decision the United States Supreme Court reversed the conviction on grounds related to free speech.[1]

In another case, involving a protest over the draft, a scuffle developed when police cleared the way for army recruiters to obtain access to a government building blocked by pickets. One of the pickets shouted to a policeman, "White son of a bitch, I'll kill you!" Again he screamed, "You son of a bitch, I'll choke you to death!" This protester was convicted for use of "opprobrious words or abusive language, tending to cause breach of the peace." His conviction was also overturned by the Supreme Court, again for reasons related to free speech.[2]

These cases are but two examples of many in which the Court has struck down prosecutions of a similar nature on the ground that such prosecutions infringed upon the rights of free speech guaranteed by the First Amendment. In these cases actual speech was involved—the words uttered were the principal reason for prosecution. In other cases the Court has expanded the concept of "speech" to include what has become known as "symbolic speech," such as flag desecration, draft card burning, and sit-

108

ins. It has gone even further, and has stretched the cloak of free speech to cover areas as remote from debate and thoughtful expression as pornography.

In addition to enlarging the definition of what "free speech" is, the Court has also moved the *application* of free speech principles beyond the public domain—to which constitutional guarantees are limited—and has held that it may cover such private areas as company towns and shopping malls. These developments appear to have been fueled by the Court's view that free speech enjoys some sort of "preferred" position in the constitutional scheme.

There are serious constitutional deficiencies in every aspect of the judicial philosophy underlying these expansions in constitutional meaning and coverage. Examination of the Court's leading "free speech" cases yields alarming results in a domain often thought to be nearly sacrosanct.

As early as 1931 the Court held that "speech" may be "non-verbal" within the meaning of the First Amendment. It did so in striking down a state statute prohibiting anyone from "publicly displaying a red flag or device of any color or form whatever, as a sign, symbol or emblem of opposition to organized government."[3] By 1966, in a case involving a black sit-in of a segregated public library, the Court had concluded that First Amendment rights "are not confined to verbal expression," but that they "embrace appropriate types of action which certainly include the right in a peaceable and orderly manner to protest by silent and reproachful presence [the] unconstitutional segregation of public facilities."[4]

In handling "symbolic speech" cases the Court has reached opposite conclusions in fact situations which would appear similar. In a 1969 case the Des Moines, Iowa school district had suspended two students for wearing black armbands to protest the Vietnam war. In invalidating the suspensions the Court held that such action could not be sustained unless the forbidden act would "materially and substantially interfere with the requirements of appropriate discipline in the operation of the school."[5] In a 1974 case, New Rider and other male Pawnee Indians had been suspended from school for wearing long hair in defiance of a short hair rule, even though they claimed that long hair was an expression of their culture, and that discipline and operation of the school were not affected. Their suspension was upheld in the lower federal courts, and by its refusal to hear the case was, in effect, approved by the Supreme Court.[6]

State statutes dealing with alleged desecration of the flag have suffered similarly disparate fates. In 1970 the Court upheld a California conviction of a man who made a flag into a vest on the ground that the danger of possible breach of the peace was overriding compared to the symbolic speech involved in the act.[7] Yet in a 1975 decision the Court overturned the conviction of a man who had sewn a miniature flag to the seat of his pants, and had been found in violation of a seventy-year-old Massachusetts statute making it a crime to treat the flag "contemptuously." The Court held that the statute was "void for vagueness."[8]

In principle, the Court has stated that it cannot accept the view that "an apparently limitless variety of conduct" can be labelled "speech" whenever the person engaging in the conduct might thereby wish to express an idea.[9] Nevertheless, the Court's expansion of First Amendment free speech rights has gone beyond symbolic speech, and far beyond tolerance of what once would have been considered offensive, opprobrious, abusive, or inflammatory language. This trend is nowhere better illustrated than in the Court's treatment of obscenity and pornography.

It was not until the Warren era, beginning in 1954, that the Supreme Court came to consider allegedly pornographic expression in terms of First Amendment rights of free speech. In the century-and-a-half prior to that time, regulation of obscenity was a state prerogative under the general police powers reserved to the States by the Tenth Amendment. Through its decisions the Warren Court created an entire new body of law in what the Chief Justice is reported to have described, shortly after his retirement, as the Court's "most difficult area." That the difficulty was vexing, indeed, can be illustrated by examining the "tests" for obscenity developed by the Court during those years.

In approaching the matter of obscenity, the Court faced two basic problems. The first was to define what obscenity—or pornography—is; the second was to decide whether it should be afforded constitutional protection as a form of free speech. In theory, the Court has held that obscenity is not a form of expression protected by the Constitution. In practice, however, the Justices have had so much difficulty *defining* obscenity, and have been so hesitant to condemn *any* form of expression, that hardly anything has been held to be sufficiently obscene to offend the Court's constitutional standards.

In an English case decided in 1868, *Regina v. Hicklin*,[10] Lord Cockburn had defined obscenity as "pornographic matter having influence upon particularly susceptible persons." That test meant, in its application, that material might be declared obscene if isolated passages would have a pornographic effect on the most susceptible. Under such a test *Lady Chatterley's Lover*, for example, might be banned for the reason that the explicit sex passages were presumed to have an adverse effect upon young readers. Youthful readers, it was thought, would be incapable of understanding the genuine love between Lady Chatterley and the gamekeeper as a part of adult experience, including the unhappy consequences to both Lady Chatterley and her lover. Nevertheless, the rule of *Regina v. Hicklin* was part of the common law of most States, and was the basis for state handling of obscenity matters until the Supreme Court preempted the field in 1957. The case was *Roth v. United States*, together with a companion case, *Alberts v. California*. The *Alberts* case applied the *Roth* ruling, dealing with federal laws, to state action as well.[11] The test of *Regina v. Hicklin* was rejected, and the Court set out on a merry chase after its own definition of obscenity.

In *Roth* the Court stated that all ideas having "even the slightest redeeming social importance" were to be protected against governmental restraint. Obscenity, however, being "utterly without redeeming social importance," was *not* to be protected. Material was to be considered obscene, said the *Roth* Court, if "to the average person, applying contemporary community standards, the dominant theme of the material taken as a whole appeals to prurient interest."

The old rule of *Regina v. Hicklin* had undoubtedly allowed states and localities to condemn genuinely artistic work by judging the work, not as a whole, but by isolated passages—and by judging it against the reactions of those most susceptible to being depraved. The results were similar in the administration of federal laws prohibiting the mailing of obscene material. It was a federal court conviction for mailing such material which gave rise to the *Roth* case. Any number of books have been held obscene under the older tests, including James Joyce's *Ulysses*, Erskine Caldwell's *God's Little Acre*, Edmund Wilson's *Memoirs of Hecate County*, and Lillian Smith's *Strange Fruit*.

The test announced by the Court in *Roth v. United States* abandoned both the isolated passage and the most susceptible person tests of *Hicklin*. Instead, the Court required in *Roth* that the work be judged as a whole, and on the basis of the reactions of the "average person," rather than those of the most susceptible. It also used "contemporary community standards," which might well be different from standards prevailing in the England of

1868. Now, if the reader so far has no clear idea what might be judged obscene according to the *Roth* test, such bewilderment may be forgiven. It would appear that the judges charged with applying the tests to allegedly obscene material had no clear idea either. In one year, not long after the *Roth* test was announced, Henry Miller's book, *Tropic of Cancer,* came before the highest courts of both New York and California. New York found the book to be hard core pornography, while California judged it a work of literary merit worthy of constitutional protection. These results suggested that perhaps a more exacting definition of the obscene would be required. The U.S. Supreme Court labored further, and brought forth new fruit.

It was held that material not only must appeal to "prurient interest" to be declared obscene, but that it must also be "patently offensive" and, beyond that, it must be "utterly without redeeming social value" as well. This was a kind of judicial slot machine theory of obscenity, in which all three tests had to register simultaneously on the middle line, or governmental authorities seeking to ban material as pornography could not win.

Then there came the "pandering" and "hard-core pornography" tests. Pandering had to do with the *manner* in which material was sold. Under this test the publisher of *Eros* magazine was sentenced to five years in prison because of the way in which he advertised the magazine. The Court agreed that the publication itself might not have been obscene, but found that it became obscene when viewed "against a background of commercial exploitation of erotica solely for the sake of their prurient appeal."[12]

The hard-core pornography test was announced in a decision overturning the conviction of a motion picture theatre operator for exhibiting allegedly obscene films.[13] The opinion of the Court stated that criminal laws in the area of obscenity were constitutionally limited to hard-core pornography. However, there were five other opinions written in the case, in concurrence and dissent, advancing the other definitions of obscenity we have noted. Perhaps the most viable of all the Court's tests for pornography was expressed, in exasperation, by Justice Potter Stewart, in considering one particularly explicit bit of obscenity: "I know it when I see it, and that's it!" Presumably this was a variation of the hard-core pornography test, and was certainly stated with more subjective candor than is sometimes the case with other Court opinions which are, nevertheless, subjective.

So difficult did the Warren Court find the problem of defining obscenity that, during its final years, it virtually gave up the effort. In one case in 1967 the Court overturned three state obscenity convictions, merely stating that the materials at issue were not obscene, but without saying why.[14] That case, in turn, was cited as the reason for reversing thirteen additional state and federal obscenity convictions in the same year, without even waiting for briefs or arguments on the merits. This was virtually to say that "anything goes."

The Warren Court preempted the field of obscenity regulation, thereby effectively preventing the States from regulating or controlling pornographic and obscene material. Having reached this state of affairs, the Court then refused to have anything more to do with the matter. With the Court's own interest exhausted, this left the field pretty much to the pornographers. States and communities had been rendered virtually powerless to protect themselves from even the most obviously obnoxious material. Beginning in 1969 the Burger Court was left to pick up the pieces.

But as it bent to the disagreeable task, the Burger Court began to indicate that its own lack of clarity—to put it charitably—would at least match that of the Warren Court. In *United States v. Reidel*[15] the Court was faced with one of the last of the Warren Court's obscenity decisions, *Stanley v. Georgia.* Therein, the Court had appeared to say that a distinction would no longer be drawn between the transmission of *ideas,* and pure entertainment, so far as adults were concerned.[16] This meant that if material were "entertaining" to an adult, even though pornographic by any of the various standards the Court had adopted from time to time, that material would fall within the protection of the First Amendment.

Based upon this reading of the *Stanley* case, a lower federal court had ruled that a federal obscenity statute prohibiting the mailing of obscene matter, when applied to willing adult recipients, was unconstitutional. Without explicitly repudiating that interpretation of *Stanley,* the Supreme Court in *Reidel* informed the lower court that it had "misread" *Stanley,* so that the questioned statute was *not* unconstitutional! Although this amounted to a complete reversal of *Stanley,* the Court did not trouble itself to explain the *reasons* for its decision. It was almost as though the Burger Court had come to the same resigned conclusion as had the Warren Court, and simply wished the whole problem would go away. But it would not, and the Burger Court, like its predecessor, was forced to try *its* hand at defining obscenity, in an effort to make some sense of its rulings in the matter.

In a 1973 case, *Miller v. California,* the Burger Court offered a definition which may be paraphrased as follows. Material was to be considered obscene if:

1. The average person, applying contemporary community standards, would find that the work, taken as a whole, appeals to the prurient interest.
2. The work depicts or describes, in a patently offensive way, sexual conduct specifically defined by applicable state law.
3. The work taken as a whole lacks serious literary, artistic, political, or scientific value.[17]

The first element of the definition is essentially a restatement of the *Roth* test. The second element clearly allows *States* to define obscenity standards, whereas the movement of the Warren Court had been towards a *national* definition. In the third element, the former requirement that work be *utterly* without redeeming social value is replaced by a test which merely requires that it lack serious value, now described as literary, artistic, political, or scientific, rather than merely as social. The case appeared to foretell a major reformulation of obscenity standards.

Chief Justice Burger, writing for the Court in another 1973 case, *Paris Adult Theater v. Slaton,* offered reinforcement to the idea that the Court was striking out in a new direction in the definition and regulation of obscenity. In the *Paris* case the Chief Justice recognized that a State has an interest in the "quality of life and the total community environment." He conceded that the experience of the two prior decades "affords an ample basis for legislatures to conclude that a sensitive key relationship of human existence, central to family life, community welfare, and the development of the human personality can be debased and distorted by crass commercial exploitation of sex."[18]

The new definition of obscenity advanced in the *Miller* case, taken together with Burger's opinion in the *Paris* case, seemed to indicate that the Court had at last concluded that States and local communities have a legitimate interest in the regulation of obscenity and pornography. However, this interpretation of the Court's intentions, never fully solidified, was put in grave doubt by the holding in a case arising in Mount Ephraim, New Jersey, decided by the Court in 1981.

The operators of an "adult" bookstore had been convicted for violation of a city zoning ordinance banning live entertainment wherein nude dancers performed before viewers in coin-operated booths in their store. The Court held that an entertainment program may not be prohibited "solely because it displays a nude human figure," adding that "nude dancing is not without its First Amendment protection from official regulation." Chief Justice Burger registered a biting dissent, complaining that citizens "should be free to choose to shape their community so that it embodies their conception of a 'decent life.' "[19]

Thus, after a decade of its own wrestling with the problem of obscenity—and despite vigorous dissent by the Chief Justice—the Burger Court appears to have reached the same dead end as its predecessor, the Warren Court. Both Courts came to agree, in effect, that regulation of obscenity and pornography should be a national concern, and that it should be taken away from states and local communities. But both Courts floundered in their attempts to be clear and effective in asserting national standards. Neither Court was able to demonstrate a solid constitutional grounding for its efforts to shield from state regulation obscene and pornographic material. About the only ray of common sense to enlighten the whole business was furnished by Justice Stewart. We, as he did, "know it when we see it." And we are coming to know that the Supreme Court has been preventing state and local governments—and the federal government as well, for that matter—from exercising their legitimate concerns in regulating obvious pornography when they, and anyone else seriously interested, can "see it" perfectly well.

In dealing with free speech the Court has also been busy on another front. In addition to expanding "speech" to cover "symbolic speech" and pornography, the Court has expanded the area in which these newly created constitutional guarantees apply. It has made those and other free speech requirements of the Constitution applicable to areas of *private ownership* and activity—areas heretofore thought not to be covered by constitutional prohibitions, since those prohibitions are directed against *governmental* action, and not against private action. In so doing, the Court has used free speech in a very curious way, indeed. The idea of free speech was to limit governmental action in certain important respects—including action by the courts. By expanding the *area* supposedly covered by free speech guarantees, the Court has, instead of following the limiting principles of the Constitution, utilized its conception of free speech to create judicial philosophies which act to expand governmental power, and has invented "rights" which are not found in the Constitution.

The key to this development is again the concept of "state action," as that concept relates to the Fourteenth Amendment's provision that no *State* shall deprive any person of the rights set forth therein. In the cases we have considered so far in this chapter, the principal question has been whether acts of a State or any of its political subdivisions, such as cities or counties, have violated any provision of the Fourteenth Amendment. The cases we are now to consider involve *company* towns and *private* shopping malls and plazas, none of which are owned or operated by States, cities, or counties. How is it, then, that the owners of these private developments could run afoul of a constitutional provision directed *only* against state action?

This particular drama opens in Chickasaw, Alabama in the early 1940s. Chickasaw was a company town owned by the Gulf Shipbuilding Corporation. Gracie Marsh was a member of Jehovah's Witnesses who had been refused permission to preach her religious views on the streets of Chickasaw. When she continued preaching anyway she was arrested by a deputy sheriff—who was, as we would now say, also "moonlighting" as the company town's paid policeman—for violating the Alabama trespass statute. She was convicted of entering and remaining on the premise of another after having been told not to remain, and her conviction was upheld in the state courts of Alabama. She appealed to the United States Supreme Court.

The Court held that Chickasaw, though privately owned, had all the characteristics of any other American town, that it did not function differently from any other town, that it was the equivalent of a public municipality, and therefore that it was subject to the same constitutional restraints. Accordingly, the conviction of Gracie Marsh was reversed, on the ground that her First Amendment rights had been violated by the—now quasi-public—town of Chickasaw. [20]

Some two decades later the company town had all but disappeared from the American scene. A new phenomenon, the shopping center, as characteristic of America now as the company town had been in prior generations, had made fortunes for developers and had become a hallmark of suburban life throughout the country. The attention of the Supreme Court, however, was drawn to one particular manifestation of this phenomenon. Weis supermarket, located in Logan Valley Plaza shopping center, in Pennsylvania, was a non-union operation. The Amalgamated Food Employees Union, Local 590, wished Weis to become unionized, so it began picketing and soliciting workers on the porch in front of the Weis store, and in the parking lot adjacent to it. The store was located over 350 feet from any public road or thoroughfare. The company applied for, and obtained from the courts in Pennsylvania, an injunction which required that union workers distribute their information only on public streets, which would have been too far away to be effective in the circumstances. Following unsuccessful appeals in the Pennsylvania court system, the union appealed to the United States Supreme Court.

In *Amalgamated Food Employees Union 590 v. Logan Valley Plaza*[21] the Court held that the shopping center was the "functional equivalent" of the business district of the company town dealt with over twenty years before in *Marsh v. Alabama*. Thus, the Court stated, the center could not "immunize" itself from picketers and protesters by creating a *cordon sanitaire* of parking lots around the buildings. The Court did not deal with the fact that the shopping center, unlike the town of Chickasaw, did not provide all of the services that a public municipality would ordinarily provide its citizens. It held, simply, that the mere fact that the mall was open to the public equated it to a "state function"—that when property is opened to the general public its *private* character may disappear, so that the First Amendment may become a restraint upon its use.

The impact of the Court's decision was considerable throughout the nation. Many state courts, particularly in California and Washington, began to allow all manner of picketers to communicate with customers in private malls, while New York courts allowed picketing in private bus terminals, and Minnesota courts allowed campaign workers to distribute literature in shopping plazas. Management of the plazas, in all of these cases, had opposed the action of the picketers, solicitors, or protesters, and subsequently appealed to the United States Supreme Court. In each case, the Court denied *certiorari*—that is, it refused to hear the case. The effect of denial of *certiorari* by the Supreme Court is to let the state court action which is being appealed stand as decided. But there was more to come.

Almost as the Court was deciding *Logan Valley*, an anti-Vietnam war group, the Call to Resistance, was active in Portland, Oregon. The protest which brought their case to the United States Supreme Court was carried on in a private, air-conditioned mall in Portland. In a situation similar to that presented in *Marsh v. Alabama*, members of the Portland police force were moonlighting as security guards at the mall. When the Call to Resistance was prohibited from distributing handbills or otherwise expressing its opinions in the mall, it sought a federal district court injunction against the corporation which owned the mall. The federal district judge could hardly be faulted for granting the injunction on the basis of the *Marsh* and *Logan Valley* cases, and for finding that the mall was the "functional equivalent" of a public business district. But the judge turned out to have been a step or two behind his restive brethren in Washington.

Three years had elapsed between the decision in the *Logan Valley* case and the time the Portland case, *Lloyd Corp. v. Tanner,* [22] reached the Supreme Court. In that interval both Chief Justice Warren and Justice Fortas had resigned, and had been replaced by Chief Justice Burger and Justice Blackmun. The *Logan Valley* case had been a split decision, Warren and Fortas having been two members of the six member majority. With the changes in the Court, the majority shifted. The resulting decision in *Lloyd,* while it did not overturn *Logan Valley* explicitly, left it a floundering cripple at best. *Lloyd* was another split decision. In it the Court agreed that speech conducted on the premises of a private shopping center *might* be constitutionally protected if there were no adequate alternative available. In that case, however, the Court found that the shopping center was interlaced with *public* streets and roads, and was not cut off from public municipal facilities. The center was therefore held not to be the "functional equivalent" of a public business district like Chickasaw, Alabama or the Logan Valley Plaza. Being wholly private property, therefore, the constitutional rights of free speech—directed, as they are, against governmental interference—did not apply.

The last act of the shopping center drama was played out some four years later, originating in the North DeKalb shopping center in Atlanta, Georgia. In the North DeKalb center numerous stores were located off an enclosed mall, and could be entered only through the mall. Striking employees at the warehouse of the Butler Shoe Company—which was located elsewhere—set up pickets at the company's retail store in the mall. The manager of the mall threatened trespass arrests, appeals were had, and the matter wound up in the Supreme Court. The Court examined its prior opinions in the *Logan Valley* and the *Lloyd* cases, and concluded, at last, that the *Lloyd* case "amounted to a total rejection of the holding in *Logan Valley Plaza.*"[23] The Court decided, therefore, that unless a shopping center takes on *all* the attributes of a public town, it remains private property, and the constitutional guarantees of free expression do not apply. We were suddenly right back where we started, thirty years before, in Chickasaw, Alabama!

And all these developments had taken place with no change whatsoever in the constitutional text upon which they all supposedly had been based. To Professor Phillip Kurland, "There is something disturbing about the proposition that a watershed in constitutional law is marked not by changes in the constitutional text, or by changes in social conditions, but essentially the result of changes in [Supreme Court] personnel."[24] Mississippi State University Professor Howard Ball has offered the opinion that, *"Logan Valley* was overturned because the Court majority's political and philosophical views regarded the 1968 opinion with disdain. It was discarded without even a decent burial."[25] Valid as these observations may be, there is an even more fundamental consideration in the Court's handling of free speech questions.

The free speech cases selected for discussion in this chapter illustrate the workings of the Supreme Court at the periphery of its authority, where some Justices would—and others would not—seek to extend the Court's power and jurisdiction. It is at the raw edges of judicial infighting that the Court reveals—perhaps more than in any other way—when it has run out of constitutional gas, and when it is pushing hard uphill to stretch its authority into new territory. In a sense seldom recognized, the Court's aggressive expansion of its own power has been inextricably bound up in its handling of the "free speech" issue. The fact is that over *fifty years* ago the Court seized upon free speech as a major vehicle by which to launch its seemingly relentless drive towards limitless power and authority.

The First Amendment requirement is that, "Congress shall make no law . . . abridging freedom of speech, or of the press." The prohibition is directed clearly and specifically at *Congress,* in a manner which one might think would make it impossible to misinterpret. Yet, the most controversial of the First Amendment issues relate for the most part to actions of the *States.* How this came to be tells us a great deal about the workings of the Supreme Court. The story—as is normally the case when we want to know the true intent and purpose of our Constitution—begins at the time of its adoption, with the evidence available from that period as to what the First Amendment was supposed to mean.

When we look to the accepted primary sources for what the concepts of freedom of speech and press were to embody—to the statements of the members of the First Congress who drafted the First Amendment, and to those of delegates to the state conventions which ratified it—we are faced with the unexpected fact that these sources do not reveal *anything* about what the purpose of the Amendment was thought to be. Nobody in these constituent bodies talked about the matter at all. Subsequent developments demonstrate that this initial lack of discussion concerning the First Amendment is to be accounted for because its provisions were taken for granted. There was at the time a general assumption that the *national* government, against whose powers the Amendment was exclusively directed, had *no authority* over speech and press in the first place. The free speech and press guarantees were included in the Bill of Rights, not to define new rights, but simply to remove any doubt at all by specifically providing that Congress should make *no law* abridging those rights.

It was at the time of the controversy over the Sedition Act, passed by Congress in 1798, that the framers of the Constitution and the First Amendment came to express themselves with force, clarity, and in detail on the meaning of the freedoms of speech and press. The Sedition Act had made it a crime for anyone to speak, write, or publish "with the intent to defame . . . or bring into contempt or disrepute" the President or other members of the government. It became evident during the controversy over this Act that the purpose of the freedoms of speech and press had been to assure to the people the right freely to examine *public characters* and *public measures,* and to communicate freely among themselves thereon.[26] According to Ithaca College Professor Benjamin Richards, "the intended purpose of the speech and press clause was just what Republican critics of the Sedition Act said it was: to safeguard the free discussion of public characters and measures to the end that capable and honorable men should be elected to public office and governmental power be scrupulously and reasonably exercised."[27]

Now comes the surprising part. It is equally clear that, intending so to restrain Congress, the Framers also intended to leave to the *States* exclusive and *unrestrained* legislative authority in the field of speech and press. The First Amendment is aimed only at Congress, and there is nothing anywhere else in the Constitution, or in any of its Amendments, to indicate otherwise. On the contrary, the Tenth Amendment specifically provides that all powers not granted to the federal government shall be reserved to the States, or to the people. If any further proof were needed it is to be found in the fact that, in approving the original Bill of Rights, the Senate had *failed to pass* an amendment approved by the House of Representatives which would also have prohibited the *States* from infringing upon the freedom of speech and press. Thus, the idea that First Amendment rights of speech and press should apply to the states was *specifically rejected* when the Bill of Rights was adopted.

It was well over a century after its adoption before the Supreme Court had occasion to explore in any detail the meaning of the First Amendment. Speaking in 1922, the Court expressed an opinion entirely in conformity with the intent of the framers. The Court said that "the Constitution of the United States imposes upon the States no obligation to confer upon those within their jurisdiction . . . the right of free speech."[28] Yet, in the now famous case of *Gitlow v. New York,* decided only *three years later,* in 1925, Justice Edward T. Sanford announced the diametrically *opposite* conclusion. Writing for the Court, Sanford said that, "We may and do assume that freedom of speech and of the press . . . are among the fundamental personal rights and 'liberties' protected by the due process clause of the Fourteenth Amendment from impairment by the States."[29]

Justice Sanford was referring to the provision of the Fourteenth Amendment that, "No State shall . . . deprive any person of . . . liberty . . . without due process of law." By styling freedom of speech and press as a "liberty" within the meaning of the Fourteenth Amendment, the Court thus "incorporated" that portion of the First Amendment to apply against the States as well as against the federal government. *Gitlow v. New York* was the first of what was to become a long line of cases similarly "incorporating" other portions of the Bill of Rights to apply against the States. This occurred even though—like the First Amendment—the *entire* Bill of Rights was designed and intended to apply only against the federal government.

Justice Sanford's statement in *Gitlow* is all the more startling for the fact that it was spun off casually, in the form of a dictum not necessary to the decision of the case. There was *no reasoning,* and *no explanation,* for what he said. There was *no examination* of the *intent* of the framers of the First Amendment, and *no discussion* as to why its application to the States was "assumed" by the Court in the *Gitlow* case. Sanford's statement was a *constitutional time bomb*—and one smuggled in by the back door at that.

The Court came to rationalize its application of the freedoms of speech and press to the States as arising from the "preferred" nature of those freedoms. Free expression, it was said, was so vital to society that the prohibitions of the First Amendment must apply to the States, as well as to the federal government, whatever the Constitution might have provided. The *Gitlow* Court, it should be recalled, was still dominated by a majority adhering to the *Lochner* doctrines of Liberty of Contract and substantive due process of law. These were the principal doctrines by which the Court, for nearly a half century—until the mid-1930s—successfully thwarted both state and federal efforts to regulate the abuses of a growing industrial society.

Liberty of Contract and substantive due process had been the result of *previous* judicial expansions of the concept of "liberty" in the Fourteenth Amendment, similar to the *new* expansion which commenced with the *Gitlow* case. The Court in *Gitlow* was doing nothing more than taking additional liberties with the "liberty" guaranteed by the Fourteenth Amendment in expanding that liberty to include free speech. In *Gitlow,* "liberty" was simply dressed in yet another new and lustrous judicial fashion, and turned loose to solicit support for yet another new and different judicial cause.

The radical new course which the *Gitlow* Court charted in 1925 was defended by such eminent Justices as Oliver Wendell Holmes and Louis Brandeis. Justice Benjamin Cardozo was perhaps the most eloquent of all in advancing the new doctrine. He termed free speech "the matrix, the indispensable condition, of nearly every other form of freedom," a freedom "so rooted in the tradition and conscience of our people as to be ranked as fundamental."[30] In those phrases, explicitly stated, is the basis of the concept that freedom of speech somehow stands above and beyond all other freedoms provided by the Constitution and the Bill of Rights, and that freedom of speech must be "preferred" to the extent of being applied against the States, *regardless* of the clear constitutional mandate to the contrary.

The phrases chosen by Justice Cardozo are noble, and rather seductive. They seemed designed to conjure a halo of eternity about them. Yet, as Raoul Berger observes, "the fact remains that the one time the American people had the opportunity to express themselves on whether free speech was 'so rooted in the tradition and conscience of our people as to be ranked as fundamental' was in the First Congress, which drafted the Bill of Rights in response to popular demand. There they voted down interference with State control."[31]

The Court's "preferred" status for First Amendment freedoms can be viewed as a doctrine which bridges the gap between the end of *Lochnerism* and the present era of even more pervasive judicial activism, which began with the Warren Court. The 1925 decision in *Gitlow v. New York* furnished the Court with the *idea*—which it did not even bother to try to justify in that decision—that it could *pick* and *choose* among the rights of the first eight Amendments to the Constitution, and at its leisure select those which it wished to dub as "fundamental" for application against the States.

The judicial doctrine which resulted from this practice was for some time referred to as "selective incorporation"—until virtually everything in the Bill of Rights had been "selected," and thereby "incorporated," to apply against the States as well as against the federal government. Selective incorporation was the beginning of the modern period of constitutional amendment by judicial decree. Thus, in *Gitlow,* the Court's alleged solicitude for individual *freedom of expression* turned out to be the *avant garde* of *judicial revolution.*

For over half a century now the Supreme Court has trumpeted elegant phrases concerning the sanctity of free expression, and has repeatedly expanded and redefined what was to be included within these "preferred freedoms." In the crucial matters considered in this chapter, the results have been neither convincing nor elevating.

The extension of newly invented "rights" of expression to such areas as private shopping malls and plazas turned out to be, not an expansion of freedom, but an *intrusion* of government. It bore a remarkable resemblance to the chief hallmark of totalitarianism, which is public intervention into every facet of existence, leaving no room for individual or group activity not officially sanctioned—or officially censored. And in the name of *free speech*! Happily, the Court appears to have sounded a judicious retreat on this small front in its war against the Constitution.

But it is doubtful whether much can be expected in obscenity and pornography rulings, where the Court's almost bizarre penchant for protecting obscene expression runs virtually unabated. Thanks to Court action—or inaction—material is easily obtainable in most cities which depicts scenes of obscene and violent abuse of women, of sexual torture, of bestiality, of mutilation, and of mayhem. George Gilder has described this array of offerings as "propaganda for degradation and viciousness that must be seen to be believed," a flood engulfing the nation's youth.[32] Following the example of the United States Supreme Court, the New York Court of Appeals has ruled that a New York law which prohibited the depiction of *children* in simulated or *actual* sexual conduct—such as sexual intercourse, masturbation, lewd exhibition of the genitals, and other overt sexual activity—was a violation of the right of *free expression* protected by the First Amendment of the United States Constitution! Those opposed to the New York Court's ruling feared that an epidemic of "kiddie porn" would follow, while one authority ventured the opinion that the case did not represent a *freedom* issue, or a *rights* issue, but a *dollar* issue. [33]

One glimmer of hope in these incredible decisions is to be found in *New York v. Ferber,* a 1983 case in which the U. S. Supreme Court reversed the New York Court of Appeals decision on child pornography. [34] The Court found the prevention of sexual exploitation of children to be a government objective of "surpassing importance," and that child pornography might, therefore, be recognized and classified "as a category of material outside the protection of the First Amendment." The Court hastened to assert that these conclusions are "not incompatible with our earlier decisions," even though most of the tests for obscenity which allow virtually anything to pass need not now be applied in regard to child pornography. The positive aspects of the *Ferber* decision must still be discounted against a deep sadness that it has taken the Supreme Court so many years to reach such an obvious conclusion.

One wonders whether, in the Court's interpretation of free speech, there is not at work a kind of constitutional equivalent of Gresham's law, in which *real freedom* is driven out by according to supposedly "adult" thrills, and to depraved "entertainment," the constitutional status of freedoms designed for serious civic purposes. William Simon has concluded that under the Court's freedom of expression decisions, "Americans are constitutionally free today to do almost everything that our cultural tradition has previously held to be immoral and obscene . . . activities that could, for the most part, be carried on just as readily in prisons, insane asylums, and zoos." [35] Professor Archibald Cox has questioned whether the Court's interpretation of freedom of speech leaves any scope for legislation "designed to protect the moral, esthetic, or patriotic sensibility of the community, or to preserve the tone of public discourse." [36]

Professor John Hart Ely reminds us that the guarantees of free expression contained in the First Amendment were "centrally intended to help make our governmental processes work, to insure the open and informed discussion of questions of which values should be vindicated at the expense of which others, and to check our government when it gets out of bounds." [37] There can be no serious doubt but that these are the great purposes which freedom of speech and press were designed to serve. Yet the Supreme Court has come perilously close to making of those freedoms something akin to a Roman circus, in which sordid entertainment and false idols divert the populace from any concern with the difficult decisions of state; in which guarantees of freedom become a shabby cover for obscene titillation; and where what is truly "preferred" has turned out to be, not fundamental protection of free institutions at all, but the enhancement of judicial power.

Behind a protective barrage of "symbolic speech," "preferred freedoms," and pornographic license, the Court has ignited and sustained its own powerful advance towards freedom's antithesis—unbridled power. For half a century now the Court has lofted freedom's majestic phrases in a pyrotechnic display of impressive virtuosity. But if we allow our glance to be diverted to the ground below, we see that the brilliance of the spectacle has not quite obscured the true movement and intent of the judicial magicians who are putting on the show.

The result of the Court's alleged—and certainly persistent—concern for the "preferred" freedoms of the First Amendment has been to use those freedoms as the primary launch pad for the Court's own orbit into realms of seemingly infinite judicial power.

IV.
TRANSGRESSION
AND
RETRIBUTION

Following the example of the Supreme Court, lower federal and state courts have joined in the crusade for a new and more enlightened society, as judicially perceived. In the process they have come more and more to resemble political, rather than judicial, agencies, and have taken on operating characteristics of political institutions. These have included solicitation by the courts of interest groups who agree with their social goals, a typically political tactic which marks, as well as any other symptom, the changed nature of the judicial process.

The results of judicial intervention have frequently been other than what was intended, the courts having acted, as often as not, without a sensible grasp of the probable consequences of their edicts. Confidence in the courts has declined as a direct fallout of their own misdirected efforts.

When the courts touch too many raw nerves in the political system, there is a natural tendency for political counter-force to marshall itself to throw back the intruder. Actions which have been taken to reverse judicial aggression in the past are instructive as to what might be expected, or possible, in the much more aggravated condition of judicial excess which we are now experiencing.

TRANSGRESSION AND RETRIBUTION

12. The Virulence of Arrogance

IN THE SPRING of 1980 Congress passed a law reviving draft registration for men born in 1960 and 1961. The President had recommended that women as well as men be required to register, and that question had been debated by Congress. Registration of women, however, was rejected, and the law requiring men only to register was enacted and signed by the President. In July of 1980 the new law went before a three-judge federal district court in Philadelphia, its constitutionality challenged by opponents of the draft, who contended that the law violated the Fifth Amendment of the Constitution. District Judge Edward N. Cahn, who wrote the opinion for a unanimous court, agreed. But before we hear the judge's opinion, let us recall a few details of the setting.

The Fifth Amendment was part of the Bill of Rights adopted shortly after the Constitution itself, and has been around ever since. For over a hundred years, beginning with the Civil War, the nation has drafted men, and men only, to serve in the armed forces. Whether it was the doughboys of World War I or the GIs of World War II, many never really wanted to go, yet most did go, and most served honorably. During all this time it never occurred to anyone that the draft violated any clause of the Fifth Amendment, or any other provision of the Constitution. Such a conclusion had to await the era of a "social" judiciary, and the opinion of Judge Cahn, issued on July 18, 1980.

Under sex discrimination rules set by the Supreme Court, Judge Cahn told us, the federal government may not treat women differently from men unless it has an important governmental reason for doing so. Moreover, the Judge observed that Congress has, over the years, provided for an expanded role for women in the military services. The Judge therefore found it "incongruous" to believe that Congress would "constantly expand the utilization of women in the military, and on the other hand endorse legisla-

tion excluding them from a pool of registrants available for induction."
This despite the fact that Congress had just debated the matter, and had
decided that, indeed, it *would* exclude women from the "pool of registrants
available for induction." "It is difficult," said the court, "for us to accept
[these] inconsistent positions of Congress."[1]

Thus a federal district court overturned a century of government policy
on the draft, freshly debated and affirmed by Congress, and assented to by
the President. Just how it came to be that, in July of 1980, this accepted
policy had suddenly become "unconstitutional" was never explained. The
court did not tell us how it made the jump in logic from its belief that the
draft policy of Congress was "incongruous," or "inconsistent" with other
congressional acts, to its holding that it was "unconstitutional." Yet that
unexamined chasm represents the vital difference between the *opinion* of
three federal judges in Philadelphia concerning the results of congressional
politics, and the requirements of a written *Constitution*. All we got from the
court was its fastidious objection to Congress taking "inconsistent positions" in legislation concerning women, which Congress has every political
right to do unless there is a clear constitutional violation.

As a corollary to this "Philadelphia story" it should be recalled that
there was then before the states for ratification the Equal Rights Amendment. That Amendment, if in effect, would have had a bearing on the case,
as it might well have had on the draft registration act in the first place. It is
as though the Philadelphia district court had grown impatient with the
troublesome process of amendment provided by the Constitution, and had
decided that its own piecemeal, hurry-up brand of constitutional change
would be preferable.

The draft act ruling of the Philadelphia District Court was later reversed
by the United States Supreme Court,[2] but the moral of the story is the
same. If the Supreme Court can indulge in the joys of inventing new
constitutional requirements, why not the district courts as well? Other
federal district courts, such as that of Judge Frank M. Johnson, Jr., in
Alabama—who, as we shall see, rearranged that State's mental health and
prison systems—have shared the fun of tinkering with the Constitution,
and have found hearty approval for their efforts, both on appeal and
throughout the segments of society which approve of aggressive judicial
activism. It would seem that the Philadelphia District Court simply
guessed wrong about what sort of judicial caprice the Supreme Court was
indulging at the time.

What the Philadelphia case illustrates is the spectacle of lower federal courts—and state courts—making themselves at home with the habits learned from their Supreme Brethren in Washington. Judicial legislation for great social purposes appears to be very infectious among those who take upon themselves this function. If the Constitution of the nation, or of a State, must be destroyed to accommodate the new dispensation, so be it, so long as the intent is good and the goal laudable. This is the essence of a revolutionary condition. That such a condition exists in the American judiciary is cheerfully acknowledged by friends of the courts who believe it to be a good thing. Social commentator Adolph Berle, who rather liked revolutions—so long as they leaned to the left—stated in 1969 that one was taking place in the United States, and that "the revolutionary committee is the Supreme Court," while a year later Robert M. Hutchins described the Supreme Court as "the highest legislative body in the land."[3]

Two other commentators favorable to the radical innovations of the courts, Theodore Eisenberg and Stephen C. Yeazell, refer, almost in passing, to "the direction in which they redistribute power." They speak of "new forms of property," which are "increasingly found in the expectation of largesse from government on some continuing basis." Thus, "the new institutional litigation is merely one product of these new relationships." The same commentators, who are professors of law at the University of California at Los Angeles, offer the thought that "one must finally evaluate such litigation in terms of its ends rather than its means."[4] This comes very close to summarizing the view of all those who support the Court's interventionist course. It is that the ends of the policies which they and the Court support justify the means of their achievement. There does not appear in such commentaries evidence of any great concern for the fate of the Constitution, as it is subjected to continuous judicial amendment in the process. Amendment by judicial fiat, rather than by the means set forth in the Constitution, is simply one of the means justified by the supposedly laudable ends of judicial policy making.

Another commentator, Professor Owen Fiss of Yale University Law School, tells us that, "To my mind, Courts exist to give meaning to our public values, not to resolve disputes." He sees the judge as an official "empowered by political agencies to enforce and create society-wide norms, and perhaps even to restructure institutions, as a way, I suggest, of giving meaning to our public values." The special competence of the courts in carrying out this function lies "in the domain of constitutional values, a special kind of substantive rationality, and that expertise is derived from the special quality of judicial process—dialogue and independence." It follows, for Professor Fiss, that the endeavor of the courts to reconstruct institutions should be seen "as but a necessary incident of that meaning-giving enterprise, as an attempt by the judge to give meaning to constitutional values in practical reality."[5]

Nor is it necessary to speculate as to where these judicial Pied Pipers would lead us. Professor Arthur Selwyn Miller, another devotee of the cult, has quite boldly stated the goal. In a book advocating increased judicial activism, Professor Miller urges that the Supreme Court be transmuted into a "Council of State," or "Council of Elders." This novel governmental vehicle should "openly and avowedly" discard the traditional admonition that judges are to interpret, not make, law. To Professor Miller it is clear enough that the Constitution has to go. But that should not be a matter of concern, as candidates for the Council would be limited to those who "openly pursue the concept of human dignity."[6] And should there arise any question as to just what the new guiding star of "human dignity" requires, we may be sure that Professor Miller and his sympathizers will be standing by to provide ever renewable definitions in their modern and ever-evolving setting. The book reveals, and even revels in, an insidious rejection of both law and the democratic process which is endemic to the whole of the activist mentality, although not ordinarily so blatantly put.

Professor Archibald Cox, as solicitor general during the 1960s, had a good deal to do with persuading the Court to adopt some of its more radical constitutional departures. In a recent book Professor Cox has concisely described both the roots and the effects of these changes:

> In the 1930's a modest view of the judicial function in con-
> stitutional interpretation fitted the new generation's desire
> for progressive social and economic reform. The legislative
> and executive branches were engaged in the redistribution
> of power and the protection of the disadvantaged and dis-
> tressed. By the 1950's the political atmosphere had changed.
> The legislative process, even at its best, became resistant to
> libertarian, humanitarian, and egalitarian impulse. At worst,
> legislatures became repressive, in the libertarian view,
> because of the Cold War, increased crime, the fear of social

disorder, and, perhaps, the strength of established economic and political power.

The "libertarians," having lost their legislative majority, moved into the judicial arena:

> A majority of the Court under Chief Justice Warren came to be influenced by an extremely self-conscious sense of judicial responsibility for minorities, for the oppressed, for the open and egalitarian operation of the political system, and for a variety of "rights" not adequately represented in the political process.[7]

We are indebted to Professor Cox, riding boldly to rescue democracy from majority rule, for putting the matter far more compellingly than a critic could. The Supreme Court came to be dissatisfied with the constitutional institutions of government, with the social policy of the political branches, and with democratic principles in general. It felt secure in a superior vision, and proceeded to apply that vision to the body politic under the guise of constitutional mandate. The policies generated in that era, save for a few hopeful exceptions, are still applied by the federal judiciary today. These policies have been identified by Professor Phillip Kurland as "an all-consuming dedication to an egalitarian ideology, a wholesale limitation upon the powers of the states, a massive expansion of the Court's power," characterized by "a lack of workman-like performance in reaching results."[8]

Professor Kurland offers the view that the Court, having "accepted with a vengeance the task of protector of the individual against government and of minorities against the tyranny of the majorities . . . failed abysmally to persuade the people that its judgments had been made for sound reasons." Among the causes of this failure has been "a judicial arrogance that refused to believe that the public should be told the truth instead of being fed slogans and platitudes." The rather pathetic conclusion emerges that "many of the Justices were incapable of doing better. They fooled not only the public but themselves."[9]

United States Circuit Court Judge J. Skelly Wright subscribes flatly to the save-the-people-from-themselves view. "If the legislatures continue to neglect their constitutional responsibilities," warns the judge, "we can only hope the Court will continue to do the best it can to fill the gap."[10] The "constitutional responsibilities" referred to must be understood to mean the "problems" invented by a leftist elite which elected representatives have had the audacity to ignore.

It has seemed apparent to some that, if the drastic constitutional changes with which we are dealing were to come about, they should have come about through the process of amendment provided in the Constitution. Yet supporters of the Court's expansion baldly assert that since the process of amendment is politically difficult, other modes of change must emerge. The reason amendment would have been "politically difficult" in the areas under consideration is, of course, that, by all the evidence, such amendments would not have had the political backing either to be proposed or to be ratified. It is evident from the complex amending procedure provided in the Constitution, and from debates at the time of its adoption, that the framers never intended that constitutional amendment should be an easy affair. But the Court has decided otherwise.

The resulting judicial amendments have been achieved by a self-styled intelligentsia which believes itself to be more sensitive, more compassionate, and wiser than others. In his remarkable book, *Democracy in America,* Alexis de Tocqueville commented in 1835 on the intelligentsia, and in particular on lawyers, which would include judges. De Tocqueville observed that they believe themselves to be more intelligent than the common run, and that this leads them to a contempt for the "judgment of the multitude." In that respect they share the aristocrats' "secret contempt of the government of the people." We now observe that lawyers, especially those holding judicial office, are among the most zealous champions of change, and the most determined opponents of constitutional restraint. Ironically, de Tocqueville considered the judiciary "the most powerful existing security against the excesses of democracy." As Walter Berns points out, "Rather than look upon the Constitution as the permanent public law of the United States, providing constraints on all the branches of government," the judges have come to see it "as a kind of letter of marque authorizing them to sail at will among the laws, striking at any they find displeasing."[11]

Lest anyone think that the "revolution" will easily abate, here is a look at the future as envisioned by a Chief Judge of the United States Court of Appeals for the First Circuit, Frank M. Coffin. The remarks were originally made at the Boalt Hall School of Law, of the University of California,

Berkeley, in February of 1979. Coffin fears that the "judge-executive," as he terms judges who take on duties of running bureaus, agencies, or departments, will be impeded by traditional judicial practices. The remedy suggested is to adopt procedures which go beyond the examination and cross-examination of witnesses according to the rules of evidence, and to allow judges to achieve "broad participation and to receive data of any sort that might be helpful in devising workable solutions" in running institutions, redistributing social and economic goods, and in performing similar functions which he would see the courts increasingly undertake. The courts' problems, according to Judge Coffin, will be intensified by a rising population pressing against limited resources, and by ever higher expectations and personal demands. This, he believes, will lead to future litigation which will be increasingly class-oriented, structure-oriented, or institution-oriented. He even suggests that litigation may become "a first cousin to single issue politics—it is but a short step from an organization with a mailing list to a class action seeking judicial relief that previously was denied by the electoral process."[12]

Judge Coffin's test for this neo-Malthusian judiciary appears to be simply whether new techniques can be found to accommodate an ever expanded judicial power. He contemptuously dismisses the debate as to whether courts *should* exercise such functions as running in a "well-worn rut of conclusionary cliches." This "rut" could be avoided if we would only devote our attention to seeking out the devices which work to make the courts' jurisdiction ever more pervasive, says Judge Coffin.

Arguments posed in the terms advanced by Judge Coffin not only assume an ever-expanding role for the judiciary, but dismiss out of hand any questioning of that expansion. In denegrating challenges to the expansionist view as "conclusionary cliches," and in use of similar terms, proponents of an ever more radical judiciary are engaging in a process which should be understood. They are reducing a great constitutional debate to "buzz word" slogans, just as the Court has reduced the complicated problems of representative democracy to the mindless incantation "one man-one vote." Such slogans have a beat, a swing, a seductive rhythm which somehow reminds one of the moronic chants heard on the Berkeley campus of the University of California during the uproarious days of the Free Speech Movement. Sloganeering not only debases, and can demolish, our institutions, but it has the same effect on our thought processes. It is well to remember that thought control is the first and essential ingredient of any sort of totalitarianism. It is the foundation of the Platonic state and the opiate by which the Platonic Guardian dulls the minds of the masses.

There is good evidence that the most ardent devotees of radical judicial expansion mesmerize themselves in their all-encompassing attempts to mesmerize others. It is not unknown for judges, savoring their novel political functions, to look up from the feast, their lips thick with the exotic sauce of new-found power, and to utter plaintive cries against those who, by asking that the judges be held politically accountable for political decisions, are, the judges say, thereby "politicizing" the courts. It is astonishing what sympathetic response they get from editors of newspapers, writers in influential law journals, and professors in tenured law school chairs. All come galloping over the hill to the defense, flailing righteously against those critics who are simply telling it like it is—that the courts have "politicized" themselves.

Consider these acts of the federal courts as reported in a 1981 survey. In South Dakota, U.S. District Judge Donald Porter ruled that ranchers must stop using certain chemicals approved by the Environmental Protection Agency to combat a grasshopper plague. In Washington Judge Barrington Parker ordered the army to upgrade less than honorable discharges of some 10,000 Vietnam era veterans found to have been abusing drugs, on the ground that the compulsory urinanalyses used to determine drug abuse were "statements" covered by the Fifth Amendment protection against self incrimination. Judge Raymond J. Pettine, in Rhode Island, forced school administrators to allow a homosexual student to take a male date to his senior prom.[13]

The same survey revealed similar examples in state courts, emulating the new departures of their federal brethren. The California Supreme Court has held intelligence tests in schools to be unconstitutional. A Florida court struck down an attempt to make functional literacy tests a prerequisite for high school grade advancement and graduation. In Massachusetts the courts required Boston to keep its school system open although it had already exhausted its budget.[14]

In all of these cases, state and federal, the courts openly interfered in decisions which had been made by properly constituted political officials, elected or appointed. On the horizon are hundreds, if not thousands, of similar suits, asking the courts to rectify, amend, or rescind acts of the

TRANSGRESSION AND RETRIBUTION

political branches of government. If the matter involved only the United States Supreme Court, it might be hoped that changes in personnel would afford some relief. But judges abound, in both federal and state courts, itching to expand the embrace of their moral superiority, and to conceive new seductions by which to term the results law.

The nature and composition of the federal judiciary was the subject of a study by Peter Brimelow, an associate editor of *Barron's,* and Stephen J. Markman, general counsel for the Senate Judiciary Committee's subcommittee on the Constitution.[15] These observers found that, following the election of 1980, the faction of American politics which lost feared that its policies might be reversed. To prevent that, the losing faction set out to use the courts—not because it trusts the *law,* but because it trusts the *judges,* who are members of the same faction—to undercut the political results of that election. This anti-conservative faction, the "revolutionaries" responsible for a legislative judiciary, was strengthened and entrenched for years to come as a result of the 1978 Omnibus Judgeship Act. That Act, which Brimelow and Markman relate had been drafted and "kept on ice for six years" by the Democrats, awaiting a Democratic President, created one hundred seventeen new federal district judgeships, and thirty-five new circuit judgeships, all lifetime appointments.

Under the Act, the authors observed, President Jimmy Carter was able to appoint nearly half the federal bench, allowing for normal attrition as well, during his single term of office. This they characterize as "a court-packing scheme unparalleled in American history." Typical of these new appointments, according to Brimelow and Markman, is Henry Pregerson who, when asked what he would do if confronted by a conflict between his conscience and the clear letter of the law, unhesitatingly replied that he would follow his conscience. Stuart Newblatt asserted in his confirmation hearing that he was and would continue to be a judicial activist. Judge to be Nathaniel Jones denounced recent Supreme Court decisions limiting school busing as the "culmination of a national anti-black strategy," and labelled congressional busing legislation as reflecting policies that "drip with racist anti-city and anti-busing features."[16]

Beneath the arrogance of such views there lies also a gross deception. One of the chief goals of the judicial revolution has been stated as the establishment of a more "egalitarian" society. The goal seems noble, for who would argue with the idea of equality? Yet we soon discover that those who administer "equality" always do so on behalf of others. They never consider themselves to be among the "equal." Thus, while equality may sound like the most democratic of concepts, it never works out that way. George Orwell observed some time ago that, on such an *"Animal Farm,"* although all animals are equal, some are more equal than others. In communist societies commissars shop for every kind of luxury at sequestered stores, while their "egalitarian" proletariat finds no meat at the public market. In America the judicial revolution claims to do for its designated beneficiaries what it is assumed they cannot do for themselves.

The American judicial revolution is based on the implicit—and usually hidden—concept that democratic society cannot address its difficulties through its constitutionally authorized political system, and that a power wiser than average must therefore intervene for the general good. This is the essential ingredient of totalitarianism, from Plato to Stalin. In the end, under such a regime, not only is democracy lost, but so is equality. The truth is beginning to dawn that when the courts claim constitutional authority for what are plainly legislative decisions, they are indulging in an arrogant affront to citizens of common sense, possessed of a reasonable understanding of the workings of government. Arrogance is a virulent disease, and in high places one of the first signs of despotism. Its presence in judicial office has the most ominous implications for the country.

The symptoms of arrogance include a callous unconcern for the sensibilities and intelligence of others. An essential part of arrogance is a feeling of superiority, whether intellectual, moral, physical, or derived from some other standard of measurement. The necessary reciprocal of a feeling of superiority about one's own status or values is a belief that those who do not share them are inferior. It is assumed that these "others"—whoever they may be—are incapable of performing correctly, and therefore must be assisted, whether they want help or not—for their own good!

Anyone who believes that the abuses initiated in the Warren era are coming to an end of their own accord would do well to review the remarks of such federal jurists as Judge Coffin, and of their academic and professional apologists. The philosophy of judicial revolution is thickly embedded, not only in the federal judiciary, but in countless state courts, including powerful state supreme courts.

It is often difficult for an average citizen, or even for a serious student of government or history, to appreciate how much pleasure it can give a judge, how much downright fun it can be, to go hacking through the institutional arrangements of a political entity, lopping here, chopping there, moralizing, sermonizing, casting the bread of wisdom upon the waters of darkness, leading the children of the night into the glories of a new judicial day. And all without the bother of elections, campaigning, explaining oneself to the ignorant, or justifying one's actions to the rabble. The courthouse becomes a kind of clubhouse, and deals are cut there not at all unlike those which formerly emerged from the dreaded "smoke-filled rooms" of the old bosses.

If this seems exaggerated, let us look at a few examples.

13.   The Madhouse and the Judge

BRYCE HOSPITAL IN Alabama was a place of last resort, where a husband or wife, a child or a parent, was sent with the lingering hope that mental affliction might be treated, and the patient returned to a useful social life. To the several thousand patients committed by law to Bryce for treatment, the hospital was more akin to the "insane asylum" of old than it was to a modern facility where recovery might be expected. Bed linens remained unchanged until they reeked of sweat and filth; clothing remained unchanged until it was virtually alive; food was gray, greasy, and scarcely edible; vomit and excrement might remain untended to for hours, if not days. Mail remained undelivered, and inmates were virtually never allowed to use the telephone. Staff pay was low, their qualifications sometimes nonexistent, and there were those among them who, on occasion, found sadistic pleasure in administering enemas with a garden hose.

The State of Alabama was responsible for the funding, staffing, and operation of Bryce Hospital, and it might be thought that the state would also be responsible for effecting an appropriate remedy. But a suit was brought in U.S. District Court for the Middle District of Alabama contending that mental patients had a federal constitutional right to some minimal level of medical treatment. Judge Frank M. Johnson, Jr. was horrified at what he saw, and concluded that there could be no legal or moral justification for failure to afford adequate treatment. And so he proceeded to fabricate yet another link in the chain of activist constitutional mythology. "To deprive any citizen of his or her liberty," he said, "upon the altruistic theory that the confinement is for humane therapeutic reasons and then fail to provide adequate treatment violates the very fundamentals of due process."[1] The case was *Wyatt v. Stickney,* decided in 1971, and it was destined to be only the first in a series of cases in the course of which Judge

Johnson issued detailed standards of care and, in effect, ran the hospital through a committee set up by the court to administer the standards.

As the case developed, it became typical of hundreds of similar cases all over the country, cases in which, for one reason or another, courts took over, reorganized, and ran schools, police departments, Indian reservations, and regulatory bureaucracies.

To be meaningful, any legal right must have a legal remedy, to be applied by a court of law if the right is violated. If Jones runs into Smith's car and damages it, Smith must have somewhere to go to determine what the damages amount to, and to see that Jones is ordered to pay them. He goes to court, and the court must have the power to enforce its ruling, which it does by threatening Jones with contempt of court, and fine or imprisonment, if he does not pay the amount ordered. The courts have provided remedies for such rights as this for centuries. If new rights are devised, however, by legislation or by constitutional amendment, different remedies may be required. And if the courts themselves invent new "rights," pressure will mount relentlessly for the invention of new remedies to follow. That is what occurred in the *Wyatt* case, and in a host of similar cases. Courts which became involved in such cases were inexorably forced to take on functions far beyond their constitutional authority, and, ultimately, beyond their own capabilities to do what they were attempting to do as well.

In his first decision, Judge Johnson gave the defendant state officials at Bryce Hospital three months to file plans describing new treatment standards, and another six months to implement them. At the end of the nine-month period, when the defendants had failed to design or implement new treatment programs, Judge Johnson held a hearing for the purpose of formulating such plans. In attendance were the original parties to the suit, and a number of "friends of the court," or *amici curiae*—as they are still termed from the days when Latin tended to govern court proceedings—including experts of several varieties, whose help was deemed necessary in the formulation of new "standards" to run the hospital. More months passed before the standards could be formulated, but they finally were, and the court issued an order for their implementation.

Federal courts do not normally interfere in the operation of state institutions; they do not administer state laws, and there was no Act of Congress or other federal legal authorization for what Judge Johnson was doing. The only authority left to which he could resort in such a circumstance was, of course, the United States Constitution. And it will be no surprise to learn that the clause relied upon was the due process clause of the Fourteenth Amendment. To commit patients to Bryce Hospital under the conditions which the court found, said Judge Johnson, was a violation of due process. When the experts finished their work, new standards were adopted relating to clothing allotments, linen, telephone and mail privileges, money to be spent for food, and qualifications of the staff.[2] All of this was required, said Judge Johnson, by the Fourteenth Amendment of the Constitution of the United States.

When the suit against Bryce Hospital was filed in 1971, the State of Alabama had been spending approximately fourteen million dollars a year on mental hospitals. Judge Johnson's decisions were responsible for raising expenditures to some fifty-eight million by 1973. The financial resources of any governmental entity are subject to practical limitation. It is evident that quadrupling the amount a State is required to spend on mental institutions is going to have an impact on expenditures in other areas. For example, the same Judge Johnson, a few years later, found the prison system in Alabama to be substandard, and issued new decrees requiring more money to be spent on prisons.

When a court orders dramatic restructuring of a State's appropriations and expenditures in particular areas, it does not have available to it the breadth of information required to determine what needs are greatest, how priorities should be ordered, or what will be lost in one sector for a gain in another. Professor Nathan Glazer has questioned whether there might not have been a relationship between poor prison conditions later found by Judge Johnson and the huge expenditures he had previously required of the State on mental institutions. Beyond that, Glazer pointed to the probable effect of the new orders of the court regarding prison expenditures upon such other public functions as schools and colleges, the ability of police to control crime, or welfare expenditures.[3]

The final decree in the *Wyatt* case placed the mental health institutions of the State of Alabama under the direction of a seven-member Human Rights Committee, to enforce compliance by Bryce Hospital and similar institutions with the new "constitutional" standards adduced by the court and its expert advisors. The court also required that a new administrator be hired to implement the program at these institutions. The court was then asked to order specific money-raising measures to carry out its requirements, but it refused to do so, saying that it owed "judicial deference" to

the state legislature in such matters. Lest it be thought that judicial deference might be carried to excess, however, the court added that a lack of
funds would not excuse failure to comply. The State was left to shift for
itself, the court making it clear that it did not know where the money
would come from, nor did it care what the effects on other state programs
might be.

After a decade or so of this sort of judicial intervention in the operation
of state and local institutions, the Supreme Court may have developed
some misgivings. In *Youngberg v. Romeo,* for example, decided in 1982,
the Court established substantive due process rights of involuntarily committed mentally retarded persons to safety, and to freedom from bodily
restraint. The Court also held that there is a right to treatment, but refused
to be specific about the extent of such a right. The Court also declined to
find a right of "habilitation," as it has been requested to do.[4]

The *Romeo* case, taken together with similar decisions, caused one
activist commentator to complain that in those cases the Court has "given a
clear signal that it does not want the federal courts overseeing the operation
of public mental health or retardation facilities," and that these decisions
have "severely limited the ability of the federal courts to develop and
implement complex institutional remedies," or "to expand the rights of
institutionalized persons."[5] Perhaps. But if the Court in *Romeo* refused to
go as far as activists would like, it nevertheless invented new "rights"
which could easily serve to expand judicial power in the future.

Conditions at the Cummins Farm Unit of the Arkansas State Penitentiary
which confronted the federal district judge for the Eastern District of that
state in the late 1960s approximated those found by Judge Johnson at Bryce
Hospital in Alabama a few years later. Isolation cells were overcrowded and
filthy, there was no rehabilitation program, surroundings were "degrading
and disgusting," medical and dental facilities left "much to be desired,"
sanitary conditions in the kitchen were deplorable, inmates were given
insufficient socks and underclothing, they had no towels, and they were
required to sleep on filthy bedding. Racial segregation was practiced as
well. In Arkansas, inmates challenged the conditions under the Eighth
Amendment of the Constitution, alleging cruel and unusual punishment.

The Arkansas District Court first heard the case in 1969,[6] and found, as
the court in *Wyatt* would find, that conditions had not substantially

improved.[7] The court therefore ordered the State "to make a prompt and reasonable start" towards eliminating the conditions complained of, which, it agreed, amounted to "cruel and unusual punishment" prohibited by the Constitution's Eighth Amendment. The Eighth Amendment, designed to apply only against the federal government, was applied against the State of Arkansas. This was done through the now familiar device of claiming its provisions to be "liberties" of the sort referred to in the Fourteenth Amendment, and thus "incorporating" those liberties within the Fourteenth Amendment to apply against the States as well. The District Court in Arkansas, as did the court in Alabama, informed State authorities that lack of funds would not excuse failure to comply, and in addition threatened to close the prisons if conditions were not remedied. Some three years later the Eighth Circuit Court of Appeals held that state authorities had still not provided a "constitutional" environment within the prisons,[8] so that yet further proceedings were required. The courts were beginning to discover that issuing a decree in such cases is one thing, but that securing compliance might be quite another.

A similar scenario has been reported by Frank M. Coffin, Chief Judge of the United States Court of Appeals for the First Circuit.[9] The setting for that drama was Boston's Charles Street Jail, which had been used to house detainees who were not on bail and who were awaiting trial. In a 1973 decision the District Court in Boston held that conditions in the jail violated the due process rights of the inmates, and that the jail must be closed.[10] The original date set for closure was June 30, 1976. In the interim, the mayor and the city council could not agree on a site for a new jail, so that nothing had been done as the closing date approached. Hence, the District Court postponed the closing for an additional year. Nothing was done during that year either, so that after delay of a few more months the judge ordered the defendants to renovate another facility, City Prison, which was to serve as an interim facility until a permanent solution could be found. After still further delays, including appeal to the Circuit Court, the Circuit Court affirmed the decision to close Charles Street Jail, setting October 2, 1978 as the date for compliance. The Circuit Court did not require any particular plan, or the appropriation of money for a temporary or permanent facility, but simply ordered the Charles Street Jail closed by that date.[11]

As described by Judge Coffin, the City of Boston faced a chaotic situation, and the ultimate necessity of even more costly facilities, if it failed to act by the final closing date. The public faced the unhappy possibility that the jail might be closed and the inmates set at large, and the inmates continued to face housing in what the court described as ill suited, makeshift quarters. The parties settled at the eleventh hour on a program for rehabilitating Charles Street Jail, which led Judge Coffin to conclude that for his reviewing court, "thankfully," there was nothing more to be done.

"Regardless of the outcome of the litigation," Judge Coffin stated, "it is clear that the District Court's role in this drama, and our role as an appellate court, were not the traditional ones of finding facts, making conclusions of law, and reviewing the abuse of discretion or clear error of law. We were working with a different calculus."[12] Professor Nathan Glazer has furnished further insight into what that "calculus" has come to be, and what the reckoning is as a consequence. Conditions in the Boston jail were nowhere near as bad as those in Arkansas, or in Alabama. However, as Glazer observed, "once one has established as precedent that inhuman conditions in jails can constitute violations of constitutional rights, one can proceed along a chain of reasoning to find ever more conditions that may be considered violations of human rights." Hence, it is suggested that a judge accustomed to traveling in these realms can easily begin to see "other possibilities for improvement, far from the original violations that excited his outrage."[13]

As if to confirm these observations, the United States District Court for the Northern District of California in November of 1980 ordered state prison authorities to improve the conditions under which maximum security inmates are held, those inmates considered most dangerous in the system. They were to be given earplugs to mitigate excessive noise, to be granted access to educational television, to be permitted to shower three times a week, to be allowed exercise periods outside their cells, to be granted the same access to telephones as the general prison population, to be given access to law books, and to be provided conjugal visits. Prison officials responded, in appealing the order, that it would force them to mix together inmates "who hate each other and in the past have tried to kill each other," pleading that, "The court has assumed the role of Warden." Surprisingly, on March 13, 1981 the U.S. Court of Appeals for the Ninth Circuit agreed with prison authorities. The court held that, while constitutional requirements must be enforced, the lower federal courts "may not institute reform programs on their own under the guise of correcting cruel and unusual punishment."[14] The Supreme Court has added its own brake to the development of "prisoners' rights," deciding, for example, that prisoners have no right of privacy, nor any Fourth Amendment protection against unreasonable search of their cells or seizure of their property,[15] and that pre-trial detainees have no due process rights to contact visits with family or relatives.[16]

But such restrictions on judicial ingenuity as these would appear to presage no general trend. On the same day in 1954 that the Supreme Court decided, in *Brown v. Board of Education,* that schools in the states must be integrated, it also decided that they must be integrated in the District of Columbia, which is governed under provisions enacted by Congress.[17] As in the States, it was some years before anything much happened as a result. In 1966 Julius Hobson, a black militant, a prominent Marxist, and a resident of the District of Columbia, brought suit against school superintendent Carl Hansen, claiming that black children and poor children in the District were being denied their right to an equal education. In its first decision in *Hobson v. Hansen,* which came to be referred to as Hobson I, the court found several practices which it disallowed: the tracking system, which separated students according to ability, was found to result in unconstitutional segregation, whatever its motive; gerrymandering of school boundaries for racial purposes was proscribed; and the practice of allowing white students to remain in predominantly white schools if they contended that transfer would cause them "psychological upset" was prohibited.[18] Most significantly, the District Court found inequality of resources and expenditures between white and black schools within the District. This finding was to lead to the more interesting aspects of the case, as the drama moved onward.

Total expenditures per pupil were approximately twice as much in the more affluent schools as they were in the poorer schools within the District. Teacher transfers were voluntary, which meant that the newer teachers, assigned to effect integration of the faculty, and who were lower paid, went to the less desirable schools. Classes in the more affluent areas were perhaps three pupils smaller than in the poorer areas, further affecting cost per pupil. Voluntary busing had led to the movement of only about five hundred elementary pupils per day out of a total of more than eighty thousand pupils. As a result, Julius Hobson returned to court, and asked for an order enforcing Hobson I. This despite the fact that the District by then had an elected school board whose majority, and whose president, were black. In particular, Hobson requested that the court require equalization of per pupil expenditures.

What followed is sometimes referred to as Hobson II, and involved a series of legal and factual arguments of great intricacy and complexity. The almost automatic remedy for supposed discrimination in school districts, integration by busing, was rejected for the District of Columbia for the reason that the school population was so heavily black to begin with that moving the few white students would have accomplished nothing. A related fact, which the court seemed loath to recognize, was that, even if expenditures per pupil at the white schools averaged a little more than at black schools, there were too few white students in the District to make any significant difference even if equalization were to be required.

Nevertheless, the court's remedy boiled down to the remarkably simplistic remedy proposed by Hobson—equalization of per-pupil expenditure. This might have involved such criteria as expenditure per pupil on textbooks, school buildings, administrative staff, teacher salaries, or other measures, all involving great uncertainties as to the end result—whether the quality of education would in fact be improved. Cutting boldly through the unknown, the inexplicable, and the unpredictable, and reducing to an absurdity the oversimplified concept already adopted, the court issued a decree which rested on a single criterion. The court flatly required simply that per-pupil expenditure on teachers' salaries be equalized.

The results of the court's decree were not what anyone had expected or desired. Such programs as demonstration schools, special resource teachers, and other efforts at superior education were decimated. A "community school" program, in which certain experimental schools elected their own boards of education locally, and remained largely free from central administration, was virtually destroyed. Whites, then blacks, fled the district by the thousands, until enrollment fell to some sixty percent of what it had been in 1961. Professor Lino Graglis observed that by the 1980s "the Washington public schools had become a last resort for poor parents who could afford nothing else."[19] It is reported that even Hobson himself at last expressed dissatisfaction with the Court's final simplistic decree, and with the results of requiring rigid adherence to nearly absolute equality of expenditure per pupil on salaries throughout the District.[20]

The range of judicial intervention into state and local affairs is astonishing both in its depth and in its detail. School desegregation cases remain the most pervasive examples. Courts have determined which students will be assigned to which school, how teachers shall be selected, what security measures shall be adopted, where new schools shall be built, and, of course, who gets bused where. But the courts have ranged far beyond the schools. In Mobile, Alabama, a federal court ordered the city to scrap its form of government and replace it with a new one, on the ground that the three member City Commission, elected at large, precluded black voters from effective participation in the electoral system. The Mayor of Mobile asserted that this was the first time that the federal government had "told a free people what kind of government they must have." In Chicago, and in numerous other cities, federal courts have ordered affirmative action in the hiring of policemen.[21] Structural changes in state and local governments have also been required by federal courts to reform such programs as medical care, housing, disability assistance, and food and drug regulations.

It is important to recognize the difference between the ordinary sort of adjudication, which the courts have always carried out, and interventionist adjudication of the kind here at issue. Conventional adjudication usually involves private rights, and arises when one person sues another. The court decides the rights and liabilities of the two parties according to applicable legal precedents, legislation, or constitutional requirements. The hearing is an adversary proceeding, with both sides presenting evidence according to established rules. The result is a one-time judgment confined by the narrow issue presented. Finally, the role of the judge is passive, in the sense that it is his task to find the facts which bear on the dispute, and to apply those facts to relevant legal requirements—but not to act as prosecutor in seeking out alleged wrongdoing, or as legislator in inventing new remedies for newly found infractions.

The operation of courts in interventionist litigation is strikingly different. The suit is likely to have been instituted by a class of individuals, such as the blacks of Mobile, Alabama, and to be directed against a class of officials being sued, such as the entire government of that city. Rather than being a mere adversary proceeding between two narrowly defined parties, the interventionist suit encourages wide participation, perhaps with extensive *amici* briefs and argument, many expert opinions, and little if any recognition of legal precedent. The gathering of evidence is not confined to facts relevant to existing rights and liabilities between the parties, but is predictive in nature, as the court seeks to formulate a decree which will operate into the future, anticipating changed conditions. The court creates social policy in a legislative manner in framing the decree, and steps into the executive area in implementing it.

It seems fair to conclude that the overall effect of judicial intervention in the administration of social policy is to reduce the discretion, authority, and effectiveness of those properly charged with running the program under judicial scrutiny. A side effect of judicial scrutiny is to make the recipient of the service being provided suspicious of the existing administration, with the expected result of further reduction in effectiveness of service. We may be particularly skeptical of the reliance courts tend to place on expert testimony in such disputes. Such witnesses have been characterized by Professor Glazer as persons who "have never taught, guarded prisons, been engaged in the custodial care of the retarded, or attended to welfare patients."[22] Reliance on their testimony, however theoretically interesting it may be, introduces another negative tendency, which is to reduce the responsibility and authority of the worker in the field, in contact with those for whom the program was designed. A corollary result, not unexpectedly, has been to increase the power of the legal profession, and of the more theoretical professions such as psychiatry, social science, and psychology at the expense of the professionals who deal directly with mental patients, prisoners, and so forth.

Despite the theoretically broad base of a class action, and despite the often sweeping effects of a resulting court decree, most of the interventionist decisions are, nevertheless, narrowly based. When Judge Johnson forced a quadrupling of expenditure on mental institutions in Alabama, for example, there was no one present who was able to inform the court what effect that might have on other state programs. This means that power and authority within a State, which are clearly political matters, have been affected, and distorted, by the courts. Nor do the courts have the organizational capacity to collect information, to balance political interests, to predict accurately—or even to guess with some probability of being correct—what the final results of their decrees will be. Furthermore, they are not organized to carry out the administrative functions which they have frequently taken on in these instances.

Thus, in Hobson II the redistribution of resources based entirely on equalization of teacher cost per pupil ignored, at the outset, other aspects of expenditure which would affect the quality of education. It had the further deleterious effect of "levelling down," for the reason that the court did not have the authority to require new spending on teacher services. Had a redivision of the pie been accomplished through legislative processes, the redistribution might well have been accomplished by "levelling up," and by improving, rather than diminishing, the quality of education.

There is evidence from a number of studies that the courts tend to prefer single factor remedies, such as busing, or the per-pupil expenditure on teacher salaries adopted in Hobson II, in supposedly reforming the behavior of governmental institutions under attack. This is understandable, and follows from the traditional function of the courts in resolving simple issues presented by conventional litigation. It suggests that the courts, even when committed to interventionist policies, resist the full implications of the task. Courts are not legislatures, even when they try to legislate. They are not mayors, school superintendents, or prison wardens, even when they interfere in the running of a city or take over the administration of a prison or school system. And there is growing evidence that their decisions, and the consequences of their decrees, demonstrate their limitations in these respects.

There is another important way in which courts drastically affect constitutional law in these cases. It is what has been described as trivialization of rights. As put by Judge Macklin Fleming, of the California Court of Appeal,

> Trivialization sets in when the language of fundamental constitutional rights begins to be routinely used by the courts to justify judicial regulation of administrative decisions of the smallest moment—with the consequence that a sort of Gresham's law operates under which bad judicial decisions drive good ones from public notice. The result, as with the boy who cried wolf too often, is to give the entire body of constitutional law a somewhat inconsequential and frivolous cast.[23]

That is to say, when the number of showers, bedsheets, and telephone calls allowed to a prisoner becomes a "constitutional" matter, one wonders just what is this thing we have called a Constitution?

In brief, in these cases the courts have found themselves encountering problems of vision, of acquisition of information, and of management and control which are for the most part alien to the judicial process. Lawyers arguing the cases seek to define the "controlling issue" narrowly, in terms of the rights of their clients. This is standard legal practice, but has quite different consequences when the decrees which result are not limited by conventional court procedures. The remedy is often something like calling for a tactical nuclear strike against a hilltop pillbox containing two soldiers and a machine gun. The problem caused by the pillbox may thereby be remedied, but at the expense of an entire area being blown away, quite possibly including those who had called for the tactical nuclear strike.

But let us suppose for a moment that courts truly are seized of the facilities, facts and wisdom necessary to create a new social order. And let us further suppose that they are good at administering it as well. What a curious situation we then have! The courts ingest problems at one end of the judicial machine, sort them out and chew on them a bit, make new laws governing their solution, and spit these edicts out the other end into their own newly created administrative apparatus for application. Happily, if any question regarding the constitutionality of such a process were to arise, the courts would also be conveniently at hand to consider that matter as well!

The most amazing thing of all is that judges who conduct these affairs believe, or say so, that they are not legislating, or amending the Constitution, but that they are only "interpreting" it. Witness Judge Frank M. Johnson, Jr., having twice rearranged the financial resources and social policies of the State of Alabama, with consequences only dimly known to him, speaking in defense of his rakishly innovative adventures:

> In summary, it is my firm belief that the judicial activism
> which has generated so much criticism is, in most instances,
> not activism at all. Courts do not relish making such hard
> decisions and certainly do not encourage litigation on social
> or political problems. . . . The basic strength of the federal
> judiciary has been—and continues to be—its independence
> from political or social pressures, its ability to rise above the
> influence of popular clamor.[24]

Does anyone, including Judge Johnson, really believe this?

In reaching out as they have, it seems quite likely that the courts have created a judicial madhouse for themselves, which is as much in need of reform as any of the more ordinary madhouses to which they have devoted their amendatory zeal. But it is evident that the courts do not intend easily or graciously to excuse themselves from the feast of new-found power to which their appetites have become accustomed. The more artful course, instead, has been to solicit accomplices to the deed—persons and groups who see in expanded judicial power a means to advance their own causes.

14.   The Court Turns Up the Pressure

WILLIAM HENRY FURMAN had been convicted in the Georgia state courts of murder during a burglary, for which he was sentenced to death. Hearing his case on appeal, the United States Supreme Court informed the country, in 1972, that, contrary to the judgment of the State of Georgia, society had "almost totally rejected" the death penalty. Accordingly, in *Furman v. Georgia,* the Court held that the death penalties of the state of Georgia, and those of all other states—as then administered—were unconstitutional.[1] Although the Court did not quite go so far as to say that the death penalty *itself,* under all circumstances, was unconstitutional, it was widely thought to be after the *Furman* decision.

Then, a few years later, Troy Leon Gregg and a companion were given a ride by two men in their car. Gregg murdered them both, execution style, while robbing them. This was another Georgia case and Gregg, as Furman had been, was also sentenced to death—under a newly enacted Georgia statute. Gregg, like Furman, managed to carry his appeal to the Supreme Court, where it was decided four years after the Furman case, in 1976. Contrary to expectations, however, the Court, in *Gregg v. Georgia,* found the death penalty to be constitutional in principle, and the new statute of the State of Georgia under which Gregg had been convicted to be valid.[2] What can account for this remarkable reversal of direction by the Court in four short years?

The theory of the *Furman* case had been that the death penalty constituted "cruel and unusual" punishment, in violation of the Eighth Amendment to the Constitution. The death penalty had, of course, been commonly practiced in the Colonies before the adoption of the Constitution and the Bill of Rights, was practiced at the time of their adoption, and had been continuously applied since. In the face of such a history, it could hardly be seriously argued that the death penalty was "unusual." And if it were held to be "cruel," the standard of cruelty obviously had to have changed somehow during the two centuries of its practice. Yet there had been no change in the legal or constitutional criteria under which the death penalty had been allowable.

What had changed were the feelings of a good number of people. The fact is that, by the time Furman's case reached the Supreme Court in 1972, the death penalty had become a *cause celebre,* around which powerful interest groups had rallied both their passions and their support.

Furman's appeal had been carried to the Supreme Court largely by the Legal Defense Fund of the National Association for the Advancement of Colored People. But consider this imposing array of groups and individuals who also filed briefs with the Court in support of Furman and the NAACP: the list includes the governors or ex-governors of nine states, six correctional administrators and prison wardens, an ad hoc committee of psychiatrists for evaluation of the death penalty, the Synagogue Council of America, fourteen religious denominational councils or groups, a group representing the major religious councils of the State of West Virginia, the National Urban League, the Southern Christian Leadership Conference, the Mexican-American Legal Defense and Educational Fund, the National Council of Negro Women, the National Legal Aid and Defender Association, the American Civil Liberties Union, and the State of Alaska.[3] Hardly anyone spoke up for the prosecution.

When the Court came to consider the case of Troy Leon Gregg four years later, there materialized approximately the same anxious groups on his behalf as had appeared on behalf of William Henry Furman. But the lineup on the other side, supporting the State of Georgia, was considerably more impressive in 1976 than it had been in 1972. And behind the new lineup was the mounting pressure of public opinion, outraged at the 1972 decision, terrified by the rising crime rate, and determined to fight the Court on the issue. One result of the 1972 decision—virtually wiping out existing death penalty statutes on procedural grounds—had been the passage of new death penalty statutes in thirty-five States, including Georgia, designed to overcome the Court's stated procedural objections. In California there had even been a referendum, in which the voters had approved the death penalty by a two to one margin. Congress had added its support by passing legislation providing the death penalty for air piracy.

Invigorated by these developments the attorneys general of many of the

States which had passed new death penalty statutes after the 1972 *Furman* decision petitioned the Court to support the State of Georgia in the 1976 case of Gregg. In addition, the Court invited the then Solicitor General of the United States, Robert Bork, to participate. The individuals and the groups remaining in opposition to the death penalty, in these changed circumstances, were shown to be far less representative and authoritative than they had seemed to be four years earlier. The result was a change in the direction of the Court which amounted to a virtual about-face.

In a provocative book concerning these two Georgia cases—and related decisions involving the death penalty—Frank G. Carrington has concluded that the 1972 case was the result of a congeries of pressure groups acting on the Court as part of a concerted and well organized campaign to eliminate the death penalty. The 1976 case, the author believes, was the result of counterpressure from various groups that had been offended by the earlier decision.[4]

Carrington's book is but one of several illuminating studies which suggest that pressure groups have for some time operated effectively upon the courts, that lobbyists have helped direct judicial policy, and that militant, and sometimes small, minorities—usually invisible to the public—have had a part in fashioning constitutional changes to conform to their own particular goals and policies, regardless of constitutional mandates.

Most Americans would be surprised—even shocked—to think that the judiciary has become subject to such activities, which we normally associate with the political branches of government. But there is growing evidence that it has. Worse, it appears very likely that the Supreme Court has solicited such pressure group participation in the judicial process for the purpose of advancing the Court's own political goals, including the expansion of its own power.

The activities of pressure groups, as traditionally understood, consist primarily in trying to influence members of Congress, or of the executive branch of government, towards the goals and purposes of the groups. From their habit of buttonholing members of Congress in the halls and lobbies of the House and Senate, representatives of pressure groups came to be known as "lobbyists." The terms "pressure group" and "lobbyist" were introduced into the language of American politics with a certain aura of suspicion and distaste, which they still carry.

A major reason for distrusting pressure groups is that they tend to operate behind the scenes, without proclaiming publicly what their programs are, who their membership might be, or how much they have paid to whom, in what form, in order to further purposes which are often in themselves obscure, if not suspect. Legislation eventually was passed to require registration of lobbyists, the disclosure of certain aspects of their operations, and to regulate lobbying and pressure groups in other respects in the political sphere. Even though we know that politics is a process which includes horse trading and bargaining, we still want to know more about what is being traded, how the bargain came about, who gets hurt, and who gets helped, when national legislative policy is being formulated.

The time seems to have come to ask the same questions regarding pressure group activity in the judicial system. If pressure groups have been as ingenious and effective in the judicial as in the political arena, we are presented with yet another dimension of expanding judicial power. By the same token, we are faced with grave and unexpected questions concerning the judicial process. How are judicial decisions made, under what influence, and for whose benefit?

Various major interest groups are said to have been particularly successful in obtaining their goals through judicial intervention. The most active of these has been the NAACP. Others include the American Civil Liberties Union, the Commission of Law and Social Action of the American Jewish Congress, the American Committee for Protection of the Foreign Born, the Emergency Civil Liberties Committee, Jehovah's Witnesses, American Jewish Committee, Japanese American Citizen's League, Congress of Racial Equality, and Protestants and Other Americans United for the Separation of Church and State.[5]

These and similar groups may work for years to effect a well-thought-out national strategy of litigation, aimed at securing through the courts some special right or consideration which had not been obtainable otherwise. These groups often initiate their own litigation, in addition to shopping around for cases in progress in which they can intervene in various ways to advance their causes. When a pressure group files its own case, the timing can be coordinated for maximum effect. For example, the American Jewish Congress usually begins its objections to Christian celebrations in public schools well before such holidays as Easter or Christmas. Were such complaints to be raised during the holiday season, a much less favorable climate of public opinion might be anticipated.[6]

The largest of the interest groups maintain legal staffs, usually in Washington, and often in other major centers throughout the country as well. In addition to seeking out cases whose fact situations seem favorable to their cause, and to timing their own lawsuits in an advantageous manner, such groups may even await the death or retirement of Supreme Court Justices before pressing certain types of litigation, in the hope of more favorable results. The names of these organizations seldom appear in the titles of the lawsuits which they sponsor. Nevertheless, the financial resources and legal staffs of judicial pressure groups have been heavily involved in a great many of the revolutionary Supreme Court decisions of recent years. The school desegration cases are an excellent example of how the technique of pressuring the Court has worked.

Brown v. Board of Education,[7] the case which sparked the Court's current interventionist revolution, did not appear on its docket as a matter of chance. Rather, the case was what has been termed "the culmination of a classic case of litigation as a form of pressure group activity."[8] *Brown v. Board* was the title case of several cases from throughout the country which the Court considered at the same time, all of which were the product of litigation sponsored by the NAACP Legal Defense and Education Fund. It has been estimated that the *Brown* cases cost the NAACP some two hundred thousand dollars to prosecute in the early 1950s,[9] an amount which would be the equivalent of well over a million dollars at current costs.

The *Brown* cases had been preceded by a series of cases running as far back as 1938, in which the NAACP first attacked segregation in higher education through appeals to the Supreme Court. The object was to secure repudiation of the "separate but equal" doctrine which the Court had previously invented to evade the requirements of the equal protection clause of the Fourteenth Amendment. That doctrine, it will be recalled, held that "separate" public facilities might be provided for different races, so long as they were "equal."

There were two great advantages, from the point of view of the NAACP, in selecting higher education as its target in the opening attack against the separate but equal doctrine. The first advantage was that demanding equal education for Negroes—and by implication for all other minorities—had an innate appeal to the American public. This country has always been devoted to education, and has entertained an abiding belief that advancement is possible through education. The second advantage was that the appeal could be made in the more rarefied halls of academe without stirring up the hornets' nest of protest which was sure to occur if the same issue were pressed too soon in the public schools where everyone's children went.

In the first case of the higher education series, the State of Missouri had provided a law school for white students only. The Supreme Court required that it also furnish Negro students with a legal education, not simply pay their tuition to attend a law school in a state where segregation was not practiced.[10] In a later case, the State of Texas had taken a different tack, and had set up separate law schools for Negroes within the state, thereby hoping to conform to the requirements of the separate but equal doctrine. The Court found no trouble in agreeing that these schools were separate, but held that they were not comparable in the quality of their education. They therefore did not meet the second requirement of the separate but equal doctrine—they were not "equal."[11] Other cases reaching the Supreme Court involving graduate schools, libraries, and other facilities of higher education in the years before the 1954 *Brown* decision yielded similar results. The Court was making it increasingly difficult to show that separate facilities—in education, at least—were, in fact, equal.

During the thirty years prior to *Brown v. Board of Education* the NAACP achieved favorable rulings in some fifty Supreme Court decisions, and participated successfully in numerous cases in the lower federal courts as well.[12] The pressure built up by these cases against the separate but equal doctrine was designed to reach the point of explosion in *Brown v. Board,* and to furnish the Court a foundation for repudiation of that doctrine in the *Brown* case. The result, rather than affording a clear and simple repudiation of the separate but equal doctrine, was the beginning of a constitutional revolution, as we have seen.

In a related issue concerning public education, such pressure groups as the American Humanist Association, the American Ethical Union, the Synagogue Council of America, the National Community Relations Advisory Council, the American Jewish Committee, and the Anti-Defamation League of B'nai B'rith have come together to persuade the Court that prayers in public schools violate provisions of the First Amendment.[13] That Amendment provides that "Congress shall make no law . . . respecting an establishment of religion." Brief prayers at school might seem to have little to do with the "establishment" of a religion, yet the Supreme Court, prodded by various interest groups, has held that any form of prayer or religious service in public schools is prohibited.

The leading case resulted from action by New York State to require the reading of a very short prayer at school, devised to be so bland an invocation of the Deity as to be non-sectarian. This prayer, the Court said, nevertheless *did* violate the prohibition against the *establishment* of religion. One of the concurring Justices conceded that the inoffensive prayer did not appear to "amount to a total establishment of one particular religious sect to the exclusion of others," but felt that the precedent, if allowed to stand, might be used to support a broad establishment of religion at some future time. [14]

Many other cases have been decided under the "establishment" clause of the First Amendment, including cases prohibiting the purchase of textbooks for parochial school children, and the transporting of such children to school on public buses. An example is the famous "released time" case. One of the grand movers and shakers of earlier days in this field was Mrs. Vashti McCollum, who sued to prevent the public schools of Champagne, Illinois from releasing children for one hour during the regular school day to attend Protestant, Catholic, or Jewish religious instruction in the school building. Mrs. McCollum has been described as one of America's "most prominent lady atheists," although even in her case organized interest groups were playing a role behind the scenes. The pressures exerted in Mrs. McCollum's case were successful. The Supreme Court declared "released time" for religious instruction to be unconstitutional. [15]

State legislation dealing with religion must now pass a three-pronged test laid down by the Supreme Court in the 1971 case of *Lemon v. Kurtzman.* [16] Such legislation, to be found constitutional, "first must have a secular legislative purpose; second, its principal or primary effect must be one that neither advances nor inhibits religion; finally, the statute must not foster an excessive entanglement with religion." There have been countless appeals to the Court resulting from its "establishment" decisions, including one from a fascinating decision by federal district Judge W. Brevard Hand, of the Southern District of Alabama, *Jaffree v. The Board of School Commissioners of Mobile County.* [17] Judge Hand demonstrates, *inter alia*, that, under the Constitution, including the Fourteenth Amendment, the federal courts have no jurisdiction to hear such cases, and that the Supreme Court was wrong in "incorporating" the requirements of the First Amendment to apply against the states in the first place!

The *Jaffree* case was reversed by the Circuit Court of Appeals and, on June 4, 1985, the Supreme Court held that the Alabama statute at issue, which provided for a moment of silence, in which a student might pray silently if he or she wished, failed to pass muster according to the *Lemon v. Kurtzman* test. The reason being that the statute had no clearly secular purpose. The excellent constitutional treatise of Judge Hand had, of course, been tossed by the wayside and was not considered.[18]

There are indications that the possibilities inherent in pressuring the courts are coming to be understood beyond the liberal oriented groups who first exploited them. It may be that the Court's abrupt reversal of direction in the death penalty cases is a harbinger of the future, as pressure groups of a different ideological stripe catch on to the game. Business-oriented "public interest" law firms are beginning to spring up, and are filing lawsuits—and briefs as friends of the court—in the same manner that minority or environmental groups have in the past. An interesting development in this regard was the lawsuit filed by Senator Barry Goldwater and a block of conservative congressmen in an unsuccessful attempt to stop President Carter's cancellation of the defense treaty between the United States and Taiwan. Although that case was lost, who can say what similar pressure groups may be waiting in the wings to evaluate the results of future presidential appointments to the Court, preparing for the opportunity to persuade a new Court majority along different "constitutional" lines?

Operating in close conjunction with pressure group assaults upon the courts—and very much in favor of yet more frequent and effective assaults—have been fundamental changes in the rules which regulate the flow of cases into the federal court system. One sometimes hears the lawyer who has lost a case in trial—or more likely his frustrated client—assert, "We'll appeal! We'll go all the way! We'll take it to the Supreme Court!" Perhaps. Cases do get to the Supreme Court, and in increasing numbers each year. But not every case a losing lawyer or disgruntled client might want to get there does—not by any means. And not every type of dispute can qualify even for trial in the lower courts. In other words, not every controversy is the sort which is susceptible to judicial solution.

Over the years courts have devised tests by which to distinguish *legal* disputes from other kinds of disputes. These tests might be thought of as hurdles which anyone—individual, pressure group, or whoever—must jump who wants to get his case to court. If the hurdles are lowered it is easier to get over them; if they are raised it is harder. As a part of its constitutional revolution, the Supreme Court has significantly lowered—and in some cases virtually removed—five such hurdles.

In legal terminology these five hurdles are known as *case or controversy;*

standing to sue; justiciability; ripeness or mootness; and the *political question* doctrine. Each of these concepts, when applied, operates to exclude certain kinds of disputes from the courts. When the barriers thus posed are lowered or removed, more pressure groups are enabled to litigate, more cases come to the courts, more types of problems are considered, more excuses for legislating and changing the Constitution are advanced, and the judges accrue to themselves more power over society. Although each of these five concepts could be subject to exhaustive legal analysis, the essence of each is rather simple.

The first concept, *case or controversy,* is governed by Article III, Section 2, of the Constitution, which states, essentially, that the jurisdiction of the federal courts therein provided for shall extend to "cases" and "controversies" at law. What this means is that there must be a real dispute between real parties having a direct interest in the outcome, and dealing with actual facts and issues. The federal courts cannot hear disputes of a problematical or abstract nature. For example, they will not render *advisory* opinions as to how a case *might* be decided in the future, in a hypothetical fact situation, for the reason that the hypothetical situation does not involve a presently existing case or controversy.

Strictly speaking, the Court has not changed the constitutional requirement in this regard. It has not said that something other than a "case or controversy" can be heard and decided by the federal courts. But changes made in the other four concepts have resulted in types of cases and controversies coming before the courts which were never envisioned when authorization for the federal court system was provided in the Constitution. The underlying purpose of the "case or controversy" requirement is to *limit* the courts to consideration of truly *legal* disputes—disputes governed by existing law, or by the Constitution.

The Constitution says nothing about the other four concepts, but all of them—save for the political question doctrine—were well developed in the common law when the Constitution was written. It was assumed by the Founding Fathers that they would continue to apply as then understood, and thus operate to exclude from the courts questions not truly *judicial* in nature. But the Supreme Court has altered these four concepts significantly. In so doing, it has lowered the barriers to judicial accessibility. It has— though it has not said so, or changed the *words* in the Constitution— basically changed the *meaning* of what a "case or controversy" is. The result has been to subvert the assumptions upon which the constitutional requirement that courts hear only cases or controversies rests, and to let into the judicial system a floodtide of cases which has revolutionized the nature of judicial proceedings.

Let us consider the concept of "standing to sue." An individual—or an organization—cannot bring a case to court unless that individual or organization has standing to sue. That is, the court must recognize the party bringing the action as an appropriate party to do so, and must allow that party to proceed with the action. Otherwise that party does not have "standing to sue," and his action cannot go forward in the courts. Among other requirements, the party bringing the suit must have a substantial real interest in it, and must be in a truly adverse legal relationship to the person or entity being sued. The traditional interpretation of this principle was illustrated in a 1923 case in which federal taxpayers had challenged expenditures by the federal government for grants-in-aid to States cooperating in a federally sponsored maternal and infant mortality program.

The Supreme Court held that the interest of an individual taxpayer in the total federal budget was "comparatively minute and indeterminable," and that the effect of the particular expenditure challenged was "so remote, fluctuating and uncertain" in relation to the tax paid by the persons bringing the suit that those persons had, in effect, no standing to sue.[19] The same principle was applied in a 1952 case in which the Court refused to review a taxpayers' suit challenging the constitutionality of Bible reading in the schools of New Jersey. The Court said that Bible reading did not affect the *cost* of education, so that taxpayers had no standing to challenge the practice.[20]

Only ten years later the Court reversed itself on the principle that if the cost of a disputed practice were insignificant, a taxpayer could not contest the practice in court. The Court changed its mind, and decided that parents and their children challenging the saying of a prayer in school *did* have standing to sue, even though the prayer did not increase the cost of education, and even though the children were not required to participate.[21] In 1963 the same Bible reading question which had been decided in 1952 returned to the Court, and that question was also decided contrary to the prior decision. The Court held that the school children and their parents were directly affected by the laws and practices complained of—Bible reading at school—and that they therefore *had* standing to sue.[22]

To pressure groups itching for social reform, and thwarted in the political processes, these decisions were a red flag invitation to strident judicial activism. By significantly expanding its interpretation of standing to sue—that is, of who would be allowed to bring cases to court—the Supreme Court solicited ever deeper involvement of the judicial system in what are essentially political and social problems. But its enlarged definition of who could bring suit in court was only the beginning of the Court's destruction of the barriers which had traditionally kept non-judicial questions out of the courts.

The hurdle which has perhaps been most drastically lowered has been the hurdle of "justiciability." This involves, not *who* can sue, but whether the *court* can act in the case. The essential question of justiciability is whether the court has jurisdiction to *hear* the suit. Jurisdiction is a concept which can readily be understood by noting the etymology of the word: the roots are "juris," meaning "law," and "dictio," meaning "saying" or "speaking." The question of jurisdiction, then, is whether the matter presented is one to which the law speaks. Is it a matter which can be resolved in court? Is it *justiciable?*

In order for a case to be justiciable, there must be involved some claim or right under the Constitution—or under applicable law—which can be addressed by the courts, and in regard to which the courts can fashion a specific remedy. The court must have jurisdiction over the persons or property involved, and must have the *power* to interpret and to enforce the legal interest at issue. If one party to a lawsuit lives in a foreign country, for example, or if property sought to be returned is abroad, there would be a serious question of justiciability. But the revolutionary aspects of the Supreme Court's alteration of the concept of justiciability lie much closer to home. The outstanding example is the case of *Baker v. Carr,* which also involved the "political question" doctrine, a concept virtually inseparable from the question of justiciability. The political question doctrine has a rather interesting history, and because it is so intricately intertwined with justiciability, the two concepts can best be considered together.

In 1841 the State of Rhode Island was still operating under a charter from King Charles II, which included no provision for amendment. Dissident groups, mainly protesting the limitations on suffrage, formed a popular convention and drafted a new constitution, apart from the existing state government. Elections were held and a second government was chosen. As a result, in 1849 the Supreme Court was asked to decide which of the two governments was legitimate. Conceivably the Court could have delivered itself of an opinion on the subject. Instead, it did its constitutional homework, and observed that, among the powers of Congress, was the power to certify a State's congressional delegation. This, the Court held, was the manner in which the Rhode Island question should be resolved—let Congress, in exercising its political functions, determine which delegation should be seated. The issue was held to be a *political question*, and not a matter in which the courts could provide a remedy. It was, therefore, not justiciable.[23]

The Court had adhered to the political question doctrine established in the Rhode Island case as recently as 1946. But by 1962, in its decision in *Baker v. Carr*, the doctrine was for all practical purposes destroyed. In that case the Court entered into the "political thicket" of reapportionment, and virtually abandoned the idea that certain matters were *political* questions which should be left to the political branches of government. Thereafter nearly anything was held to be "justiciable" which a majority of the Justices might choose to consider. There was no longer a predictable requirement that the matter be governed by existing law, or by the Constitution. The judges simply began to change the law to fit the cases they wanted to decide.

The last hurdle, that of "ripeness or mootness," can be thought of as related either to standing to sue or to justiciability. A case is "ripe" for determination only if some *right* has been affected in regard to which the court can, at the time of the suit, fashion a *remedy*. If there is no present remedy available, the case is said to be moot. For example, in segregation cases the plaintiff may have been a child in school at the time a case was commenced, who had graduated or left school before the case could come before the Supreme Court for review. Under the ripeness-mootness doctrine the Court would say that no controversy remained, for the reason that no relief could be granted, in that the plaintiff was already out of school. Such a case would be declared *moot*, and would not be accepted for review.

Strict application of the mootness doctrine might well have altered considerably the presentation and determination of discrimination cases, and of similar cases involving not only the original plaintiff, but others who might find themselves in the same situation. Once the original plaintiff dropped out of the suit, for whatever reason, there was a danger that the entire action would be declared moot. But pressure groups wishing to press on with such claims—together with judges who were anxious to find justification for hearing them—turned to another legal device which satisfied their purpose, the *class action* suit.

The *five barriers* which traditionally had kept political and social issues—issues which were not truly *legal* issues—out of the courts had been lowered or demolished. Yet something *more* was still required to open the halls of "justice" to the most comprehensive of *social* questions. The class action suit was the device struck upon by courts and pressure groups alike to accomplish this purpose. The *class action* suit had been developed and used at common law, but—like the constitutional specifications of "case" or "controversy"—its use came to be *expanded* by the courts in a manner which changed the kind of case the courts would agree to hear. The expanded use of the class action suit can be illustrated by returning to our previous example of mootness—the case in which the child who originally alleged discrimination has since left school, so that no relief can be granted, and whose case is therefore declared to be moot.

If the same kind of suit is originally filed, not only on behalf of the child presently in school, but on behalf of all children similarly situated, the action can be made virtually perpetual. The idea is that, whatever *individual* students might drop out of the suit, for whatever reason, all of the others in a similar situation—whether individually identified in the original suit or not—remain. That is what is now done in a typical class action suit.

Once the courts accept such a class action suit, it does not make any difference if the original plaintiff graduates or leaves school. The rest of the "class"—not referring to the class in school, but to other students also allegedly discriminated against—remains active in participating in the suit. A live "case" or "controversy" remains to be determined, the matter is "justiciable," the rest of the class has "standing to sue," the case does not become "moot" but remains "ripe" for determination, and it can proceed on appeal no matter how long it takes.

Class action suits, largely carried on by pressure groups, are like waters from the Fountain of Youth to otherwise dying causes. Such suits have been immensely successful in combating discriminatory practices, particularly in the southern states. They have also been utilized to achieve high damages in consumer fraud actions—where everyone who bought a product under attack is theoretically joined in the "class" undertaking the suit—in job discrimination suits, and in many similar actions.

But the inventiveness of the courts—in partnership with the interest groups seeking to expand their own influence through expansion of the power of the courts—was not quite exhausted. Having altered or eliminated the five former barriers to judicial inquiry, and having expanded the class action suit to encompass much that might not yet have been included in the judicial embrace, the Court appears to have feared that some constraints still remained. The doors of the judicial palace had to be flung open the last few degrees to accommodate all true "friends of the court."

The final device hit upon to allow and even to entice full pressure group involvement in the judicial process was an expansion of the use of the *amicus curiae* brief. Under the rules of the Supreme Court, organizations or individuals not a party to the original suit may in some circumstances be allowed to file briefs in support of one or the other of the principal parties. Under current rules, consent is often given by the Court to file *amicus* briefs where the applicant claims an interest in the decision, or where the brief to be filed presents arguments or other material which would not otherwise come to the attention of the Court. This practice vastly expands pressure group involvement in the judicial process, by allowing pressure groups to select cases by which to advance their purposes without themselves having to wait for an opportunity to initiate their own litigation.

Among the most active organizations in using the *amicus curiae* brief have been the American Civil Liberties Union, the American Jewish Congress, the AFL-CIO, and the National Lawyers Guild. An excellent example of the use of the *amicus* brief was seen at the beginning of this chapter—the long lists of dignitaries and organizations filing such briefs in the death penalty cases, *Furman v. Georgia* and *Gregg v. Georgia.*

All of these changes in what might *seem* mere technical requirements of the Court, and which have remained all but unknown to the general public, have allowed pressure groups to bring to bear their very considerable resources in selecting test cases, and in prosecuting those cases through the court system to the Supreme Court. At the same time many, if not most, members of the general public who might be affected never know when a case involving their interests is working its way through the court system. They lack the resources, the expertise, and the access to basic information concerning court activities which pressure groups keep constantly at their fingertips. Parents interested in neighborhood schools may know nothing of judicial action in regard to busing until they are told, after the case is all over, that they now have to put their children on buses to be taken to some other part of town to school. Citizens favoring the death penalty or prayers at school may know nothing of judicial action in these areas until the Supreme Court announces its decision, and no chance remains to affect the outcome.

To counter the revolutionary effect of changes in these procedural con-

cepts, some southern states passed legislation seeking to prevent pressure
group organizations from instituting litigation, or from sponsoring litigation already in process. Those statutes sought to deny interest groups
standing to sue in such cases. The legitimacy of these state statutes was
challenged by the NAACP, which received a favorable ruling from the
Supreme Court in the 1963 case, *NAACP v. Button*. [24] There the Court held
that the NAACP objectives were not a technique of resolving private
differences, but a means for achieving the lawful objectives of equality of
treatment by all government—federal, state, or local—for members of the
Negro community. The Court added, significantly, that such action "is thus
a form of political expression." Leaving no doubt about its *political* interpretation, the Court asserted that, "For such a group, association for
litigation may be the most effective form of political association." [25] The
state laws at issue were therefore declared to be unconstitutional. Whatever
one may feel about the goals of the NAACP, these statements of the Court
are as direct an admission as could be imagined of the *political stance* the
Court has adopted, and of the clearly political *consequences* of its decisions.

A disturbing aspect of opening the judicial process to types of action
which formerly would not have been entertained by courts has been the
sheer *quantity* of cases which has resulted. There has been an immense
increase in litigation of all kinds. The courts have seemingly invited anyone
with a grievance of any sort to come in and try his luck. Judge Ruggero J.
Aldisert, of the Third Circuit Court of Appeals, has suggested that this
rush to the courts is symptomatic of a change for the long term which has
serious implications. Half in jest, half in earnest, he has projected the
increase in federal court cases between 1960 and 1974—which was
approximately sixty percent—to the year 2010. By then the caseload, at
the same rate of growth, would be such as to require 5,000 federal
appellate judges, whose opinions would fill 1,000 *volumes* each year. This
compares to approximately 170 appellate judges today, and some 600
district court judges. Judge Aldisert sees this engulfing tide of lawsuits as
resulting from demands of new litigants for judicial resolution of problems
that have traditionally been accommodated by the political branches of
government—the legislative and executive—or by private entities. [26]

Judge Aldisert suggests an even more disquieting result of the vast
increase in pressure group litigation. Some of the more skeptical members
of the judiciary, he tells us, are saying, "Scratch the surfaces of coalitions

and you will find more legal and public relations professionals with healthy fees than private citizens sincerely persisting in the causes."[27] If this is true, the Judge has pointed to yet another hidden factor in the shaping of constitutional policy. He has indicated that there are *pressure groups behind* the *pressure groups*, pushing on for yet more legal and constitutional innovations. There exists in such a chain of events the possibility of a "hidden government," far more difficult to detect and regulate than any traditional type of political pressure group operating in the legislative or executive arena.

Martin Shapiro, Professor of Law at the University of California, Berkeley, has observed that it is *marginal* groups, who find it impossible to gain access to the political branches of the government, and highly *organized* groups who may have lost out in the political branches, which the Court presently tends to serve. Thus, the Court may be considered a clientele agency, with these groups as its principal *clients*. Shapiro fears that, as a result, the Court "exhibits the characteristics of other agencies of government. It is subject to lobbying by a wide range of groups, some of whom find it essential, others merely a supplementary source of representation." Shapiro goes even further, suggesting that "if it wishes to act effectively in the long run, the Court must reserve its major effort for its particular clientele."[28] It is Shapiro's thesis that the opinions of the Court in supporting its clientele groups enhance their standing and power, and that these groups, in turn, then support the Court.

In an even more alarming analysis, Professor Shapiro has carried his investigation of courts and pressure groups a step further. There is evidence of what he terms an "iron triangle" of interaction among the federal *courts, pressure groups,* and agencies of the federal *bureaucracy*. The tendency is for agencies to anticipate the policy views of the courts in reviewing their actions, for the courts to promote the legal positions of the pressure groups, and for the pressure groups to use the protection and promotion of the courts to further their goals with the agencies.[29]

The result is a closed system in which major policy questions are resolved through a court-interest group-agency accommodation over relatively long periods of time. This can have serious repercussions on national *policy*, and upon political *responsibility*. The process, Shapiro concludes, tends to create single issue political movements. A major result of the single issue movement is diminution of the control the President has over government policy. In the end there is a further *fragmentation* of political responsibility, and a further obscuring of the sources of political power and decision making. Neither of these results is conducive to responsible democratic government.

In his provocative book, *Disabling America,* Richard E. Morgan suggests that hidden interest groups have played a major, perhaps decisive, role in the recent constitutional revolution. School busing, Morgan finds, "was foisted on a nation taken unaware by a small set of interlocking interest groups, judicial, academic, and bureaucratic idealists intoxicated by the rhetoric of governmentally managed social change."[30] Morgan agrees that the recent Supreme Court agenda could never have commanded a majority in the country, and still does not. Rather, he sees what he terms the "rights industry" as having appeared "armed with an impressive constitutional rhetoric, operating through courts and administrative agencies to create rules and regulations in the empty policy space between majorities, and then saying, in effect, to Congress and the country, 'come get me if you can.' "[31]

Arthur Bentley, as long ago as 1908, suggested that the judicial branch of government is as susceptible to group pressure as are the executive and legislative branches. Researchers Karen O'Connor and Lee Epstein have recently confirmed that this is so, and that, moreover, group pressure has been exercised on the courts far more pervasively, and for a much longer period of time, than had previously been supposed. They note that, by 1968, "those exploring the role of interest groups in litigation had well-documented the pervasive role that particular interest groups played in the judicial forum," adding that research had by then "indicated that politically disadvantaged groups used either *amicus curiae* briefs or test cases to influence the Supreme Court's policy-making in highly salient areas of the law."[32]

O'Connor and Epstein found that, of 306 important constitutional cases studied, from fifty to sixty percent or more were sponsored by organized groups. Even more interesting was their finding that, in cases sponsored by such groups, other interest groups had filed *amicus* briefs in nearly forty percent of them. In all, the authors conclude that "the majority of cases resulting in important policy declarations were the product of organized interests."[33] The authors also found that interest group use of the courts "has been a common method of lobbying employed by interest groups to affect policy throughout the Court's history," and that such activity is "not a phenomenon idiosyncratic to the decades of the 1970s."[34] Interesting, however, was their further observation that such activity had reached a peak in the Burger Court era, indicating that more groups are catching on to the idea.

A great deal more investigation is required before we can fully understand what the results of pressure groups upon the Supreme Court and the federal court system have been. But it begins to appear that the vast *reallocations* of public *resources* and political *power* which have been ordered in recent years by the Supreme Court have sprung in significant degree from *hidden*—or at least obscure—*pressures* brought to bear on the Court. These pressures have helped to make of our Constitution something which formerly it was not. Pressure group ingredients, unknown to the public, have been churned through the judicial process to emerge at the other end as freshly minted "constitutional law."

It is clear, at the very least, that pressure groups have come to play a much greater role in judicial policy making than has been generally recognized. The courts have manipulated their own internal workings to make it easier for the political and social interests they have chosen to serve to gain access to their processes. Barriers which once existed to deflect and set apart from the courts disputes not appropriate for judicial consideration have been weakened or swept away by the Supreme Court. The chief beneficiaries have been well organized pressure groups, aware of these crucial changes, fully prepared to take advantage of them, and perhaps even implicated in inducing the changes in the first place.

The destruction or weakening of the limiting concepts which formerly governed standing to sue, justiciability, ripeness or mootness, and the political question doctrine have radically altered the type of *case* or *controversy* which the courts will now entertain. Heavy use of the *amicus curiae* brief and of the *class action* suit by pressure groups has greatly accelerated this process.

Barriers which once prevented non-judicial questions from reaching the courts also prevented the courts from aggrandizing their own power by invading realms not contemplated for them in the constitutional scheme. The barriers which have been *destroyed* were an integral part of the system of *separation* of *powers* and checks and balances which was built into the Constitution. Their removal has been instrumental in allowing clandestine access to the judicial process by favored groups of the Court, and in expanding judicial power into areas reserved to politics by the Constitution.

In all of this, there is at least one thing of which we can be certain. If the Court has been seduced by siren calls from without, the Court itself is guilty of putting on its finest silks, applying its most fetching perfumes, and leaving the door unlatched. It has been said that the history of a legal system is the history of the demands made upon it. It seems quite likely that it may also be the history of the demands solicited by the system itself. The demands upon the Court during the past quarter-century have been both radical and intense. The reason, in no small part, is that the Court itself has turned up the pressure.

15. Social Fallout

THE UNITED STATES Supreme Court, in conducting its affairs, cannot avoid adopting a stance, setting a tone, or creating an aura. There is a priestliness about the Court, and it plays the role of exemplar, whether consciously or not, and whether or not the Justices would have it that way. In the early days of the American Republic, Alexis de Tocqueville observed that in this country social problems tend to become legal problems. It may also be that the process works in reverse: that court decisions devolve back into society as political and social problems. Law and the courts play a role in American society unique to the Western world. The final and supreme enunciator of law, the Supreme Court, exerts an influence throughout our society beyond that of the highest courts in other countries. This chapter offers some examples, and some speculations, as to how recent Court actions may have affected the way we feel about ourselves, and our expectations from society, not only by the decisions reached, but by the examples set.

The decisions of the Supreme Court are an important part of this country's response to its total environment, national and international. The work of the Court becomes a part of the texture of world society, and helps to determine whether the pattern for existence shall be of law, or of lawlessness. In recent years, throughout the world, the tide has run strongly towards lawlessness—either the random lawlessness of rightist dictatorships, or the much more insidious, purposeful, and dogmatic lawlessness of communist dictatorships. Freedom, for which law is an indispensable underpinning, is a battered concept in most of the world today.

If the world about us seems to be in a state of disintegration, so also in our own society we have been buffeted by winds of internal dissolution, and have seen basic institutions questioned or rejected at an unprecedented pace. The presidency, once strong and vigorous, has suffered assassination and resignation, and, at least in the years between the death of President Kennedy in 1963 and the election of 1980, failed to remain the rallying point of national will and policy which it once was. In such an environment the idea of law, and the stability law provides, might have served as the inspiration for a renewal of faith in our institutions. The courts might have provided a steadying course through turbulent years, and a haven of stability in a maelstrom of social upheaval. But that is not what happened. Instead, beginning in 1954 with the school desegregation case, *Brown v. Board of Education,*[1] the Supreme Court inaugurated the judicial revolution which was to characterize the Warren era. Beginning with the *Brown* case we have, in addition to other onslaughts which the country has sustained, experienced an unprecedented attack on our institutions by the Supreme Court as well.

Since 1954 we have been constantly told by the Court that not only our institutions, but our behavior, are unacceptable by the Court's standards, and that both are, therefore, unconstitutional. The Court's attack has been directed against such critical elements of society—the home, the schools, morality, representative political institutions, criminal justice—that it may be justifiable to characterize it as an attack against society itself. That, after all, is the essence of a "revolution." The symbolic victim of the Court's attack has been the Constitution, once the guardian instrument of American democracy. An essential instrument of the Court's revolution has been its repeated distortion of the Constitution through "interpretation" in order to justify its own revolutionary fervor.

Let us consider what social repercussions these judicial assaults upon our institutions may have had, given the setting in which they have occurred. What attitudes or actions have been stimulated? What hopes or fears have been engendered? Do Americans look at themselves and their country differently as a result? Do they have different expectations of their government and of other social institutions? Admittedly there is no ineluctable line of causality running from Court decisions to any mathematically inevitable societal reaction. But there are some interesting indicators.

One of the most egregious elements of the judicial revolution involves administration of the criminal justice system, particularly in regard to the use of evidence said to have been obtained illegally. It appears to be undisputed that, as Court decisions have progressed from the elaboration of one esoteric rationale to another—each designed to protect the accused by excluding evidence of his guilt—the rate of violent crime has been rising dramatically. This has occurred not only in the cities, but in the suburbs, and even in rural areas. We do not know with certainty that the Court's changes in the criminal law and the rising crime rate represent precise cause and effect phenomena. But there is some intriguing evidence as to how people feel about the matter.

A typical report in the *Los Angeles Times* demonstrates widespread fears among adult Americans concerning the possibility of their becoming victims of violent crime.[2] Fifty-five percent of women fear being raped; twenty-four percent of the population fears being beaten up; twenty-three percent worry that they will be robbed; seventeen percent fear that they will be murdered. The same study shows that forty percent of all Americans feel unsafe in their everyday environments—their homes, neighborhoods, business districts, and shopping centers. Over half of those interviewed keep guns as a result. Eight out of ten feel that the criminal justice system is ineffective, while nearly two-thirds say that police should be given more power to question suspects.

An equally interesting question concerns the perception of the potential criminal regarding the nature and consequences of his acts. We seem to know very little about this, although *Chicago Sun Times* columnist Roger Simon has furnished some provocative thoughts. Simon reiterates the generally accepted statistic that half of all violent crimes in America are committed by juveniles from ten to seventeen years of age. These are not "kid stuff" crimes, but murder, armed robbery, and rape. One of the challenging aspects of Simon's report is that such crime is by no means confined to the ghetto. On the contrary, there is evidence that much of it occurs in the middle class suburbs. Even more interestingly, the evidence is that middle class parents go to great lengths to hide such crimes, and that many crimes therefore go unreported, and unpunished. Simon's column is directed primarily at hidden suburban juvenile crime. But the moral he draws seems generally applicable. It is that, when parents do nothing, the children who commit such crimes learn a lesson: "they learn they can get away with it."[3] Is the lesson any different when the criminal courts become a "revolving door" from crime to technical deficiencies to release?

A *Los Angeles Times* reporter writes of overhearing the following conversation at the Farmers Market in that city, relating to a gang of young robbers reportedly at large in the San Fernando Valley:

"They could catch them if they really wanted to," one man said.

"It wouldn't make any difference," another replied, "The judge would just give them probation."

The reporter noted that there was no argument, and that often there is not when such a conclusion is drawn.[4] What results might be expected, one wonders, from a developing belief that crime will go unpunished, or that the punishment, if any, will be relatively light?

One answer to such questions, as he saw it, was furnished by the Sheriff of Colusa County, California, in February 1981. He resigned, saying that he found it no longer possible to work within a system which the public now rarely respects. He described a judicial system going "steadily downhill." A veteran of seventeen years in the sheriff's department, and Sheriff since 1974, he charged that, "We now have a high court [in California] that has become a monster that devours all common sense and makes guilt or innocence a secondary issue. I have seen criminals go free, not because they were innocent, but because of the procedure used when handling their case." In the departing Sheriff's opinion, the courts have created "a legal farce that becomes more and more unreal every day."[5]

The Sheriff's opinion was echoed in the resignation, in the same year, of a twelve-year veteran judge of the California Court of Appeal. Justice George E. Paras stated that he could no longer serve "under the domination" of the state's Supreme Court. Justice Paras described that court as "an authoritarian body which rules our state like a little junta, exercising little regard for precedents, statutes, constitutions or the will of the people." Two other California judges also resigned at about the same time, stating similar reasons.[6]

Speaking before the American Bar Association in February of 1981, Chief Justice Warren E. Burger said that the United States is "approaching the status of an impotent society" because of its inability to stop crime. The Chief Justice termed crime a "day-by-day terrorism" which infects every large city, making its citizens "hostages within the borders of our own self-styled, enlightened, civilized country."[7] In the face of these realities the spectacle of endless appeals, technical acquittals, and early paroles, even of those convicted of the most vicious and violent crimes, continues. The *Los Angeles Times* has suggested editorially that there are cases in which even those considered unlikely to commit another crime should not be paroled, where the crime for which they were convicted was particularly heinous. "A longer prison term," the *Times* believes, "would serve as a warning to other potential offenders that serious crimes bring serious consequences, and that society's first duty is to protect the innocent."[8]

Another area of intense reaction to court decisions has been in the sensitive matter of pornography. Pornography may be difficult to define, and perhaps even more difficult to control, as judges have sometimes alleged. Yet state and local governments managed to keep it out of the public eye until prohibited from doing so by the courts. Some would say that there is no need to control it, while others would contend that when court decisions thrust rows of pornographic publications onto every corner newsstand, and allow every other sort of pornographic entertainment, some social result will follow. An example arose a few years ago in Los Angeles. That city had passed an ordinance requiring "adult" picture arcades to close during the early morning hours. The purpose was to prevent patrons from masturbating in the arcades, thus intensifying health and police problems. Excretia also appears to have been involved. The case went to the California Supreme Court. In a four to three decision, the Court, in an opinion written by the Chief Justice, found that the ordinance infringed upon the First Amendment right to free expression. The majority felt that, "While this governmental purpose may be laudable, the means selected for its accomplishment fail to meet the strict standards required by the Constitution."[9] One wonders whether it ever occurred to Thomas Jefferson that the prohibition of public masturbation during a pornographic display might impair freedom of speech.

A more serious consideration is the relationship between violent erotica and violent crime, particularly rape. A study of the National Pornography Commission in the early 1970s concluded that there was no link between pornography and violent sexual acts. A more recent study by Dr. Edward Donnerstein reaches quite the contrary conclusion. His study indicates that after seeing scenes where a stronger male attacks a weaker female, sexually and violently, men are more apt to endorse rape, and to view it as a non-violent act. He suggests that this kind of pornography leads to "an incredibly unrealistic view of what aggression and rape are."[10] A new presidential commission, appointed in 1985, reached similar conclusions.[11] In the meantime, there is little indication that the courts, in virtually endorsing pornography, have any idea at all as to what results might follow, or have even thought about it.

In the view of Professor Wallace Mendelson, in such matters as crime and pornography, and in other areas as well, the courts not only have failed to convince the public that their views are sound, but have also raised difficult enforcement problems. These problems tend to breed lawlessness in policemen and other law enforcement agents who ignore court requirements when they sense that the community sides with them, and against the courts. Mendelson warns that by "ignoring or discounting deeply felt fears of a crime ridden society, the Justices invite disrespect for themselves and the law."[12]

Writer Thomas Sowell has attacked the entire basis of judicially inspired social reforms. Sowell characterizes the courts, as well as the federal bureaucracy, as having set up a "caretaker industry" which is "essentially a denial of other people's humanity." Whether or not one agrees with Sowell, his conclusion is thought provoking. "It is a healthy sign that those assigned these sub-human roles have bitterly resented it," Sowell feels, though he warns that "it may ultimately prove a social and political catastrophe if their anger at judicial and bureaucratic heavy-handedness finds a target in Blacks as scapegoats."[13]

Another example of social fallout from activist court decisions is the idea that there is a judicial remedy for every sort of difficulty. This idea has led to extensive filing of a new type of lawsuit, concerning "disputes of the heart." In one such case, Tom Hansen, a man of twenty-six, sued his parents for $350,000 because he objected to the way they had brought him up. In another case a woman sued her husband for $35,000 for failing to carry out his husbandly duty of cleaning the snow off the sidewalk, after she slipped and broke her pelvis. She says, however, that she still loves him and does not believe the suit will create any problems. A rejected suitor has sued his ex-fiancee to recover the expensive tokens of his love. Some states prohibit such suits, and the case of Tom Hansen was thrown out of court. There are other states in which the courts seem more receptive, even though courts everywhere are heavily overburdened.[14]

Most courts, state and federal, criminal and civil, have a huge backlog of cases. In many state courts civil actions cannot be set for trial for as many as two to four years after they are filed. A judiciary which is overburdened, or which overburdens itself by soliciting yet more lawsuits through judicial activism, can create serious social repercussions for that reason alone. Commentator Richard Y. Funston observes that a lack of appreciation for the institutional limitations of the judicial system, leading to increased opportunities for retrial and appeal, has contributed to an "alarming backlog of criminal cases." He reminds us that the guarantee of the Sixth Amendment of "a speedy trial" has more than one purpose. The public, as well as the accused, has an interest in speedy justice, in that justice delayed may be justice subverted, by the accused as well as by the state.[15] Former Chief Justice Burger has expressed similar views. Endless motions, appeals, and retrials, often based on the most specious of technicalities, not only further burden overworked courts, but they are also the stuff of which such people as the resigned Colusa County Sheriff fashion their disgust.

New Hampshire Supreme Court Justice Charles G. Douglas III reports the prospect of a declining confidence in the federal judiciary as the courts proceed to take over the administration of more schools, prisons, and mental health institutions. The difficulty, Douglas suggests, is that the courts will fail to solve all of the problems presented through federally applied judicial "wisdom." "The new role of a federal judge," says Douglas, "is that of the power broker between contending interest groups. He then appoints masters and experts to carry out voluminous judicial decrees that read like a chapter out of the Internal Revenue Code, but 'may turn out to be pretty thorough-going failures' that will harm the federal image."[16]

These forebodings of Justice Douglas, written in 1978, had already been borne out by pollster Louis Harris two years earlier. Harris found that in 1976 only twenty-two percent of those polled said they had "a great deal of confidence" in the Supreme Court. The figure ten years earlier had been fifty-one percent. The principal public feelings behind this drastic change appear to be related to the "law and order" question, and to unfulfilled expectations. Harris found a widespread feeling that court decisions have led to an era of permissiveness in which the guilty go free on technicalities. Unfulfilled expectations were reported ranging broadly from disappointed litigants to those who felt that institutional changes being administered by the courts were not turning out as well as had been hoped.[17]

As to institutional changes run amok, let us take a final look at school segregation. For years the Los Angeles school system has been the object of segregation litigation. When the school district was found to be segregated by a state superior court judge in 1970, 49.9 percent of the pupils were white. By mid-decade this figure had dropped to thirty-seven percent, and by the end of the decade white enrollment was 23.7 percent. Mandatory busing was ordered by the superior court to begin in the fall of 1978, when white student enrollment was at 29.7 percent.[18] Similar results have been reported from Boston, Washington, D.C., and other cities where the courts have attempted to run the schools.

In California, the state Supreme Court, at one time even more politically inclined than the United States Supreme Court, had required, in Los Angeles and elsewhere, more strict desegregation measures than those imposed nationally. In 1979 the voters of the state took matters into their own hands. Proposition 1, a state constitutional amendment, was initiated and passed by a two to one margin. The Amendment said, in effect, that unless the U.S. Constitution required it, the courts and other authorities in California should not impose busing in the schools. In November 1980, an intermediate state Court of Appeal ruled that Proposition 1 was constitutional. After the expenditure of tens of millions of dollars and the generation of intense acrimony on both sides, and still without achieving its aim, forced busing appeared to be all but dead in California. The Speaker of the California Assembly, Willie Brown, a black, was quoted as saying, "I'm recommending to black folks in this state that they abandon the defense of busing."[19] Brown described the issue as "a waste of everybody's time," while the black Mayor of Los Angeles, Tom Bradley, recognized that, "Most parents, whatever their color, whatever their background, wherever they live, don't want their kids transported back and forth across the city."[20] And then the issue was appealed to the California Supreme Court.

Attorneys for the Los Angeles School Board had assumed that the California Supreme Court would reverse the appellate court, and hold Proposition 1 to be unconstitutional, but felt they could win in the U.S. Supreme Court. Pro-busing advocates were equally confident of the results in the California Court. On March 11, 1981, the California Court issued its ruling, which astonished friend and foe alike. It refused to hear the case. The appellate court decision remained in effect, and forced busing in California was at an end, at least so far as the state courts were concerned.

The reaction to the California Supreme Court's refusal to interfere further in busing was a sobering lesson in the extent to which judicial politics can ultimately influence our patterns of thought. If anti-busing forces were astonished at the ruling, pro-busing forces were enraged. The California Court was accused of having "succumbed to the ugly conservative mood that's sweeping our state," of having been "overcome" by a "conservative tide," of having been "swayed by the perception of popular opinion," and of producing "a sense of dismay."[21] A true sense of dismay can easily be achieved by reflecting for a moment on what the outrage, or jubilation, was all about.

The people of California had amended their state constitution. They had amended it to provide for no more busing than the federal Constitution "required." That is, no more than the U.S. Supreme Court was presently willing to say it required. It was this state *constitutional amendment,* carefully and narrowly drawn to meet current federal standards, which nearly everyone expected the California Supreme Court to declare "unconstitutional." The Cause of Busing was to triumph, whatever the state constitution said, even if freshly amended to say it by a two to one vote! A majority of a seven-person state Supreme Court—there were actually two vacancies at the time of the ruling—was expected to invalidate what the people of the state had just legitimately done to amend their constitution. Such was the faith in law in the State of California after a quarter-century of judicial politics.

The constitutionality of California's constitutional amendment, Proposition 1, was also decided by the U. S. Supreme Court, in 1982. The Court upheld the California amendment while voiding an apparently similar effort by voters of the State of Washington.[22] Even though the two cases, taken together, indicate that the Court has not finally made up its mind to repudiate its long line of busing decisions, it may be fair to assume that the victory for anti-busing forces in California will lend strength to similar forces elsewhere. Eventually this will require the Supreme Court to review the school buses in full dress fashion. All indications are that the Court is going to have to reverse itself, and to admit to a failed social policy dressed up as constitutional dogma. In that case, the "constitutional" history of busing will have run something like this: from 1789 to the late 1960s the Constitution did not require busing; from the late 1960s to the 1980s the Constitution did require busing; from the 1980s onward the Constitution does not require busing. In the meantime, nothing in the Constitution which is supposedly the basis for these interpretations of the Supreme Court has changed. What does such a string of pronouncements over a relatively short span of years say for the Court as the guardian of the Constitution? What does it say about the Constitution itself? Or about the legitimacy of the courts, or about the rule of law?

Another interesting aspect of social fallout from the recent Court decisions relates to the kind of "rights" which have been created by the Court. As rights were developed at common law, they were ordinarily thought to be the reciprocals of duties or obligations. The same held true for the political philosophy upon which our Constitution is based. If certain individual rights were recognized, there were also civic duties required. Freedom within society implied a commitment to society, and to its agreed upon methods of operation and change. Author Daniel Boorstein has raised the possibility that inordinate concern with rights threatens, finally, to obliterate any consideration of reciprocal obligations. New "rights" invented and granted by the Court fit into Boorstein's analysis.

Boorstein traces the development of what he terms a "minority or veto psychology" in the country, with small groups having more power than ever before, and espousing a belief in the intrinsic value of dissent. "Professional dissenters," Boorstein states, "do not and cannot seek to assimilate their program or ideals into American culture. Their main object is to preserve and conceal their separate identity as a dissenting minority." This represents a significant change in American climate. "The ideal ceased to be that of fitting into the total society and instead became the right to retain your differences," with the assumption becoming that "the only 100 percent American is only partly American." Boorstein fears that dissent "has tended to become the conformity of our most educated classes." He leaves us with the unsettling thought that, "Disagreement is the lifeblood of democracy, dissension is its cancer." These observations are all the more prophetic when it is considered that they were made as early as 1967.[23]

Alexander Hamilton wrote in Federalist No. 25 that "every breach of the fundamental laws, though dictated by necessity, . . . forms a precedent for other breaches where the same plea of necessity does not exist at all." An ominous confirmation of this observation is reported from the Nixon era, relating to the "changing" Constitution which the Court has pressed upon us. A Deputy Assistant Attorney General, conducting a workshop on governmental concepts, advised participants that "separation of powers is obsolete." He urged his audience that the Constitution is "flexible," and suggested that,

> Your point of view depends on whether you're winning. The
> Constitution isn't the real issue in this; it is how you want *to*
> *run the country,* and achieve national goals. The language of
> the Constitution is not at issue. It is what you can interpret it
> to mean in the light of modern needs. In talking about a
> "constitutional crisis" we are not grappling with the real
> needs of running the country but are using the issues for the
> self-serving purpose of striking a new balance of power . . .
> Today, the whole Constitution is up for grabs.[24]

Whether or not this interpretation of the fundamental law was approved, tacitly or otherwise, as presidential policy, it has, in effect, been endorsed by Justices of the Supreme Court as judicial policy.

Sir Thomas More is one of the famous martyrs of English history. He stood to his death for the idea that law, not will, should govern. He died when he got in the way of Henry VIII on the question of divorce, which Henry wanted so he could have a new wife. To More, divorce was against the law. Henry wanted one anyway. In Robert Bolt's play, *A Man for All Seasons,* More and a young man, William Roper, discuss the meaning of law:

> ROPER: So now you'd give the Devil benefit of law!
> MORE: Yes. What would you do? Cut a great road through the law to get after the Devil?
> ROPER: I'd cut down every law in England to do that!
> MORE: Oh? And when the last law was down, and the Devil turned round on you—where would you hide, Roper, the laws all being flat? This country's planted thick with laws from coast to coast—man's laws, not God's—and if you cut them down—and you'd be just the man to do it—d'you really think you could stand upright in the winds that would blow then?[25]

In the passion for change it is all too easy to forget the ends that may result when the means of the law are brushed aside; and that the wind sometimes reaps the whirlwind.

16.   Courts Under Siege

ON TUESDAY, NOVEMBER 4, 1986, the voters of the State of California were presented with the question: "Shall Rose Bird be elected for the term provided by law? Yes/No." The people of the state replied with a resounding "NO!" by a margin of nearly two to one, the first time in the history of the state that a Supreme Court Justice had been removed from office. In addition to rejecting the Chief Justice, the voters also ousted two of her radical colleagues by landslide percentages of sixty to forty and fifty-seven to forty-three. Nationally we have witnessed Chief Justice Rehnquist subject to charges of "insensitivity" to minority and criminal rights, in a desperate, though ultimately futile, effort to prevent his confirmation. Seventh Circuit Court of Appeals Judge Daniel A. Manion, enthusiastically endorsed by liberal and conservative alike in his home state, won confirmation only by the narrowest of margins. The case of Robert Bork is fresh in mind. To some it seems that the judicial pot has never boiled so fast or furiously.

All of this might have been anticipated, and in fact was, after Ronald Reagan won his first landslide victory in 1980. Following that election a Justice of the California Supreme Court called for the establishment of a permanent statewide organization to combat what he characterized as the coming "political onslaught" against judges. One response to his plea was that the Justice "has good reason to be uneasy because the tide has definitely turned."[1] Liberals cry out that conservatives, led by President Reagan, have injected politics into the realm of the judiciary. And so they have—in the very best American tradition.

Defenders of the Warren-Burger era courts charge that the independence of the judiciary is under attack. The fact is, however, that we are not witnessing an "attack" by political forces against the judiciary; rather what is happening is a *counterattack* by political forces to reform a judiciary which has ventured across the forbidden line from the realm of law into that of policy-making, and even constitution-making. The courts in this country have engaged in similar forays in the past. In periods when it was perceived that political leadership was weak, the judges have eagerly leapt in with political decisions designed to fill the vacuum. When this has happened the people have inexorably struck back through their elected representatives. That is what is now occurring at the federal level; and on the state level, at least in California, it has occurred with a vengeance.

The U. S. Supreme Court has mounted frontal assaults against the political branches of government upon four separate occasions in our history. And on each occasion the Court has, sooner or later, found itself under siege by counterattacking political forces. Strong, even vitriolic, attacks have been launched against the Court by Presidents Jefferson, Lincoln, and Franklin Roosevelt, as well as by members of Congress and the public. On each of the first three occasions the Court was forced, in varying degrees, to alter its course, and to withdraw from its illicit political conquests. We are now in the midst of the fourth, and by far the most extensive, era of judicial invasion of the political arena, and are witnessing a mounting political reaction, with the issue yet to be resolved.

The actions of the Court in all four of these eras were intimately entwined with the politics of the day. The Court has repeatedly demonstrated that when it believes the political machinery to be weak it will attempt to gain by bald aggression the political power it perceives to have been relinquished, or allowed to languish. When national political alliances weaken, and when presidential leadership falters, the Court strikes. When political power is rejuvenated, the legislative and executive branches act to regain the ground lost to the Court. When a realignment of political forces gives rise to renewed presidential leadership, the people strike back through the political branches.

The first confrontation, which initiated the ongoing struggle between the political branches and the judiciary, occurred in 1803, centering on the case of *Marbury v. Madison.*[2] In that case, as we have seen, Chief Justice Marshall claimed for the Court the power of judicial review. He then exercised that power to declare unconstitutional a portion of the Judiciary Act of 1789. President Thomas Jefferson believed that the "crafty chief judge,"as he put it, had usurped for the Court a power which the Constitution did not intend, and that as a result the whole structure of constitutional democracy was threatened. The Jeffersonians mounted a massive political counterattack, which was undoubtedly aimed ultimately at Marshall. But rather than charging directly at the Chief Justice himself, an oblique tactic was chosen for the assault. Impeachment charges were brought against Justice Samuel Chase, a member of the Marshall Court, in 1804. Chase was a vulnerable target. As a judge during trials involving the infamous Sedition Act, he had stacked juries against Republican defendants and had shown open contempt for even the most distinguished attorneys representing them. Even before his appointment to the Supreme Court, Chase had been described by Alexander Hamilton as "universally despised" for having tried to corner the flour market. The Resolution of Impeachment, brought by the House of Representatives, was laid before the Senate for trial on December 7, 1804. Twenty-three votes were required for conviction, and the Jeffersonian Republicans had twenty-five seats. Yet, in a trial which lasted two months, the Republicans could muster only nineteen votes to convict. Chase returned to the bench and served until his death in 1811. Jefferson termed impeachment a "farce," while Henry Adams later concluded that the case proved impeachment to be an impractical thing for partisan purposes.

If the impeachment move against Chase failed in its immediate aim of removing him from office, perhaps it did not fail in its strategic purpose. That was to serve notice to the Federalist judges, John Marshall in particular, that the political branches, and not the courts, were running the country. John Quincy Adams asserted that the assault on Justice Chase "was unquestionably intended to pave the way for another prosecution, which would have swept the Supreme Judicial Bench clean at a stroke."[3] The effort had come close enough to success to cause Chief Justice Marshall grave concern for the independence of the judiciary. Marshall enjoyed an exceptionally long term as Chief Justice, which ended only with his death in 1835. Yet, never again, following its use in *Marbury v. Madison,* did he exercise the power of judicial review to strike down any other act of Congress.

The battle between Jefferson and Marshall was a reflection of a fundamental political realignment taking place in the country. The old Federalist power, defeated by Jefferson in the election of 1800, had been founded upon a coalition between the industrial Northeast and the slave-owning South. Jefferson succeeded in breaking that coalition by a reorientation which united the South with the new West. The Federalists had lost out politically and knew it. Their last ditch effort had been an attempt to pack the court system with Federalist sympathizers, and John Marshall was anchor man for the defense. But that effort was not enough. As the new Jeffersonian Republican coalition took hold and prospered, its adherents appointed new members to the judiciary, including the Supreme Court. Under the presidency of Andrew Jackson the coalition not only changed its name from Republican to Democrat, but further consolidated and deepened its hold on American politics. There was no chink through which the Supreme Court could pry into national policy making functions in the vigorous political atmosphere which existed from Jefferson's presidency to the end of Jackson's second term, in 1837.

But the coalition of South and West which had underpinned the Jefferson-Jackson era came unglued after Jackson, and began to disintegrate over the slavery issue. The slavocracy of the South gradually came to dominate the Democratic party, and the West rebelled. The increasing southern domination reflected itself in the judiciary, where pro-slavery opinion had become deeply embedded. On the Supreme Court there were five pro-slavery Justices, led by Chief Justice Roger Taney. It was that majority which, by the margin of a mere five votes to four, decided *Dred Scott v. Sandford*, in 1857, the case in which the Court held that Negroes were inferior persons, forever banished from the possibility of citizenship, even if freed.[4] And, for only the second time in its history, the Court declared an Act of Congress unconstitutional—the Missouri Compromise. In so doing, it destroyed the difficult political compromises concerning slavery in the territories of the West by which Congress had sought to avert civil war.

The *Dred Scott* decision provoked a storm of outrage in the North and West, which continued unabated into the presidential election of 1860. Abraham Lincoln knew how wrong the decision was, and knew the mood of the country. In one of his famous debates with Douglas he attacked the judicial politics which the decision represented:

> Familiarize yourselves with the chains of bondage and prepare your limbs to wear them. Accustomed to trample on the rights of others, you have lost the genius of your own independence and become the fit subjects of the first cunning tyrant who rises among you. And let me tell you, that all these things are prepared for you by the teaching of history, if elections shall promise that the next *Dred Scott* decision

and all future decisions will be quietly acquiesced in by the
people.[5]

Chief Justice Taney and the slavocracy had the votes to win the day in
Dred Scott, but they lost the war. Not just the Civil War, which the case
surely did nothing to avert, but the "war" between the judiciary and the
political branches which the case engendered. The new Republican party
of Lincoln not only defeated the Democratic party in the election of 1860,
but accomplished a second major realignment of sectional forces in the
country. Lincoln brought together the Northeast and the West, putting
himself in the White House and isolating the South. Through Lincoln's
election, the *Dred Scott* decision was repudiated and the stage was set for
the war against slavery.

In his first inaugural address, Lincoln pursued his attack on the Supreme
Court. Speaking in the presence of the aging Chief Justice Taney, who had
just administered to him the oath of office, the new President charged that,

> . . . if the policy of the government, upon vital questions
> affecting the whole people, is to be irrevocably fixed by
> decisions of the Supreme Court, the instant they are made,
> in ordinary litigation between parties in personal action, the
> people will have ceased to be their own rulers, having to that
> extent practically resigned their government into the hands
> of that eminent tribunal.[6]

Chief Justice Taney continued on the Court in virtual disgrace until his
death in 1864 at the age of eighty-seven. At his death the Court was left at
the lowest level of esteem and effectiveness in its history. In the years
immediately following the Civil War, the Court was unable to pick up the
shattered pieces or to regroup its inherent power effectively. Moreover,
those years were dominated by the politically powerful Reconstruction
Congress, which forced military government upon the defeated South, and
brought impeachment proceedings against President Andrew Johnson for
opposing its policies. Such a Congress was in no mood to tolerate judicial
opposition. Congress revealed its contempt for the Supreme Court by
changing its size three times within seven years, for what were obvious
political reasons. Despite such treatment, there were signs in 1868 that the
Court might, in a pending case, declare unconstitutional the acts of Congress by which "Reconstruction" had been imposed upon the South.
Congress acted quickly and effectively.

The case involved an appeal by a Mississippi newspaper editor, William McCardle, related to the Reconstruction Acts. It had already been argued before the Supreme Court, but not yet decided, when it became apparent that a vote against the constitutionality of the Reconstruction Acts, and military rule in the South, might result. In a bold move, Congress hurriedly passed legislation removing jurisdiction of the case from the Court. The legislation was vetoed by President Andrew Johnson, against whom the House of Representatives had already brought impeachment proceedings, and was repassed over the President's veto. While the Court could have decided the case in the meantime, it did not. When it did finally approach its decision, the Court was forced to consider whether Congress had effectively deprived it of jurisdiction. In the end, Chief Justice Chase held for a unanimous Court that it had no power to examine the motives of Congress, and that the Constitution had "by express word" given Congress the power to make such exceptions to the appellate jurisdiction of the Court. The Court, therefore, declined to rule on the issue of the case, or upon the constitutionality of the Reconstruction Acts.[7]

According to constitutional scholar Carl Swisher, the *McCardle* case was one in which "[t]he Supreme Court seems to have acted on the principle that discretion was the better part of valor."[8] Had the Court declared the Reconstruction Acts unconstitutional, Congress was in a mood, and had the power, to do great harm to the Court in retaliation. The political reality of the early post-Civil War years continued to justify the belief of competent observers of the day that the Court could not survive the political crisis which the *Dred Scott* decision had visited upon itself and the country.[9]

However, quite the opposite turned out to be the case. With the end of Reconstruction and the regeneration of civil government in the South, the inordinate power which Congress had exercised during the Reconstruction period receded. At the same time, no effective presidential leadership developed. For twenty years, from the end of Grant's second term in 1877 to the inauguration of McKinley in 1897, no President served more than one term. The country was in political turmoil, political leadership was weak, and the Court moved in.

But it did not move all at once. Marshall in *Marbury v. Madison,* and Taney in *Dred Scott v. Sandford,* had struck thunderbolts from the blue. Yet each case turned out to be a single shot, however much that shot might have reverberated through the society of its time. As the Court gathered new strength in the latter years of the nineteenth century, it also absorbed a philosophy which was to launch it upon a far more fundamental and sustained attack against the political branches of government. What the Court was absorbing, as expressed by a growing number of dissenting Justices, was the *laissez faire* theory of economics. That doctrine, in essence, held that government, federal or state, should not interfere in the operation of the burgeoning free enterprise system.

The hallmark case of the new era, and the decision in which *laissez faire* was made holy writ, was *Lochner v. New York,* decided in 1905, the case in which the Court held that the State of New York could not constitutionally regulate the maximum hours of workers in an occupation considered injurious to health.[10] That finding of the Supreme Court set the conditions for a war against national and state economic policy which was to last for some thirty years.

But the Court had begun to gain new strength even before the *Lochner* decision. As early as 1895, and for reasons different from those relied upon in *Lochner,* the Supreme Court had held the income tax to be unconstitutional. That decision invalidated a century of precedent to the contrary and eventually required adoption of the Sixteenth Amendment, in 1913, to secure its reversal. Similarly, *Lochner* reversed a century of precedent recognizing that economic and social policy was a matter for the political branches, not the judiciary, to determine. Once the *laissez faire* doctrine had been fully embraced, the Court turned its attention firmly away from the rights of the political majority, and the injunctions of the Constitution, and towards the "rights" of businessmen in the new industrial economy, rights which do not appear in the Constitution, but which the Court itself was busy creating.

This development on the Court was orchestrated against a continued disintegration of the earlier, sectional political alignments, and a failure of any new and effective political alliance to emerge. Professor Wallace Mendelson holds the view that, towards the end of the nineteenth century, "[t]he agrarian West and the industrial Northwest were frozen in a union that neither could dominate by merely political processes." What might have been a natural realignment between the West and South had been soured by war and Reconstruction. That impasse opened the way for judicial "mediation," which Mendelson observed "on a grand scale."[11]

As cases in the vein of *Lochner v. New York* effectively deprived both the urban laborer and the western farmer of the fruits of their political representation, by invalidating legislation enacted on their behalf, William

Jennings Bryan dreamed of a new sectional realignment. However, his effort towards that end, launched in the election of 1896, depended primarily on a western farm revolt, which was not destined to win the day. As one commentator put it, "reform associated with shaggy agrarians could not carry a swiftly industrializing nation." Neither Bryan nor anyone else was able to hit upon a political realignment which could effectively challenge the entrenched autocracy of the Supreme Court, and nothing happened to upset the autocracy of the Court until the early 1930s, when a radical new political alignment, quite unlike that dreamed of by Bryan, occurred during the first term of Franklin Roosevelt.

The balance sheet of judicial review tells the story in the meantime. Prior to the Civil War the Court had struck down but two congressional acts as unconstitutional. From the Civil War to 1937 the Court struck down seventy-six acts of Congress, and hundreds of acts of state legislatures.[12] Yet, the Court had never successfully demonstrated during this period that its *laissez faire* economics had any viable connection to the Constitution, and the illegitimacy of its claim that it had became more obvious as the years passed. At the same time, a vigorous political undercurrent was washing against the foundations of judicial supremacy.

Prior to the time of Franklin Roosevelt, national political alignments had formed out of an amalgamation of sectional alliances. What had occurred by 1936 was the rise of urbanism, which had become a nationwide phenomenon, although more heavily felt in the Midwest and East. From this new phenomenon Roosevelt fashioned a new kind of alliance, a powerful amalgam of urban interests, upon which the New Deal was built. Once the strength of the new alliance began to assert itself, *Lochnerism, laissez faire,* and the autocrats of judicial politics were doomed. But not without a titanic battle between the President, the Congress, and the country on one side, and a stubborn, but increasingly isolated, Supreme Court majority on the other.

In his *Lochner* dissent Justice Holmes had observed that the case had been decided "upon an economic theory which a large part of the country does not entertain." As the first Agricultural Adjustment Act, the National Recovery Act, and a host of other New Deal measures were struck down, the economic theories of the Court became even less "entertaining." Indignation mounted, and the cry against the Court became intense, rivalled only by the outrage directed against the *Dred Scott* decision three-quarters of a century earlier. After his landslide reelection of 1936, a triumphant President was ready to sound the death knell of *Lochnerism* and all its trappings. The attack was levelled in a "fireside chat" delivered by Roosevelt on March 9, 1937, designed to prepare the country for the knockout punch the President had in mind.

The President addressed the nation in terms reminiscent of the excoriating language used by Lincoln against the Taney Court. Roosevelt asserted that the Court had cast doubts on the ability of the elected Congress to protect the nation against economic and social catastrophe through legislation. "We are at a crisis in our ability to proceed with that protection," said Roosevelt. He further charged that, in blocking economic legislation, "The Court has been acting not as a judicial body, but as a policy-making body." The President drove his indictment home, denouncing "the claim made by some members of the Court that something in the Constitution has compelled them regretfully to thwart the will of the people." Rather, Roosevelt accused, "it is perfectly clear, that as Chief Justice Hughes has said: 'We are under a Constitution, but the Constitution is what the Judges say it is.' " In his final condemnation, the President laid his charge exactly on the constitutional violation of which the Court was guilty: "The Court in addition to the proper use of its judicial function has improperly set itself up as a third House of Congress—a super-legislature, as one of the Justices has called it—reading into the Constitution words and implications which are not there, and which were never intended to be there."[13]

Roosevelt's decisive stroke was his famous, or infamous, "court-packing" plan. The President proposed that Congress provide that an additional Justice be appointed for every Justice then serving on the Court who was over seventy, of which there were six. Congress had changed the size of the Court before for political motives, and there was no reason why it could not do so again. Age, of course, had little relevance to the real issue. The plan was simply a tactical device to allow the President to appoint enough additional Justices presumably to furnish a majority vote to abandon *laissez faire* and *Lochnerism*. But Roosevelt's plan was not well received, even by many who disagreed with the prevailing philosophy of the "Nine Old Men," as the Court was often termed at the time, and Congress defeated it. However, as had Jefferson's attack on the Marshall Court, the threat proved to be sufficient to accomplish the President's purpose. Justice Owen Roberts, one of the five man majority which had voted to kill the early New Deal measures, changed his vote in a series of key cases in the months following Roosevelt's assault on the Court, allowing such crucial measures as the Social Security Act, an amended Farm Bankruptcy Act, and the National Labor Relations Act to become law. Roberts' change in view has often since been characterized as the "switch in time that saved nine." It also saved the New Deal, and allowed implementation of the overwhelming mandate which Roosevelt had received from the people of the country in the election of 1936.

Only after decades of effort preceding his own first four years in office could Roosevelt achieve what Lincoln and Jefferson had accomplished against a usurping judiciary within a few years. Even so, it took a combination of the arrival of a strong President, a realignment of political power in the country, an economic crisis of unprecedented proportions, and the militant tenor of the times for the people of the country and their duly elected political representatives to achieve victory over a recalcitrant majority of but five Justices. The imperious power of the Supreme Court could be illustrated no more effectively.

As it had following its previous retreats from policy-making excesses, the Court remained relatively quiescent for some years, but not for as long as it had following *Marbury v. Madison* or *Dred Scott.* The case which signalled the resurgence of judicial activism was, of course, *Brown v. Board of Education,* decided under the then newly appointed Chief Justice, Earl Warren.[14] Although *Brown v. Board* was decided in 1954, it was not until the 1960s that the Court hit full stride. Once again, the power of the Court reached its zenith just as the country fell upon an era of weak political leadership, which coincided with a period of great ill fortune in national and international affairs.

First came the Kennedy assassination. Then President Johnson let an unpopular war get out of hand and was compelled to withdraw as a candidate for reelection. Watergate and the forced resignation of President Nixon accentuated the accumulating legacy of leadership in difficulties. President Ford proved too weak to defeat the virtually unknown challenger, Jimmy Carter, who in turn was tried and found wanting. The political vacuum of those years, 1963 to 1980, is one which matches closely the vacuum existing at the end of the Grant administration. Then, too, for some twenty years no President was able to serve two full terms.

Like the *Lochner* Court before it, the Warren Court plunged headlong into the political thicket, and for a long while feasted on the berries. However, in its pleasure it had also stuck thorns in its side, the infections of which presently began to show. The deep public resentment against school busing is most apparent. The one man-one vote slogan, together with its implementation, has not produced the results which had been assumed. Concerned with increasing, often senseless, crime, the public is losing patience with the arid fastidiousness of the courts in excluding supposedly illegally obtained evidence in criminal prosecutions. The Court's contraceptive and abortion decisions have been justified by reference to such ethereal "penumbras" and "emanations" from the Constitution that is it impossible to take them seriously.

There may yet be vitality, and even prophecy, in an observation of Justice Brandeis made many years ago. He perceived that, while a judge may advise, and while he may persuade, he may not "command or coerce." In Brandeis' opinion a judge "does coerce when without convincing the judgment he overcomes the will by the weight of his authority."[15] Since its decision in *Brown v. Board of Education* the United States Supreme Court has been relying primarily on coercion by authority, and not on persuasion by argument based on good judgment.

There are indications that many Americans—judges, government officials, policemen, and citizens alike—are beginning to appreciate the constitutional implications of what the Court is doing. The matter was summarized well in an opinion by the Utah Supreme Court. Pointing to the use which the United States Supreme Court has made of the Fourteenth Amendment, the Utah Court characterized it as having been employed to

> . . . extend and engraft upon the sovereign states, limitations
> intended only for the Federal government. This has resulted
> in a constant and seemingly endless process of arrogating to
> the Federal government more and more powers, not only not
> granted to it, but expressly forbidden to it, and in disparage-
> ment of the powers properly belonging to the sovereign
> States and to the people.[16]

This is a thoughtful observation which not only describes what the Court has done, but complains about it in valid constitutional terms. The Utah Court added that the judicial history of recent years "is a clear vindication of the forebodings of the founding fathers and their fears of centralization of power."

There is a fundamental distinction of great importance between the Warren era and the *Lochner* era. The *Lochner* syndrome, by comparison, was much more benign. There the Court merely butted its head against actions which had already been taken by other branches of the federal government, or by state governments, and declared them unconstitutional. Though it sought to destroy any sort of social or political regulation of the burgeoning industrial system, the acts of the *Lochner* Court were relatively discreet and limited. The power of the Court was exercised only after government had affirmatively exercised its own power.

By contrast, the Warren usurpation operated in a generative, rather than a reactive, manner. It did not wait for government to pass a law which it then struck down as abhorrent to its social philosophy. Rather, it solicited a clientele, received countless proposals to create new "rights," and finally chose those "rights" it wished to enshrine as "constitutional." When Justice Roberts changed his mind, the Court changed its ways—New Deal legislation was upheld, and the *Lochner* philosophy was dead. It is difficult to imagine so definitive an end to the much broader and more pervasive judicial transgression which has characterized both federal and state courts beginning with the Warren era, and continuing relatively unabated throughout the era of the Burger Court as well. But there can be no doubt that counter-pressure is building, or that courts at all levels are beginning to feel the heat.

Whether the landslide election, and reelection, of Ronald Reagan in 1980 and 1984 signalled the beginning of another historic realignment of political power, as did the elections of Jefferson, Lincoln, and Franklin Roosevelt, remains an open question. At least one hallmark of such periods of political rejuvenation, the vigorous political drive to remove a usurpatious judiciary from the roles of legislator and constitution maker, is clearly apparent. And the typical cry of revisionist judges, as they are relentlessly flushed from their constitutional cover, is that their judicial independence is being endangered. So it is.

And so it should be. For the reciprocal of judicial independence is judicial *responsibility*—the responsibility of the judiciary to its constitutional function. It is only through faithful exercise of that responsibility that the judiciary can fairly claim the independence which it so cherishes. When the courts conceive and impose entire social agenda, as the U.S. Supreme Court has done over the past three decades, or when they reject or emasculate legitimately enacted legislation, as had been the habit of the Court in the *Lochner* era, they have thereby foresaken their legitimate claim to independence.

Returning to the California example, it had been the habit of the Rose

Bird Supreme Court to behave much like the *Lochner,* Warren and Burger Courts, even with a vengeance. The principal case against Bird and her two Associate Justices was the court's refusal to enforce the death penalty in criminal convictions, even though voters in 1972, and again in 1978, had approved the death penalty by overwhelming margins. In over fifty cases Rose Bird had not voted to affirm that penalty once, and the court itself had affirmed it in only three cases. In one case the penalty was overturned because "use of a voter registration list produced a statistically improper jury panel."[17]

The death penalty was but the leading edge of the judicial arrogance which inflamed Californians. Other opinions of Chief Justice Bird had included findings that legislation prohibiting public employees from striking was in violation of the prohibition against involuntary servitude of the Thirteenth Amendment, abolishing slavery; and an equal protection argument which would have invalidated the popular Proposition 13 property tax limitation;[18] and rejection of referendum efforts to overcome blatant gerrymandering by the Democratic dominated legislature.[19] A host of such specious, and obviously ideological, opinions fueled opposition to the court in California.

San Francisco Chronicle Columnist Guy Wright expressed typical citizen reaction against Chief Justice Bird and her court. Wright took no part in the first referendum concerning the Chief Justice, when originally appointed, in which she then only narrowly missed being recalled. This time Wright's interest was intense, not only in regard to Bird, but to the other two radical Justices running for confirmation with her. Wright charged that these Justices had "turned the state Supreme Court into a political boiler room," that they had "abandoned any effort at judicial sincerity," and that they had made of the court "an embarrassment for everyone who cares about the law. They should be recalled."[20]

The citizens of the country as a whole do not have the advantage of being able to vote directly to oust usurping judges which the state constitution has provided for the people of California. And so, for practical purposes, the political counterattack at the national level must center on filling judicial vacancies with men and women who hold the concept of law, and the principles of the Constitution, above partisan advantage or policy preference. Basic constitutional principles have been at issue in the bitter confirmation battles over President Reagan's appointments to the federal courts. The Manion and Rehnquist confirmations revealed the frayed desperation of radical defenders of judicial imperialism, though not the hysterical fury which was instigated to defeat the nomination of Robert Bork, a matter to which we shall return in the final chapter.

Those who favor judicial policy making are rarely willing to say so candidly in public. Their attack, rather, is for having been "insensitive" to this or that constituency, for having once owned property whose deed contained a restrictive covenant, or for having belonged to a club which excluded women. When such charges as these, rather than adherence to law and the Constitution, are advanced as the touchstones for judicial acceptability, we have wandered far afield from any manageable principles of constitutionalism.

The hairbreadth confirmation of Judge Manion to the Seventh Circuit Court of Appeals illustrates well the shabbiness of the opposition. Having little more to go on than some typographical errors in old briefs, the defense mustered a list of law school deans to attest to Manion's incapacity for the office. Paul Houston of the *Los Angeles Times,* suspecting that few, if any, of these deans had ever met Manion, or had an opportunity to evaluate him, did some investigation. He found that in South Bend, Manion's home town, there was across the board support and respect for the man, and so reported to two of the signatory deans. Their replies are illuminating.

Dean Paul D. Carrington, of Duke University, said, upon hearing the praise Manion had received from associates in Indiana, that he was reminded of the "false views" which had been generated regarding Judge Clement F. Haynsworth, when he was nominated for the Supreme Court in 1969. Dean Arthur N. Frakt, of Loyola (Los Angeles) felt "a little sheepish," adding that, "If it turns out he [Manion] is someone of substantial ability, I would feel it was unfortunate he got caught up in this."[21]

Alexis de Tocqueville observed that the power of the United States Supreme Court is enormous, but that it is, in the end, the "power of public opinion." He described the Court as "allpowerful as long as the people respect the law; but they would be impotent against popular neglect or contempt of the law." Tocqueville added that "if the Supreme Court is ever composed of imprudent or bad men, the Union may be plunged into anarchy or civil war."[22] We have already experienced the Civil War, abetted in no small measure by the Supreme Court's *Dred Scott* decision, and it may be fair to characterize the present turmoil over the judiciary as a forceful, necessary, and legitimate political attempt to arrest the further advance of judicial anarchy.

V.
LAW IN
A FREE SOCIETY

In American society law is an integral part of a social contract, which seeks both to provide necessary government power, and to limit that power to agreed upon uses. The roots of the American social contract, the Constitution, are embedded deeply in the centuries of Anglo-American legal development which were required to achieve such a concept. Activist judges ignore the precious and fragile nature of the social contract, and threaten its existence.

The Constitution provides for a system of separation of powers in order to control government. Assumed in that system were certain internal judicial restraints which had operated for centuries to limit the kind of disputes which courts would hear and decide. The radical expansion of judicial power in recent years has been facilitated by a renunciation of these restraints as courts reached out to achieve non-judicial goals.

Underlying the endeavor to restrain power is the fundamental difference between government and law—between gubernaculum *and* jurisdictio. *The power to govern carries with it the tendency to threaten individual rights, and it is the great function of law to prevent government from doing so. That function is in danger of being lost when the courts of law themselves begin behaving like arms of government.*

The concluding chapter of the book considers responsibility for judicial lawlessness, and possibilities for reinvigoration of our constitutional system, together with its potent, yet fragile, guarantees of individual freedom.

17.　The Social Contract

IT IS OF great significance for American social and political development that the Constitution was born out of a period of ferment and ambivalence, of practicality and idealism; an era in which strands of political realism crossed and intertwined with philosophical concepts, some of which eventually ran in a similar direction, some of which pulled another way, in a tension which is as yet unresolved. The idea of a social contract, by which to knead society together, permeated the atmosphere of the time; but so did the contrary concept of justifiable social disintegration, which fired the spirit of the American Revolution.

There is something to be said for the view that, in the vortex of the American revolutionary period, one set of choices was made in 1776, when the Declaration of Independence was signed, and quite another set in 1789, when the Constitution was ratified. A fundamental "self-evident truth" enunciated by Thomas Jefferson and the signers of the Declaration of Independence was that "all men are created equal." They are also endowed with certain "inalienable rights," which include "life, liberty and the pursuit of happiness." These sweeping assertions, however, were accompanied by an extensive list of specific complaints against the Crown, so that in the Declaration there is a conjunction of the ideal and the practical which should not be overlooked.

Fifty-six delegates from the thirteen Colonies signed the Declaration of Independence. Of these, only six were present at Philadelphia thirteen years later to sign the Constitution. Benjamin Franklin was there; Jefferson was not, and disapproved of the secrecy of the Convention. Such a revolutionary firebrand as Thomas Paine stayed away because he "smelled a rat," while others were absent for similar reasons. The resulting Constitution, it is often said, therefore lacked the idealism of the Declaration, and concerned itself only with the prosaic machinery of government.

An examination of the concepts embodied in the two documents reveals that they are closer in spirit, and even in practicality, than might be supposed. But the most interesting question is whether, or to what extent, the principles upon which the two documents were based remain valid and viable today. If there has been an erosion or repudiation of underlying principles, does the Declaration of Independence have continuing value as a guiding ideal? More significantly, is the Constitution still a workable social contract at the 200th anniversary of its adoption?

The idea that "all men are created equal," and that they are "endowed with certain inalienable rights," necessarily raises questions about the origin of man, and about the state of nature in which his origin occurred. What is the basis for this assertion? By what authority can such a proposition be supported? What does "equal" mean? What "rights" are "inalienable," and where do such "rights" originate? The answers to these questions have a great deal to do with our view of society and government, with how we perceive each other, with how we arrange the institutions which arise out of the social contract, and with what we expect of those institutions.

Three principal political writers had advanced ideas about the social contract by the time the framers of the American Constitution met to create one. They were two Englishmen and a Frenchman—Thomas Hobbes, John Locke, and Jean-Jacques Rousseau. The work of Rousseau was the freshest, his book, *The Social Contract,* having been published in 1762. It was a work more in tune with the generalities of the Declaration of Independence than with the practicalities of the Constitution; more akin to revolutionary rhetoric than to the patient growth of legal and contractual relationships. Rousseau's work was based on assumptions about the state of nature, the formation of society, and the development of the individual in the social order which have had a profound, and arguably pernicious, effect upon American society.

Penetrating illumination has been thrown on the work of Rousseau by the perceptive contemporary writer, Robert Ardrey, who is concerned with the biological origins of the social contract. Ardrey's book, which he also titled *The Social Contract,* is dedicated to the memory of Rousseau. A few moments with Ardrey and Rousseau are well spent, for the doctrines of Rousseau, which permeate activist Court decisions, are, in the opinion of Ardrey, false.

Rousseau's point of departure is to posit man as a part of nature, and to contrast this pristine "natural" man with the man to be found in the society of the eighteenth century. Rousseau charged that, "Man is born free, yet everywhere we see him in chains." In nature, said Rousseau, man had been happy and good; but in society he had become depraved and had been rendered miserable. With this judgment, as Ardrey puts it, "the Age of the Alibi was launched: Nature made me happy and good, and if I am otherwise, it is society's fault."[1] What Ardrey demonstrates is that Rousseau "could hardly have been more disastrously wrong" in his assumptions about man in a state of nature. The question is whether wrong assumptions have not led to even more disastrously wrong social programs, as those assumptions have insinuated themselves into the judicial psyche, and as they have been effected through judicial legislation.

Ardrey represents a new kind of anthropology, which might be termed anthropological biology. As the term suggests, it is an amalgamated science which attempts a deeper reach into the origins of the species than either anthropology or biology might achieve separately. Ardrey attempts to link the known use of artifacts and techniques by early man with the development of his biological functions and capacities. The "state of nature" which results is instructive when compared with the state of nature assumed by those who influenced American thinking at the flashpoint of revolution and constitution making.

As Ardrey sees it, for eons there was no such thing as an *individual*. There was only a hunting tribe, organized to stalk and kill the beasts which were its food, in a situation where failure meant starvation. The quality for which evolution opted during these millions of years was superior *social* responsibility. Not only responsibility, but utter conformity. Any display of individuality would have meant death in the small communities of fifty or so in which Ardrey believes our ancestors lived, while they hunted in compact bands of only ten or twelve.

Total submission to society was necessary for the reason that these bands of hunters did not possess the weapons with which to make their kill at a distance. They had stone axes, perhaps metal ones later on, spears, and daggers. Group cooperation—social responsibility on pain of death—was required to make the kill without being killed. It was only some 30,000 years ago that the bow-and-arrow was invented, and not until some 10,000 years ago, after the retreat of the Wurm ice sheet in Europe, and the Wisconsin ice sheet in North America, was widespread use of this deadly new weapon achieved. Then, for the first time in human history, a single hunter off on his own could make a kill, and thus, of his own initiative, secure the means for survival. It was not until this point had been reached, barely ten millennia ago, that the possibility of the individual was achieved.

These rudimentary yet crucial developments in the rise of man from a socially coerced beast of prey, who ate his meat raw, to the possibility of becoming civilized seem tedious in their pace, slower than the drift of continents, compared to the race of modern innovation. Even the half-millennium or so of Anglo-American constitutional development is an afternoon's interlude by comparison.

The contribution of Ardrey is most fascinating in the connection he makes between these developments and the structure of the human brain components: the reptilian, the cortex, and the neocortex. The reptilian, the most ancient, functions to establish territory, find shelter, hunt, mate and breed. The cortex is a kind of "thinking cap" which has grown around the reptilian brain, developing approximately one hundred million years ago. It is capable of learning, of wider emotions, and of the sense of smell. The neocortex, whose development was completed only some half-million years ago, is capable of foresight, memory, symbolic language, and conceptual thought. As a matter of brain interaction, it appears that the neocortex has difficulty communicating with the cortex and the reptilian brain, which together are called the limbic system. Hence there is a tendency for those ancient brain structures to bypass or override the more sophisticated capabilities of the neocortex, especially in situations of stress.

This leads Ardrey to an analysis of the individual in society which is quite at variance with that of Rousseau. "Social order," says Ardrey, "is contained in our animal past and is ingrained in the patterns of our animal sub-brains. The individual is the creature of the human future, and we still do not know quite what to do about him."[2] As to equality, Ardrey concludes quite bluntly that, "A society is a group of unequal beings organized to meet common needs."[3] That is to say, men are created, not equal, but *un*equal.

If Ardrey's analysis is correct, the idea of Rousseau that the individual was the beautiful ancient reality, and society the later ugly oppressor, is just the reverse of what happened in human evolution. The fact is that the error of Rousseau's premise is implied in his solution, which is an amazing one considering his delicate solicitude for the pristine individual, frolicking joyously amongst the delights of nature.

Rousseau posits, as the cure for the ills to be found in a debauched society, a "general will," in which the individual surrenders all sovereignty; in which private property is abolished; and in which, presumably (although we are never told quite how), the individual regains the antediluvian grace of which society has supposedly robbed him. And how is this miracle to be wrought? By the individual *submitting completely to society!* This is a version of the social contract which Ardrey describes as "scarcely a contract at all, but a document of surrender of the individual to the group."[4] Rousseau's remedy for an oppressive society is an even *more* oppressive society—a return to the true state of nature which Rousseau had never understood.

It is an irony which haunts us still that Rousseau, attempting a kind of charming reincarnation of the Garden of Eden, leads us directly to the gates of the gulag. As does one of the two English philosophers in the background of American constitution making, Thomas Hobbes. Hobbes wrote his great book, *Leviathan,* during the mid-seventeenth century, as the Colonies in North America were being established. That Hobbes takes us along the same path as does Rousseau is an irony compounded, when we consider that Hobbes' starting point could hardly have been more different from that of Rousseau.

Hobbes also begins with a particular view of man in a state of nature. But what a nature Hobbes envisions! To him, nature is "force and fraud," where "every man is to every man a wolf." In nature there are "no arts; no letters; no society; and which is worst of all, continual fear, and danger of violent death; and the life of man, solitary, poor, nasty, brutish, and short." Hobbes is appalled at nature, and to him almost anything would be better. The root cause of the chaos he sees is that nature is "without a common power to keep them all in awe," which Hobbes proposes to remedy by the creation of Leviathan, a sovereign and all-powerful government.[5] To Hobbes the absence of such a government is virtually the dissolution of society, a return to the horrors of nature, a calamity to be prevented at all costs, no matter how oppressive the government.

It is amusing as well as ironic that Rousseau and Hobbes arrive at the same desolate prescription for a social contract, starting as they do from totally different visions of nature—Rousseau, the extreme optimist about nature, Hobbes, the extreme pessimist. The result in each, so far as government is concerned, is to put aside patience, to eschew moderation, and to reject any possibility of limitations on power. Each, from a different perspective, became transfixed by a devotion to the State. Each came to feel an almost holy call to "save the State" (whatever state) from one perceived peril or another, real or fancied. Each, in fact, feared freedom; each was terrified of a governmental vision less perfect than he believed his own to be; of a social contract not of his own coercive will and making.

It is significant to note that the idea of *equality* is not at all incompatible with the prescriptions of either Rousseau or Hobbes. Be it Leviathan or the General Will, the tentacles of government stretch into every recess and private place of either philosopher's vision. There is no room left for deviation where the State is supreme in all things; there is no room for variation, for personality, for creativity, even for humor. In short, there is no room for individuality, which is the antithesis of equality. But there is plenty of room for equality, even absolute equality—for everyone, that is, except those who pull the levers by which Leviathan is manipulated.

The framers of the American Constitution knew the danger of raw power, and took the greatest of pains to guard against it. Yet they did not repudiate the great cry of equality, or the other idealistic sentiments expressed in the Declaration of Independence. Rather, in the Preamble to the Constitution, they expressed a purpose "to form a more perfect Union, establish Justice, insure domestic Tranquility, provide for the common defense, promote the general Welfare, and secure the Blessing of Liberty to ourselves and our Posterity. . . ." Phrases such as "Justice," "domestic Tranquility," "general Welfare," or "the Blessing of Liberty" can be read to express an idealism nearly as universal, and thus as imprecise, as any in the Declaration of Independence. Surely the two documents share more in spirit than many have supposed, and are not truly incompatible. They also share in practicality.

The Declaration had emphasied ideals, but had also meticulously listed specific grievances in justifying the rupture with the mother country. The Constitution took note of ideals in its Preamble, but emphasized specifics, and the workability of institutions, in the provisions it made for government. The Preamble of the Constitution seems, in this view, to serve as a bridge between revolution and government, forging a seamless weld between the two great documents of the American Revolution. Even Thomas Paine—whom John Adams characterized as, "The filthy Tom Paine," came to appreciate what the Framers had accomplished.[6] Paine emphasized the difference they had set between a *government* and its *constitution,* insisting that a constitution is antecedent to government, and that any exercise of authority beyond the limits defined in a constitution is an exercise of "power without right." Paine pointed out that in a state where there is no distinction between the constitution and the government, there is no constitution, and he was able to accept the American Constitution on the basis of such considerations.

In rejecting the prescription of Hobbes and Rousseau that all power be lodged in a sovereign lawmaking body, the framers found themselves in agreement with the thinking of the other English philosopher who had given consideration to the qualities of the social contract, John Locke.

Like Rousseau and Hobbes, Locke also presupposes a state of nature, from which he proceeds to construct his social contract. Locke's nature is characterized by "peace, good will, mutual assistance, and preservation," in which all valuable human attributes are already possessed by the "free, sovereign" individual. This hardly describes the bloody meat eaters which our ancestors in all probability actually were. Nevertheless, there is an element in Locke's view essential to the kind of government which the founders wished to create. Locke, holding that the individual derives his rights from nature, necessarily regards *government* as *not* being the source of those rights, but as *fiduciary* in character. The task of government is to make secure rights which already exist, not to be the bountiful dispenser of the goods of life. Government is therefore to be *limited*.

It would appear that none of the philosophers whose views on the state of nature were available to the American revolutionaries was entirely correct. Locke was right, up to a point. Mutual assistance and preservation certainly did characterize early man, and perhaps occasionally peace and goodwill. But a "free, sovereign" *individual,* already in possession of certain rights, would have been impossible. Perhaps Hobbes came closest. Life in nature would not have been "solitary," but it would surely have had a good chance of being "poor, nasty, brutish, and short." Rousseau missed the mark entirely. Luckily, the founders followed Locke most closely.

And now, unluckily, two centuries later, how much there is of the pall of Leviathan, and of the specter of the General Will, in the elitist view that free men in a democratic society are incapable of minding their own business, and so must have it minded for them. Such a view, whether it emanates from the academy, the intellectuals, or the courts, is as fundamentally anti-democratic and unconstitutional as could be imagined. It rejects the liberating hypothesis of Locke that government is not a source of rights, but their guardian; lodged in the judiciary, such a view is capable of destroying the last best defense of freedom, an independent court system. The ghost of Rousseau haunts us in yet another fashion, in the belief that, if there are flaws and faults in an individual, it is not his doing, but a wrong inflicted by society.

The "Age of the Alibi" has been given constitutional sanction by the Supreme Court in its many-faceted attacks on the social institutions which the Court appears to imagine have inflicted individual wrongs. In its constant meddling with the Constitution, the Court joins in a fraternal spirit with both Rousseau and Hobbes; it fears freedom, questions liberty, despises the capacity of a democratic society to judge for itself, happily imposes its own General Will, and with gusto begins to build its own Leviathan.

If the assumption of the Declaration of Independence that all men are created equal is false, must we then acquiesce when our judiciary tries to pound us all into the same mold anyway? If judicial interference in the schools has nearly always led to a "levelling down," is that not also the result of most of the other judicial adventures we have been following as well? We must surely make something of equality other than the literal statement we find in the Declaration of Independence. It *is* self-evident that we are endowed with "life," but with "liberty"?—not in a state of tribal, animal-hunting nature. Surely Locke was wrong there, and Hobbes right. It may be that the "pursuit of happiness" is the point of genius in the Declaration. The mere fact of existence opens up possibilities which can be enhanced, altered, and pursued to the best of our abilities.

The recent bent of the Court represents a drift far to one extreme in the dynamic tension which is built into our constitutional system. The Declaration of Independence tends towards impossible ideas; the Constitution reminds us to keep our eye on defined and limited processes, and not to sacrifice our institutions to the elusive goals of passing idols, since we are very likely to change our minds later on. But the Court has disengaged itself from the constitutional balance wheel, and has allowed itself to be pulled towards false dreams of perfection, to be pushed by a false guilt of imperfection. The Court forgets that the framers of the Constitution carefully left the *ends* of government out of that document, and provided only for an open *means,* a *process* by which, if left intact, the "pursuit of happiness" can be continuously refined, dreamed about or redefined in any way we wish.

There is another aspect of the state of nature as Ardrey sees it which is of great moment in considering the restraints of a constitutional system. As we come to understand the ancient origins of the brain, and the eons during which it was soaked in savagery, we ignore at our peril the "state of nature" which still exists, in the brain's cortex and reptilian portions, the limbic system, in ourselves and in those around us who constitute society. We can think of the neocortex as a device which somehow attempts to imprint a new path of behavior on the ancient blood-strewn trails of the limbic system. In the same manner, a constitution is an attempt to fit a pattern of order over the howl of the mob; an effort to control the ancestral passions of the hunt and the kill.

A constitution is an artificial device in the truest sense of the word. It is an unnatural attempt to restrain natural instincts; an artifice fashioned by master craftsmen out of a pattern invented by their own art. Constitutionalism, with its subtleties and restraints, is a product of the neocortex, an effort to seal over and suppress the deep rumblings of the limbic system, ever threatening to erupt through the civilized sophistication at the surface.

Curiously enough, a very similar apprehension concerning the destructive potential of the human psyche was expressed at the dawn of Western civilization, in the drama of ancient Greece. Greek drama can be viewed as a combination of religious preaching and political exhortation, made entertaining by the skill of the dramatist. Underlying the earliest plays, those of Aeschylus, is a fear of chaos—a terror inspired by looking too intently into the savage core of the human psyche. This is no better illustrated than in his great trilogy, the *Oresteia*. Agamemnon, having sacrificed his daughter to obtain favorable winds for his voyage to Troy, is slaughtered on his return by his wife, Clytemnestra, and her lover, Aegisthus. Vengeance is wreaked, and the gods are propitiated for that slaughter, when Orestes murders his mother for the deed, a crime which, in its turn, drives Orestes mad. He is pursued by the Eumenides, with snakes for hair, until he finds refuge in the temple of Athena at Athens. It is only there, under the law of the City, that the terror runs its course, and the cycle of retribution comes to an end. Orestes recovers, and order once more gains ascendency over chaos.

The Greeks developed nothing like a constitutional system as we know it, and their understanding of law was rudimentary. But their instinct, indeed their experience, concerning the state of nature is as relevant as today's science. Their recognition of the vital necessity to tame the eruptive forces lodged in the human psyche was awesome in its reach, and terrifying in its dramatic expression.

The value of Greek insights, in their ancient-modern congruity, and as related to the difficulty of forming institutions to tame brute nature, is underscored in the long and arduous process which has been required in Anglo-American history to transform embryonic constitutional ideas or practices into institutions truly capable of restraining power. The taproot of the American Constitution touches the year 1215, and a meadow called Runnymede, between Staines and Windsor, west of London, in what is now County Surrey.

In the English midlands rebellious barons had laid siege to castles loyal to the King, and in May of 1215 their forces had entered London itself. The condition of the country was explosive, and unpredictable. Voices of moderation, led by the Church, beseeched the King to recognize the just grievances of the insurgent lords, and to negotiate a settlement with them, lest the kingdom be engulfed in full scale civil war. The King relented, and articles of settlement were drawn up.

One can easily imagine the medieval array of flags and pennants, of colorful tents and polished armour, the trumpet flourishes for the King and his party, and the drum rolls for the barons, as the antagonists filled the meadow to meet and settle their differences—the sight, for all its splendor and pageantry, yet barely concealing the coiled springs of war. There at Runnymede, persuaded by force as well as by reason, by the Holy Church and by his own fear for his throne, King John, on a fine June day in the year 1215, set the great royal seal to the articles which had been agreed upon between himself and the barons of England—which came to be known as Magna Carta.

The Great Charter arose out of a feudal society of the sort which had pervaded Europe for centuries, a system characterized by *status*. Society was organized into rigid classes—almost castes—in which the position of the individual depended upon that of the group or family into which he was born. This determined his status, which could change little, if at all, during his lifetime. Dukes remain dukes, bakers remain bakers, shoemakers remain shoemakers, and peasants till the land unto eternity.

In part the agreement reached between King John and the barons at Runnymede was but an affirmation of the ancient feudal rights of the barons, based on their status. But Magna Carta was also the dawn of a new era, for the Great Charter was also a *contract,* bargained for and agreed upon between the parties. It has often been said that the movement from feudalism to the modern state was a movement from *status* to *contract.* In one sense that movement began at Runnymede in 1215, but in a more fundamental sense the true development and acceptance of the idea of contract had to await structural changes in society. Thus, in fact, Magna Carta might more appropriately have been known, in 1215 and for long thereafter, as the Great Promise, rather than the Great Charter, for the contracts made by it proved difficult to enforce.

Central to any governmental system which aims to provide freedom for the individual is an acknowledgment that individual rights must be accorded formal recognition and institutional protection. In Chapter 29 Magna Carta expresses the rudimentary requirements of limited government and individual rights:

> No free man shall be taken or imprisoned or deprived of his
> freehold or of his liberties or free customs, or outlawed, or
> exiled, or in any manner destroyed, nor shall we go upon
> him, nor shall we send upon him, except by the lawful judg-
> ment of his peers or by the law of the land.

Here, in 1215, are the essential ingredients of *due process of law.* Yet, centuries passed before an enforcing agency could be developed of sufficient strength to make such rights stick.

Sir Edward Coke, Lord Chief Justice, engaged in a titanic struggle with King James I over just this issue in the early seventeenth century. The question, as put by Coke, was a choice between the *rule of law,* the common law of England, and *despotism,* the rule of the King beyond law. In his courageous effort to impose law on the despotic King, Coke enhanced the standing of Magna Carta by developing the theory that it was a "law fundamental" which James could not transgress. Coke pointed out that Magna Carta had been confirmed over thirty times by the Kings of England. He argued, therefore, that, as fundamental law, judgments and statutes against it "shall be void." This was one of his great contributions, so far as American constitutional law is concerned. Out of such a concept grew the idea of a superior fundamental law, running back to one particular document, binding King and Parliament alike, and having a verifiable content which can be applied to test the ordinary proceedings of governmental institutions.

For all of its rich history, however, England never developed institutional restraints on the sovereign power of the King, or of the King in Parliament, or later upon Parliament itself, comparable to those fashioned in the

Colonies, and embodied in the Constitution at Philadelphia. Lord Coke could fulminate against Royal power for a time, but by 1616 he had become too irritating, if not too dangerous, so that King James removed him from his judicial offices. It was not until after 1700 that Parliament passed a Tenure of Judges Act, assuring the independence of the British judiciary, and forming a solid basis for judicial protection of individual rights in England.

It was only a few years after James I dismissed his Lord Chief Justice that the Pilgrims of the Mayflower drew up an agreement among themselves as to how they intended to run the new Colony which they were establishing:

> In the name of God, Amen! We whose names are under-
> written, the loyal subjects of our dread soveraigne lord,
> King James . . . doe by these presents solemnly and mutu-
> ally in the presence of God, and one of another, covenant
> and combine ourselves togeather into a civill body politick,
> for our better ordering and preservation . . . and by vertue
> hearof to enacte, constitute, and frame such just and equall
> lawes, ordinances, acts, constitutions, and offices, from time
> to time, as shall be thought most meete and convenient for
> the general good of the Colonie, unto which we promise all
> due submission and obedience.[7]

The Mayflower Compact represents a significant, if painfully delayed, step forward from Magna Carta as a model for true constitutional government. There is evident in the Compact a subtle yet crucial transformation from a relatively simple two-way contract between King and subjects to the more complex idea of a mutual covenant among free individuals, agreeing to govern themselves in a society to whose formation they give their consent.

These and similar developments which occurred prior to the American constitutional period might be described as the unconscious phase of constitution-building, a phase which lasted at least five hundred years in Anglo-American history. It is easy to take constitutional arrangements for granted; and it requires some act of will even to attempt to project oneself into the protracted, often painful process of their creation. However, reflection upon this long evolutionary process reveals both the immense historical obstacles to arriving at what has happened, and the felicity of the result. It also provides a glimpse of how fragile are the institutions of freedom, and how easily they can be lost or destroyed.

The contract proposed at Philadelphia, and accepted by the parties thereto, was to provide a process by which government could function, and at the same time guarantee the maintenance of freedom from government power. Both in the original Constitution, and in later Amendments, there was virtually no concern with the *substance* of policy or the goals of society. That was the genius of the document. It is what made the Constitution possible, and what has allowed it to endure. Hannah Arendt suggests that the American Revolution "actually proclaims no more than the necessity of civilized government for all mankind."[8] Professor John Hart Ely has observed that "only rarely has our Constitution attempted to tell elected officials what substantive values to favor or disfavor, and when it has tried, most often the attempt has been doomed." The result is that, "What has distinguished the American Constitution, and indeed America itself, has been a process of government, not a governing ideology."[9]

Until recently the two most important exceptions to these principles had been slavery and prohibition. Slavery was protected in the original Constitution; Civil War and a later Amendment were required to eradicate it. Prohibition, adopted by one Amendment, had to be repealed by another. The one institution produced a tragedy, the other something more closely resembling a farce. Now the Supreme Court has injected a whole series of social policies into the Constitution, contrary to the intent and nature of the document. This has been done, for the most part, in the name of protecting some minority or another. James Madison had something to say about that approach to the Constitution as a social contract.

Madison pointed out that the idea of the Constitution is not only to divide the functions of power within government, but to divide society itself, in order to assure a *pluralistic* polity in which no dominant majority would threaten tyranny. Madison articulated this purpose as "comprehending in the society so many separate descriptions of citizens as will render an unjust combination of a majority of the whole very improbable, if not impracticable." He warned against an alternative way of securing the rights of the minority by "creating a will in the community independent of the majority." That method, he argued, furnishes a "precarious security," for the reason that "a power independent of the society may as well espouse the unjust views of the major, as the rightful interests of the minor party, and may possibly be turned against both parties."[10] Madison put no trust in Platonic Guardians.

The nineteenth century English political philosopher, John Stuart Mill, expressed a similar view:

> The disposition of mankind, whether as rulers or as fellow-
> citizens, to impose their own opinions and inclinations as a
> rule of conduct on others, is so energetically supported by
> some of the best and by some of the worst feeling incident
> to human nature, that it is hardly ever kept under restraint by
> anything but want of power. . . .[11]

It was just such a view of human nature which led to the bargain struck in the Colonies in 1789. The American social contract is an agreement to withhold from public officials of whatever office the power to impose "their own opinions and inclinations" upon the country as required rules of conduct.

In injecting social and political values into the Constitution, the Supreme Court Justices are doing exactly what Mill warned against, and what the Constitution sought to prohibit—imposing "their own opinions and inclinations" upon the country, in the guise of constitutional law. In so doing, the Court is dangerously close to becoming that "power independent of society" which Madison feared: a power which "may as well espouse the unjust views of the major, as the rightful interests of the minor party, and may possibly be turned against both parties."

The possibility of a social contract, solemn and enduring, was won in the Anglo-American world only through centuries of struggle, and was based, at least in part, on ideals or beliefs which can no longer be defended. Men are not created equal, but unequal; they are not "endowed" with liberty, but must struggle for it; the individual did not spring full-blown from an ancient sylvan glade, but clawed his way slowly out of eons of tribal savagery; and the race still carries, in its animal brain, and in its social fabric, all the blood, lust, and chaos implanted in it along the way.

The social contract is a promise we make to each other during a period of good behavior to try not to revert to some of our worst and ancient habits. A constitution is conceived to put obstacles in our way if we lose control and decide to let loose anyway. Certain rights which we once believed we were endowed with turn out, instead, to be goals we have invented for our own achievement. The concept of the free individual, living in a state of happiness, is not an Eden lost, but an ideal to be pursued, a future to be sought and cherished. If some of the "givens" which we once counted on seem now less sure, the work of the Constitution, which has nevertheless allowed us to continue to strive in freedom, is all the more sacred.

The tensions of the Revolutionary period which were left unresolved were left purposely so. The central vision of the Declaration of Independence is the "pursuit" of happiness. And even that document, in all its idealism and self-assurance, does not presume to define the goal. In a spirit of perfect harmony, the Constitution also foregoes the setting of goals, and provides instead a process by which to pursue the elusive, and ever changing, vision of a happy life.

The American Constitution is written in the belief that human affairs can be so ordered that we need endure neither Chaos nor Leviathan; that we need submit neither to anarchy nor to the General Will of self-appointed Guardians. Where power is unrestrained, the vision of a good life becomes a mirage, and then a bitter parody of human aspiration. The protections against the abuse of power in the Constitution were hard won, not only in our own Revolution, but in concept and practice over many centuries. Its limits on power, and its protections for real freedom, do not attract too many new friends in a world of cynical revolutions and resulting gulags. There is no assurance that our constitutional guarantees will not one day be swept away in the name of some seemingly more glorious and idealistic goal. Of anyone who would set us on such a course we should inquire, meticulously, as to the nature of the new vision, and we should assess carefully the costs and risks of the enterprise.

18. The Process of Restraint

IN ESTABLISHING FOR the Supreme Court the power of judicial review, in *Marbury v. Madison,* Chief Justice Marshall in effect proclaimed the Court to be the special guardian of the American social contract, the Constitution. The Supreme Court, and the court system as a whole, seemed well equipped to perform such a function, and in much of its work has continued to do so satisfactorily. But the Court's role as an effective guardian of the social contract had depended to a great extent upon the operation of certain well established principles limiting the scope of its power; upon procedural requirements which restrained the Court from overreaching the accepted limits of judicial authority. This amounted to a *process* of judicial restraint which has, to a large extent, now been abandoned.

In discussing the collusion between the Court and pressure groups in Chapter 14, we discovered how the Court has destroyed long established procedural concepts which had operated to exclude from judicial consideration issues which are in the province of the executive or legislative branches of government. We saw that the Court has abandoned its former reluctance to entertain "political questions;" that it has broadened the "standing to sue;" that it has made more kinds of disputes "justiciable" in court through such devices as allowing extensive class action suits, and considering fewer cases to be "moot;" and that it has extended the reach of its rulings by permitting wider use of the *amicus curiae* brief. The result has been to include within the constitutional classification of "case or controversy"—indicating the assigned jurisdiction of the courts—matters which were never intended to be there.

There are other devices of restraint of equal importance which the Court has also flouted or ignored. These include the well established principles by

214

which written documents have long been interpreted in Anglo-American law, principles which apply whether the documents be ordinary contracts, legislative enactments, or formal constitutions.

Examination of the principles of contract or statutory interpretation reveals how perfectly their application accords with the grand strategy of the Constitution—to limit all public power, including that of the Court. Whether it be Magna Carta, the Mayflower Compact, the American Constitution, or some similar document, the seminal characteristic of such documents is that they are, in essence, contracts. They are a species of the genus by which humankind moved from medieval to modern arrangements in society and government. The contract which is the Constitution, therefore, can—and should be—subject to the elementary and accepted principles of contract interpretation.

The point of departure for contract interpretation is in the words of the contract. The first principle is to read it and see what it says. If the words are, in the term of legal art, "clear and unambiguous on their face," there is no need to go further. We know what is meant and have only to do as the contract says. Essential ingredients at this point of contract interpretation are integrity and restraint. The First Amendment serves as an excellent example. That Amendment says that *Congress* shall "make no law" abridging freedom of speech, press or assembly, or establishing a religion. The meaning could hardly be more clear or unambiguous; the listed prohibitions apply to Congress, and to Congress only. Yet, in 1925, over a century and a quarter after the adoption of the First Amendment, the Supreme Court, in *Gitlow v. New York,* "assumed" that the prohibitions concerning speech and press applied also to the States by way of the Fourteenth Amendment. In *Gitlow,* as we have seen, the Court did not so much as trouble itself with an explanation of this revolutionary assumption.

Another principle of contract interpretation is that any word or phrase which might be ambiguous should be read in the context of the entire document, and should be given a meaning which comports with the general intent of the document. Candor and integrity are required in ascertaining what that intent is. In the case of the Constitution there can be no honest doubt but that its master intent was to *control* and *restrain* power. One of the most heinous offenses of judicial revisionism is that the allegedly ambiguous phrases upon which the Court has relied to invent new constitutional philosophies have not been read in the context of this clear and obvious purpose. The "due process" clause of the Fourteenth Amendment has spawned the most notorious of such misuses of the Constitution. Following its gratuitous assumption in *Gitlow v. New York,* the Court gradually "incorporated" not only the provisions of the First Amendment, but ultimately nearly the whole of the Bill of Rights, to apply against the States as well as against the federal government.

Read in context with the identical clause in the Fifth Amendment, and in the absence of any expression of intent to "incorporate" any of the Bill of Rights, the due process clause of the Fourteenth Amendment was, and is, not in the least ambiguous so far as applying those rights against the States is concerned. Rather than honoring the Constitution as amended, the Court created its own storm of ambiguity in the shadow of which it could go about imposing its will on the Constitution and the country.

The basic aim of honest contract interpretation is to determine—and give effect to—what the parties who made the contract *intended.* Otherwise the contract they made is stolen from them, and comes to mean something else. If the intent is arguably ambiguous on the face of the document, there are two generally accepted principles by which the interpreting authority may seek to ascertain the true intent. These are to discover the intent *expressed* by the parties outside the contract itself at the time it was made, and to discover the meaning the parties themselves have given to the contract in *practice.* In the case of the Constitution, evidence of its intent can be found in the Federalist papers, in the debates of the constitutional convention, or in the ratifying conventions in the States. The general intent of the main provisions of the Constitution and its Amendments is not really difficult to ascertain. Yet the Court has repeatedly displayed utter indifference to such intent.

Perhaps the most egregious, and one of the best documented, examples is the Warren Court's disposition of the history of the Fourteenth Amendment in *Brown v. Board of Education.* Faced with unrefuted evidence that the framers of that Amendment had no intention that it should apply as the Court wanted to apply it, the unanimous decision of the Court was simply to refuse to "turn back the clock" to consider what the framers of that Amendment had meant or said. The manner in which the Court has come to dismiss questions concerning the intent behind important provisions of the Constitution is as alarming as the fact of what it has done. Both the Court majority and its apologists have come to dismiss references to the intent of the framers with a sort of indulgent little smile—perhaps a condescendingly sympathetic sneer—indicating that there is something the matter with anyone who would even raise such a question. A bit antiquated and out of touch, one is given to understand. But these vignettes of contempt are really a mask to hide the face of thievery—to conceal the fact that the meaning expressed and intended in the Constitution has been stolen away through "interpretation."

If the revisionists, embarrassed at the discrepancy between their work and that of the founders, turn to the next principle of contract interpretation—the meaning the parties have given to the document in practice— they may at first seem more comfortable. There is a great deal of precedent for what the Court is up to today. That is because it has been up to the same tricks for some time now, and can point to strings of its own cases to prove it. But in order to rely on this principle, it must be shown that the practice was adopted by the *parties* to the contract—not merely by someone interpreting it for them.

Let us remind ourselves once again that the most elemental quality of a contract is *mutual agreement* between or among the *parties* to that contract. Without mutual agreement there is no contract. And without mutual agreement to *change* the contract, there is no legitimate change. The "amendments" which have been announced by the Court in recent years were argued by lawyers in quiet chambers, and adopted by the Court in closed sessions of what some apologists, as we have seen, have been pleased to term the "Revolutionary Committee." In none of this was there any agreement by those whose assent is required to make constitutional change valid—the Congress, the States, and the sovereign people of this country. Not only have we not consented, but we are only beginning to become aware of what has been done. Silence may sometimes imply consent, but silence in *ignorance* does not.

There can be no legitimate claim that what the Court has done might derive from an accepted practice. Quite the contrary is the case. What the Court has done in school prayer cases, in reapportionment, in applying the exclusionary rule, in abortion, and in other matters is to say that practices of a century or more are no longer to be allowed. The Court has told us in case after case that what everyone had always believed the Constitution to mean is not what it means at all. Any argument that the Court's doings are based on an accepted practice thus turns out to be transparently fragile, and shatters upon examination.

These principles of contract interpretation—that the clear and unambiguous meaning of contract language should be effected; that ambiguous words or phrases should be read in the context of the entire document; that the expressed intent of the parties should be observed; and that the practice of the parties should be respected—have long been accepted as a part of the law of contracts, and should be accepted as part of the "due process of law" according to which the Supreme Court interprets the greatest of our contracts, the Constitution. One would think that the Supreme Court, of all our institutions of government, might be expected to be the most sensitive in honoring accepted legal principles. And yet, in interpreting the document which is the foundation of our national polity, the Court has ignored or repudiated the elementary procedures of contract interpretation. Had these principles been observed, the shape of constitutional law today would be quite different from what it is.

If the objection be raised, as it might be, that a *social* contract should not be subject to the same rules of interpretation as ordinary contracts, we can turn for analogy to the principles of statutory interpretation. In its origins and adoption, statutory law, it is true, is more akin to a constitution than is an ordinary contract. Statutes are enacted by authorized *representatives* of the parties to the social contract—members of Congress or the state legislatures—whereas ordinary contracts are made between private parties. Yet, the principles for interpretation of statutes are very similar to those for the interpretation of contracts. It is still the duty of a court to ascertain the *intent* of the legislature, to examine the *history* of the act, to determine what was proposed, what was discussed, what changes or compromises were made, and what final meaning was *agreed* to. This is the same set of considerations we dealt with in discussing the origins of the Fourteenth Amendment in an earlier chapter of this book. The Fourteenth Amendment, in origin though not in ratification and adoption, was a *legislative* act, and in that sense similar to any other statute.

It has long been accepted that the words of a statute must be given the meaning attributed to them by those who drew the act, at the time it was drawn. Yet it is sometimes the case that the words of a statute can be construed to mean what a later proponent *wants* them to mean, even though such was demonstrably not the original intent of the legislature. It is the recognized rule that if such a later construction can arguably be found within the words of a statute, but still not within its *intent,* that construction is not to be held to be "within the statute." The framers of the Constitution understood this very well, and so expressed themselves on numerous occasions.

James Wilson, a leading participant in the constitutional convention, who later became Supreme Court Justice Wilson, said that, "The first and governing maxim in the interpretation of a statute is to discover the meaning of those who made it." Jefferson, as President, pledged to administer the Constitution "according to the safe and honest meaning contemplated by the plain understanding of the people at the time of its adoption— a meaning to be found in the explanations of those who advocated . . . it." Chief Justice Marshall, who participated in the Virginia ratification convention, recognized, in speaking to that body, that if a word was understood in a particular way when the Constitution was framed, the constitutional convention "must have used it in that sense."[1]

An example would be the universally understood meaning of the term "due process of law" as used in the Fifth Amendment. That term was meant to apply to the procedures used in court, and never to any legislative enactment. Did that plain understanding trouble Chief Justice Taney when he wished to find a rationale for declaring the Missouri Compromise unconstitutional? Not at all. No more than the same phrase, with the same meaning, in the Fourteenth Amendment troubled the *Lochner* Court when it invented "substantive due process," or later Courts which found baths for mental patients or visitation rights for prisoners to be part of "due process of law"!

Finally, whether we put the discussion in terms of *contract* interpretation, or in terms of *statutory* interpretation, the result is the same. The purpose of either is to discover the *intent* of those responsible for the framing of the document. In either case this is done through application of commonly accepted principles by which courts have long been guided in interpreting written instruments. Whether the courts accept such guidance depends upon whether they are willing to practice self-restraint, and display integrity, in doing their work. Chief Justice Warren's handling of the history of the Fourteenth Amendment in *Brown v. Board* evinced a conspicuous lack of both traits. The attack on the schools which followed was a perfect example, not of judicial restraint, but of Romantic madness. Once judicial meddling set in, and the buses began to roll, the pull of perfection and the push of guilt drove courts at all levels to excesses which have kept the schools in turmoil ever since. Rousseau would have smiled upon such a marvellous example of his handiwork.

Judicial self-restraint must necessarily begin with an unwavering perception on the part of the judges that they are but *one element* of the constitutional scheme, and that the grand design of which they are a part is to *limit* governmental power, *including theirs.* They are not free to pluck "emanations" of their own fancy from "penumbras" of their own manufacture, as the Court with unabashed license did in *Griswold v. Connecticut.* Nor are they authorized to focus narrowly upon isolated phrases of the Constitution—in a kind of constitutional scrabble game—to see whether some particular phrase, taken by itself or rearranged with other phrases, can be redesigned to accomplish what may seem to them a laudable goal. On the contrary, judges are required—if they are to live up to their oath to *defend* the Constitution—to operate within the realization that the whole purpose of that document is to provide for a process of restraint in the exercise of power.

It is an odd thing that, in principle—and emphatically, if one is to believe their words—Justices of every stripe express agreement on all this: it is the Constitution which must control, and all of their decisions must be firmly anchored in that document. It is even accepted that more recent decisions of the Supreme Court itself should not control over the provisions of the Constitution where there is a conflict. Chief Justice Burger "categorically" denied that what the Court has most lately said should control over the Constitution; Justice Frankfurter agreed that the "ultimate touchstone of constitutionality is the Constitution itself and not what we have said about it;" while even the arch-interventionist himself, Justice William O. Douglas, wrote that a judge "remembers above all else that it is the Constitution which he swore to support and defend, not the gloss which his predecessors may have put upon it."[2] Harvard's Raoul Berger agrees, yet comments rather somberly upon the assertions of these Justices:

> Like Chief Justice Burger and Justices Douglas and Frank-
> furter, I assert the right to look at the Constitution itself,
> stripped of judicial encrustations, as the index of constitu-
> tional law and to affirm that the Supreme Court has no
> authority to substitute an "unwritten Constitution" for the
> written Constitution the Founders gave us and the people
> ratified.[3]

Various other commentators have felt differently about the document conceived nearly two centuries ago in Philadelphia, and have not hesitated to say so. We have heard the Constitution referred to as "archaic;" we have been told that it consists of "absolute artifacts of verbal archaeology;" we hear that it is "strictly a matter of concern only to theoreticians;" it is asserted that the Constitution expresses the "idiosyncratic purposes of the Framers," and even that to seek its intent seriously is "filialpiestic" irrelevance.

It may be that some of the eighteenth century terms in which our basic documents of government are couched are quaint, perhaps even archaic sounding, to the modern ear. Consider the solicitude of Thomas Jefferson and those who labored with him on the Declaration of Independence for the "decent respect to the opinions of mankind," which required them to explain to the world what they were doing. How charmingly naive! One thinks of powdered wigs and a minuet, of a Haydn trio or a Mozart quintet, flawlessly executed in a chandeliered drawing room. Imagine a Khomeini, an Amin, a Castro, a Hitler, a Mao, a Khadafy or a Gorbachev thinking in terms of a "decent respect" for the opinions of mankind! It would be "counter-revolutionary" to the tyrants of the twentieth century to refer to the idea of a government "deriving their just powers from the consent of the governed"—except for a good belly laugh. It is no longer, "We the People" who "do ordain and establish" governments. The "people" need not trouble themselves in an era where ministrations for their benefit are so readily available—from those who "know best." There is more than a hint of such thinking in decisions of the Warren era, and the virus has since worked its way insidiously into the nation's judicial system at all levels.

Those who labored on the Constitution at Philadelphia, and the literate and intelligent colonists who, by their ratification after vigorous and sometimes acrimonious debate, cemented themselves together as a nation, truly *did* possess a civility which might today seem strange. Yet, if some would now dismiss the fruits of their labor with a quick grimace and a flick of the wrist, it is a dismissal without discussion. The argument has yet to be made that the Framers lacked strength, courage, or foresight. Nor is it likely to be maintained without a blush that they failed to understand the abuses of power, or that, collectively, they did not comprise one of the most remarkable groups of men ever to come together to draw up an instrument of government. It is only that somehow, mysteriously, without our quite knowing why, their work has come to be declared "archaic" by so many "liberal" thinkers.

In the event, however, that we do not agree with that assessment, there is much in our constitutional tradition by which to guide our thoughts. Some twenty years after *Marbury v. Madison*, Chief Justice Marshall again addressed the subject of *constitutional* interpretation, in an equally famous case, *Gibbons v. Ogden*.[4] The case dealt with the power to regulate commerce, which had been vested in Congress by the Constitution. If the power were to be broadly construed, Congress could establish a uniform national system for commerce among the States. If narrowly construed, there would be the risk of unreasonable state barriers to commerce, of trade restrictions, and even of the kind of commercial chaos which had been one of the principal conditions leading to the constitutional convention in the first place. Marshall looked to the great purposes of the Constitution, and to accepted principles of *contract* interpretation:

> As men, whose intentions require no concealment, generally employ the words which most directly and aptly express the ideas they intend to convey the enlightened patriots who framed our constitution, and the people who adopted it, must be understood to have employed words in their natural sense, and to have intended what they have said. If, from the imperfection of human language, there should be serious doubts respecting the extent of any given power, it is a well-settled rule, that the objects for which it was given, especially, when those objects are expressed in the instrument itself, should have great influence in the construction . . . We know of no rule for construing the extent of such powers, other than is given by the language of the instrument which confers them, taken in connection with the purposes for which they were conferred.[5]

In his decision in *Gibbons v. Ogden* the power of Congress "to regulate commerce . . . among several states" was upheld by Marshall as clearly *expressed* and *intended,* and state claims which would have interfered with that power were disallowed.

The last sentence in the passage quoted says, in itself, almost all there is to be said about the function of a court in interpreting a written constitution: "We know of no rule for construing the extent of such powers, other than as given by the language of the instrument which confers them, taken in connection with the purposes for which they were conferred."

Interventionist courts, from *Dred Scott* to the present, have taken quite a different view of the Constitution. Despite their lip service to it, these courts have claimed for themselves, not the power to *interpret* the Constitution, but the power *to govern.* An excellent example of this is furnished in a comment by Court of Appeals Judge J. Skelly Wright, quoted in a previous chapter. Judge Wright advances the view that the need for judicial action is strongest in the areas of the law where political processes have proved "inadequate," and where problems have been "neglected" by politicians. Wright concludes that, "If the legislatures continue to neglect their constitutional responsibilities, we can only hope that the Court will continue to do the best it can to fill the gap."[6] In a more recent speech at Harvard Law School, Judge Wright conceded, happily, that some judges "have gotten carried away" in wielding such power, implying that some constraints might be appropriate after all. One can imagine a celestial twinge of recognition on the faces of the Founding Fathers, and almost hear a murmur of hope that their "idiosyncratic purposes" might not have missed the mark so far after all.

But the ghosts of the Founding Fathers should not be too sanguine before hearing from Professor Archibald Cox. As Special Prosecutor during the Watergate affair, Professor Cox was removed from that office in the famous "Saturday night massacre," which in turn caused the resignation of the Attorney General and other officials. In his book, *The Role of the Supreme Court in American Government,* Professor Cox argues that the cause of the downfall of the "Imperial Presidency" of Richard Nixon was his contempt of legal and constitutional processes. Yet, in the same book, Professor Cox appears still to place himself among those who are not equally concerned about an Imperial Judiciary. Constitutional adjudication depends, in his view, upon a "delicate, symbiotic relation" between the Court and the people:

> The aspirations voiced by the Court must be those the com-
> munity is willing not only to avow but in the end to live by.
> The legitimacy of the great constitutional decisions rests
> upon the accuracy of the Court's perception of this kind of
> common will and upon the Court's ability, by expressing its
> perception, ultimately to command a consensus.[7]

This comes perilously close to saying that what is constitutional is whatever the Court can get away with; that the Court has full license to tinker and meddle so long as it guesses right about its risk of being ignored, impeached, or amended out of business.

What does such a view have to say if some new, yet still marvelously "symbiotic" Court majority, based in a different constituency, should decide, for example, that free speech is a bloody nuisance? Or that certain groups of voters are subversive and ought to be disenfranchised? Or that public funds should no longer be wasted on trials of the obviously guilty, who should therefore be taken directly to jail? If the Court seeks only to "command a consensus" there is nothing whatsoever to prevent that consensus from resting on freshly invented "reasons of state," which could as easily serve to justify the obliteration of all constitutional government as to preserve it. There are no guidelines to restraint left in such a constitutional philosophy as this.

The view expressed by Professor Cox affirms how easily it is that passions—often deeply embedded in the psychic makeup of a judge—can influence the process of his decision making on vital constitutional issues. Sometimes emotions may be consciously forged into a new "symbiosis." At other times, as we know, a judge may not even be aware of the operation of such forces. Emotion charges in where reason should rule— the limbic system erupts to neutralize the neocortex. Deeply felt beliefs of right and wrong form screens around the mind which allow to pass only data which tend to support views already held—*judgments* already made— and to exclude any material which might lead to a contrary conclusion. Justice Black engaged in some such exercise in his reapportionment opinion in *Wesberry v. Sanders,* rejecting constitutional history to reach a preordained conclusion.

What we must ask of the judges is that they become *aware* of the screens, that they endeavor to remove them, and that they admit all the evidence which fairly bears on a constitutional issue, however repugnant that evidence may seem to them. The traditional way in which judges have been trained to excise their own prejudices, and to compensate for their own inadequacies, is through observation of the principles of contract and statutory interpretation, and the other processes of restraint which we have discussed. They all were schooled in the principles of ripeness and mootness, of what constitutes a case or controversy, in the dangers of adjudicating political questions, and in matters of justiciability and the standing to sue. They all know how properly to interpret a written contract. They know well that faithful adherence to the requirements of these tested judicial processes would conform to the constitutional purpose which they are appointed and sworn to serve. When these principles and processes are not honored, restraint is lost.

When judges loosen or disregard these restraints, their decisions are no longer related to the Constitution. The Constitution becomes simply whatever the Court says it is—in which case the Court's ultimate authority is no more than its own opinionated urges and causes.

19. Gubernaculum and Jurisdictio

THE SUBJECT OF this book is restraint on the power of government, which is necessarily coercive. The courts themselves, at their best or at their worst, are a part of the governmental power structure. While the ultimate authority of the courts may rest upon a general willingness to obey their judgments, in the meantime there are bailiffs and sheriffs, prisons and fines for contempt, to deal with those who would flout the law as spoken by the courts. The genius of Anglo-American law, and particularly of the American Constitution, is that, even though courts partake of sovereign governmental power, they have come to be separated from the coercive powers of government in a manner which has left them uniquely fitted to act as guarantors of the right of free people to claim significant immunity from what might otherwise be total government control. The limits on legislative and executive power laid down in the Constitution are boundaries which it is within the constitutional authority of the courts to police and to enforce. What we are faced with in activist jurisprudence is a breaking down of the distinction between the authority of the courts to police these boundaries, as a matter of law, and the tendency of the other branches of government to ignore the constitutional limits placed on government in exercising coercive power. This happens when the courts, rather than policing the other branches of government, begin taking on coercive powers themselves.

Let a good friend of activist judges, Anthony Lewis of the *New York Times,* speak, as he is wont to do, unabashedly as to what the Supreme Court has really been up to. Lewis has boasted that Chief Justice Warren "was the closest thing the United States has had to a Platonic Guardian, dispensing law from a throne without any sensed limits of power except what was seen to be the good of society." Oddly, such glowing praise

225

seemed tinged with a nagging doubt, even from Lewis. He added, "Fortunately he was a decent, human, honorable, democratic Guardian."[1]

The decisions to which Lewis refers are those treated in this book, and all of them can fairly be subject to the comment Professor John Hart Ely made of the abortion decision in *Roe v. Wade*. They are wrong. They are wrong not because they are *bad* constitutional law, but because they make no attempt *to be* constitutional law. They make no attempt to be *law* of any kind.

Such departures by the Court have not as yet been subject to any effective tests or controls by which to judge their validity, or to reverse them when wrong, yet the issue is clear enough. The lines are drawn between an elite which thinks it "knows best," which includes not only activist judges, but their supporters in the academy, the media, and intellectual circles, and the institutions of law and representative government for which our Constitution provides.

The true purpose of courts can be vividly perceived by recalling, as if in reverse image, the function courts are made to perform when any fully socialist system comes to prevail. In such a system the courts do not serve as protection against a tyrannical minority (or majority), nor to guarantee the rights of persons. Rather, they function to advance the ends of the state, as a means to disguise the uses of illegitimate power, as willing instruments of tyranny and oppression. Law vanishes, and the courts become thoroughly political institutions. Such a use of "law" has been vividly documented in what British historian Paul Johnson has termed Fidel Castro's "first unambiguous act of tyranny" after gaining power in Cuba in 1959. A "war crimes" court had acquitted a number of Batista air force men for lack of evidence. The president of the court was soon thereafter found dead, was replaced, and a new trial found the defendants all guilty. Castro explained that, "Revolutionary Justice is based not upon legal precepts but on moral conviction."[2]

The Supreme Court has led the American judiciary in a similar direction. The Court has not been coerced by a Castro or forced by an Ortega; it has not been neutered by a Hitler or bludgeoned by a Stalin. No, the Court has only been seduced by its own insatiable proclivity for "doing good." The "conscience" of the judge, his "moral conviction," has been invited to take the place of a conscientious search for the meaning of the law, or of the Constitution, as legitimately enacted or adopted.

The rise of interventionist jurisprudence, and its departure from the norms of law, suggests what may be a largely unconscious, yet potentially lethal, drift of our entire political system towards the embrace of statism. If the late eighteenth and the nineteenth centuries seemed to present the cheerful prospect of expanding liberty, and an ever more successful pursuit of happiness, the twentieth century has moved somberly in the opposite direction. The plague of communist-fascist ideology has already engulfed much of the planet. The milder, hence perhaps more deceptive and seductive, liberal-socialist variant has deeply infected Western patterns of thought. This drift has been brilliantly illustrated by Paul Johnson, in his stimulating work, *Modern Times*.[3]

Johnson points to the concept of relativism as perhaps the chief source of twentieth century disruption, bloodshed and violence. He traces the origins of the relativistic view to the proof of Einstein's theory of relativity. When this idea began to appear in popular culture, older beliefs and faiths disintegrated. It came to be believed that there were no longer absolutes of good and evil, of knowledge, or of value, any more than there were perceived under the Einstein theory to exist absolutes in time and space. The effects have been cataclysmic.

One of the most devastating results has been acceptance of the concept of "social engineering," which Johnson demonstrates was most effectively inaugurated by Lenin. Lenin intended this concept as an operational device by which to advance the root and branch destruction of the institutions of Western society which stood in the way of his expressed goals, and which his heirs have not altered. Social engineering is directly related to the Romanticism of Rousseau, and to the idea of the perfectibility of man on earth. When the vision is vivid, fire is in the eyes, and all power is in the state, nothing said for existing institutions can stand in the way of the "progress" to come.

Social engineering was a preeminent aim of the Warren Court, reflecting a similar revolutionary infection deep within elements of American society. A common point of departure of all modern tyranny has been an initial intent (or at least an alleged intent) to do good. The elusive *end* then becomes compelling, and if the *means* to that end are the destruction of all limits on the power of some individuals to coerce and control others, we tend not to notice. Until it is too late.

The Supreme Court has "engineered" out of existence one constitutional restraint after another, slowly at first, at an accelerating pace during the last few decades, in the name of causes which it perceived as worthy.

When Chief Justice Warren was faced with a constitutional argument supporting a position which would have thwarted the particular policy he was at the time intent on imposing, his habitual question to counsel would be, "But is it good?" Not, "Is it the law?" Or even, "Is it what the Constitution says?" Under such a standard, what is the "good" to be sought in any particular case? Where is it to be discovered, and how defined? And if the policy at hand is "good," but not constitutional, does it not follow (as it did for Warren) that the Constitution, when measured in opposition to some Justice's concept of the good, is *not* good?

It is difficult to imagine a more devastating attack on constitutional government than that inherent in Warren's apparently well-intentioned question. Such an approach to the Constitution is the end of the line for the rule of law. We know how the rule of law ended in communist Cuba, as it has in all other communist, or "Marxist," states, yet it is not always easy to see the same image in similar threats of a more domestic variety. What are we to make, for example, of the growing disregard in leading law schools for even a pretense of constitutional justification for judicial activism? Professor William Kristol has adopted a phrase from the *Communist Manifesto*, "They Disdain to Conceal Their Views and Aims," as the title of an arresting article discussing this movement.[4] Kristol reports evidence of widespread abandonment of any deference to established forms of government in the most radical precincts of legal education. As one sympathizer has admitted, this drive is animated by "a deep hostility to liberal legalism and the capitalistic economic and social structure with which liberal legalism is associated."[5] There is a heavy dosage of Marxist criticism and socialist sympathy. So much so that, for the most radical, "democracy means socialism, not elections,"[6] and so it is that Kristol concludes that proponents of such attacks on established legal institutions now "disdain to conceal their views and aims."

If it be true that many judicial activists would not espouse quite such a radical departure from legal norms, still Professor Kristol has pointed accurately to the direction in which they are all heading. The prospect is chilling, and causes one to ponder once again the wisdom of those in Philadelphia who knew so well the lust for power lodged in the human psyche, and sought, two centuries ago, for devices permanently to curb its abuses. Has the lure of privilege, or the will to dominate, been much attenuated in the interim? Has the neocortex gained noticeably in its evolutionary struggle with the animal passions of the limbic system in a bare 200 years? Or, as these things sometimes appear to change, is it still much as the French proverb has it, *"Plus ca change, plus c'est la meme chose"?* Is it that the more change there appears to be, the more things, in truth, remain the same?

Despite the barrage of judicial policy making which we have lately endured, it is obvious that the framers of the Constitution intended, not to enshrine policy in that document, but to provide a means through the political system by which policy should be adopted—and changed—from time to time. Professor John Hart Ely notes that, "As a charter of government a constitution must prescribe legitimate processes, not legitimate outcomes, if like ours (and unlike more ideological documents elsewhere) it is to serve many generations through changing times."[7] Chief Justice William Rehnquist once observed that the limitations which the Constitution places upon both federal and state governments "were not themselves designed to solve the problems of the future, but were instead designed to make certain that the constituent branches, when *they* attempted to solve those problems, should not transgress these fundamental limitations."[8]

Yet transgress the Court may, whenever it declares unconstitutional an Act of Congress. Judicial veto brushes aside all of the complex considerations of the political process, and suspends the theory of democratic responsibility. This is an exercise of power not to be undertaken lightly. The determination of as few as five Justices can obliterate the political product of some 535 members of Congress, together with all the political and social input which had led to the adoption of the Act to be voided. These responsibilities of judicial review are serious enough when the Court simply confines itself to *reviewing* Acts of Congress—in the manner in which judicial review has traditionally been understood.

When the Court goes further, and allows itself to leap from review to the *creation* of social policy, it is not simply overruling, it is *displacing,* the political process. It is substituting itself for the 535 members of Congress, for the Executive in exercising its correlative legislative functions of checks and balances, and for the whole remaining apparatus of political decision making. This includes the political parties, related interests of state and local governments, and many similar functions and aspects of the political system. Such acts by the Court are, in any meaningful sense, simply indescribable within the uses and understanding of constitutional restraints. They are blatantly and flatly *outside the law.*

Although he accepted implicitly the traditional processes of restraint, it was Chief Justice Marshall who, if unintentionally, laid the foundation for today's rejection of those restraints. Yet Marshall, even as he asserted for the courts the power of judicial review in *Marbury v. Madison,* took great pains to *define* and *limit* that power. He held that "the province of the court is, solely, to decide the rights of individuals," therefore its province was "not to inquire how the executive, or executive officers, perform duties in which they have a discretion." He believed that, "Questions in their nature political . . . can never be made in this court."[9] He then demonstrated the reasons why the Court would, he believed, be so restrained.

Marshall affirmed that only the *people* have an original right to establish a constitution, and that that right "is the basis on which the whole American fabric has been erected." He reminded us that the exercise of that original right was "a very great exertion," which by its nature ought not, and could not, be frequently repeated. He recognized that, "The principles, therefore, so established, are deemed fundamental: and as the authority from which they proceed is supreme, and can seldom act, they are designed to be permanent."[10]

Marshall then explicated the very essence of a constitutional process: "To what purpose is power limited, and to what purpose is that limitation committed to writing, if these limits may, at any time, be passed by those intended to be restrained? The distinction between a government with limited and unlimited power is abolished, if those limits do not bind the person on whom they are imposed, and if acts prohibited and acts allowed, are of equal obligation." Marshall concluded, therefore, that, "It is a proposition too plain to be contested, that the constitution controls any legislative act repugnant to it," for, if this were not so, "the legislative may alter the constitution by an ordinary act."[11]

Can anyone find in *Marbury v. Madison* the faintest whisper of a hint that the *Supreme Court* may alter the Constitution by "an ordinary act," when *Congress* is *prohibited* from doing so? On the contrary, to Marshall it was apparent "that the framers of the Constitution contemplated that instrument as a rule for the government of the courts, as well as of the legislature. Why otherwise does it direct the judges to take an oath to support it?"

Why, indeed?

"This oath certainly applies [to judges] in an especial manner, to their conduct in their official character," said Marshall. "How immoral to impose it on them, if they were to be used as the instruments, and the knowing instruments, for violating what they swear to support!"[12] What

Marshall was telling us, and what all too many of his successors have failed to heed, is that the grand design of the Constitution—its farthest reach—is to provide a *process* by which to *restrain* the exercise of *power.* It was never intended—as the Court has come to use it—that the Constitution should serve as an excuse for the repudiation of restraints on the judicial process which were assumed and accepted by all, or as a foundation for judicial policy-making.

Edward Gibbon observed, in his great work on the decline and fall of the Roman Empire, that "the discretion of the judge is the first engine of tyranny."[13] "Discretion," used in this sense, is whatever a judge thinks is right, for whatever reason, or for no reason. A judicial decision based on *discretion* is at the opposite pole from one based upon *law,* or upon the Constitution. Can we say with certainty that some future Gibbon will not point to the year 1954, and to the decision in *Brown v. Board of Education,* and say, "In that year, and in that decision, with the best of intentions, the engine of tyranny was set in motion"? Or one might choose, instead of *Brown v. Board, Lochner v. New York,* or *Dred Scott v. Sandford.* Even, heaven forbid, *Marbury v. Madison?*

When we find the Court emerging from the shrouded half light of some newly cast "penumbra," bearing heretofore undiscovered "emanations" from the mysterious interstices of secluded constitutional recesses, we are coming full circle back to something very like the smokey precincts of the Oracle at Delphi. But even the ancient Greeks who worshipped at the Delphic shrine brought with them a profound concern for the concept of restraint. They lived under the motto, "Nothing in excess." This motto reflects one of the deepest fears in ancient Greek civilization, a fear mirrored in the companion motto, "Moderation in all things." The Greeks believed that if will or passion were carried to excess, retribution was sure to follow. To the goddess Nemesis was assigned the duty of meting out swift and terrible punishment to those guilty of excess. There was a special word—hubris—to describe that quality of excess which called down the vengeance of the goddess. The concept of hubris, together with the retribution of Nemesis, formed the original basis of tragic drama. Greek tragedy, and the theatre itself, were invented out of these concepts.

To the Greeks, the essence of tragedy is a strong and good individual who goes too far, asks too much, crosses the forbidden border, and, in so doing, arrogates unto himself the qualities of the gods. Then Nemesis strikes. Oedipus learns that he has slept with his mother, and blinds himself. Clytemnestra and her lover murder her husband, Agamemnon, and in retribution she is killed by Orestes, her son. The Greeks, only barely civilized, had a profound fear of savagery. Their tragic drama may be seen as a paean to ordered society, and a sermon to those who would, through excess, risk return to disintegration and chaos. Yet, for all the religious origins of Greek drama, tragedy operates directly out of human nature, and requires no divine intervention. The twentieth century is filled with hubris, and the wreckage of Nemesis is everywhere. In country after country the abuse of power has brought crashing down the horrors of revolution, and in most cases revolutionary excesses far worse than those replaced. We learn again, and then again, how quickly still the mask of law may slip from a savage face.

This country, in 1776, was blessed by monumental good luck in following the precepts of the Greeks, whether consciously or not. The American revolution was a revolution of moderation. The results of that revolution, following the characteristics of the event itself, were balance and toleration. The machinery of government fabricated at Philadelphia is a miracle of craftsmanship, what one commentator has termed "a sunburst of political genius," which has endured longer than any other formal governmental structure today in existence. But it is not immortal, and it is not indestructible. The mainspring of the constitutional machine, the separation of powers, is simple and strong. But it can be broken.

There is not much in the hot media format of the "Now" society or the "Me" generation to induce one towards contemplation of what the future may bring. Past and future tend to become equally irrelevant in the "Red Hot Now." Yet history tells us repeatedly that those who do not prepare for the future may have none. Or, as the philosopher George Santayana has supposedly put it, those who do not remember history are condemned to relive it. In the perspective of Anglo-American history one might expect that the court system, and particularly the United States Supreme Court, would be preeminent among those institutions taking a longer range view of society. The procedures by which courts operate, the history of the development of law, the reasoned deliberation followed by a written opinion explaining the decision—all present an opportunity ideally suited to the exercise of perspective. But that is not what has emerged from the Court.

What we have had, instead, is a "Now Generation" of Justices, who seem to have forgotten, or to have repudiated, their constitutional past. As the judicial wrecking ball has swung against one social institution after another, and as the Court has virtually laid siege to the social foundations, in all of its explanations of what it has done there does not appear much reflection as to what the long term results might be. There is a grave danger that one result may be a loss of confidence in the Supreme Court, and in the capacity of the judicial system to police the Constitution fairly. In 1942 Max Lerner commented on the unique status of the American Constitution, and of the Supreme Court, in the minds of Americans:

> Talk to the men on the street, the men in the mines and
> factories and steel mills and real-estate offices and filling
> stations, dig into their minds and even below the threshold
> of their consciousness, and you will find in the main that the
> Constitution and the Supreme Court are symbols of an
> ancient sureness and comforting stability.[14]

Is there anyone who can say with assurance that the same faith remains today?

There is an even greater danger, which is the danger of a loss of faith in constitutionalism itself. There is the possibility that we shall lose the very understanding of what a constitution is, and of what its purposes are, upon which confidence in the system must rest. For assistance in grasping the fundamentals of this prospect there is perhaps still no more perceptive and sensitive an analysis of the irreducible essentials of constitutionalism than that advanced by the late Professor Charles Howard McIlwain.[15] Two words sum it up: *gubernaculum* and *jurisdictio*.

Gubernaculum is the power to govern. In our system that would include the Congress, the Executive, and the agencies operating under the executive branch. The term encompasses all of the political, policy-making, and legislative powers which are entrusted to government. *Jurisdictio* is the province of law administered by independent courts. Its most important feature is the enforcement of individual rights against government power. In order to exercise this responsibility, it is utterly essential that courts remain independent of the governing power. The courts must be able to stand against a king or a president, a dictator or a junta, a parliament or a congress, whenever *gubernaculum* seeks to intrude upon *jurisdictio*.

Jurisdictio is uniquely designed for the settling of *private* disputes, and for the protection of *individual* rights against the encroachment of public power. Professor McIlwain puts it this way:

> If *Jurisdictio* is essential to liberty, and *jurisdictio* is a thing
> of law, it is the law that must be maintained against arbitrary
> will. And the one institution above all others essential to the
> preservation of the law has always been and still is an hon-
> est, able, learned, independent judiciary.[16]

Jurisdictio is the power of the courts to guard rights which have been won
or granted, and which have been embodied either in ordinary law or in the
more permanent law of the Constitution.

We know that rights are never won forever, and that it is in the nature of
government, sooner or later, to find reasons to encroach upon them. This
includes governments of elected representatives of the people as much as it
includes the lords and kings who governed in the past, or the false saviors
who abound in the present. Professor McIlwain concludes his provocative
study on constitutionalism with the following passage:

> We must leave open the possibility of an appeal from the
> people drunk to the people sober, if individual and minority
> rights are to be protected in the periods of excitement and
> hysteria from which we are unfortunately not immune. The
> long and fascinating story of the balancing of *jurisdictio* and
> *gubernaculum,* of which I could give only the barest outline
> here, should be, if we could study it with an open mind, of
> some help in adjusting and maintaining today the delicate
> balance of will and law, the central practical problem of
> politics now as it has been in all past ages. The two funda-
> mental correlative elements of constitutionalism for which
> all lovers of liberty must yet fight are the legal limits to arbi-
> trary power and a complete political responsibility of gov-
> ernment to the governed.[17]

The framers of the American Constitution knew that in order to assure
"legal limits to arbitrary power" the only answer was a judiciary completely independent from political domination. Their understanding was
that the great and independent powers they conferred upon the courts
would be used to police the boundaries of the Constitution, and to guarantee that the legislative and executive branches did not encroach upon the
rights of the people. They knew their history, and they knew the necessity
of what they did.

But it never occurred to the Founders that the courts would ever claim the kinds of power—usurped from the sphere of *gubernaculum*—which they have now come to exercise. As one follows the course of the decisions which have led to this pass, it becomes ever more apparent that something has gone terribly wrong. However earnestly the Court may have labored, the result is strange and disquieting. The fearsome doubt grows that we are confronted with a product which is alien to the entire enterprise which the Court was designed to serve. There is absent in these decisions any connection to the legal and constitutional *culture* which is the grounding of the Constitution, and of the powers of the Court. The Court's newly discovered "principles" are not of the law, but of the will; not the result of defined and bridled power, but of power which has broken the constitutional mold, imperious and unpredictable. With hardly any display of fundamental thought, and emanating at times pristine ignorance of the whole matter, the Court has gone about repudiating the principles of our social contract, and savaging its structure.

The institutional imbalance which has developed is akin to that which faced the barons of England in 1215. Except it is the judges, and not the King, who are today's usurpers. Nor is it unlike the struggle between Lord Coke and James I. Except that now it is the agency of the law, the Court, and not the agency of power, the Throne, which is the villain. Lord Coke held up the law to the King and said that the King was wrong. For this he was contemptuously dismissed. Today, those who hold up the Constitution to the Court and say that the Court is wrong are dismissed with similar arrogance. Today, as in the England of Coke and James I, there is no agency of government exercising the authority to correct a dangerous abuse of governmental power.

We face the results of judicial self-control in a state of utter collapse. In their pressing charge towards higher justice, the Justices have thrust aside the patient implements of judicial restraint; they have annulled the limitations placed upon them by the Constitution. The social, political, and legal forms from which the power-taming concepts of *jurisdictio* and *gubernaculum* were shaped have been shattered, to be replaced by—we know not what.

20.   Liberty Under Law?

"JUDICIAL POWER, AS contradistinguished from the power of the laws, has no existence. Courts are the mere instruments of the law, and can will nothing."[1] That was the constitutional deal as Chief Justice John Marshall saw it, and as it was universally understood when the Constitution was written. In return for life tenure on the bench, and the absence of direct intervention by any other branch of the government, courts would play a limited and objective role in the constitutional system, and would abjure any policy-making function. A century later Charles Evans Hughes, soon to become Chief Justice, still claimed the Court to be "about as far removed from political influence as any human institution could possibly be."[2]

But in imposing a conservative veto upon congressional actions in the past, and in legislating a liberal-socialist agenda in recent decades, the Court has not kept the faith. The judiciary, which was contemplated as a bastion of stability and order, has fallen victim to the "social engineering" which has characterized the disruptions of the twentieth century. The Court, while displaying an almost innocent insolence, has drawn itself into a stance of royal arrogance quite outside the structure of the Constitution. We have lately addressed the problem of an Imperial Presidency. We must now address the problem of an Imperial Judiciary.

In order to preserve the unique functions of the executive and the legislature—and at the same time guard against excess—each of those agencies is endowed with some part of the powers of the other. When the President becomes too "Imperial," Congress can pull on the constitutional reins; when Congress exhibits either inability to act or a proclivity to become too powerful, the President can play his constitutional cards. Both the executive and the legislative branches are also subject to the review of the courts, and their abuses can be checked in this way as well. Moreover, the abuses of both the executive and the legislature can be restrained or reversed by popular elections.

None of this applies to the Supreme Court, or to any of the judges of the lower federal court system. They are presently restrained effectively neither by Congress nor by the President, and they are appointed for life, untouchable through the ordinary political or electoral process.

The framers knew that the sirens of some invented necessity or other sing sweetly from every rock and crag of government. And yet, in providing for the checks and balances of government, it would now appear that they left a gaping breach in the constitutional defenses against abusive power, one through which the Supreme Court, fired by ever changing visions of "justice," has charged time and again. The founding fathers failed to provide specifically for an institution whose job it was to check judicial power run wild. The Congress and the President were subject to clearly stated checks and balances—the Supreme Court was not.

The reason for the omission was that the framers wished to avoid the possibility of legislative or executive interference with the necessary independence of the courts. But the utterly crucial basis for this reasoning was an assumption that the courts would continue to operate as they had in the Anglo-American system for centuries. Nothing in the whole theory or history of separation of powers would make any sense if it were to be assumed that courts of law could usurp the power of Congress to legislate, or the power of Congress, the States, and the people to amend the Constitution.

How do we get courts to stop legislating? How do we get the Supreme Court to admit that it has no authority to amend the Constitution, and to cease doing so? How do we make it clear that the Justices are not to be point persons for a political agenda? How do we convince the judicial system that it is beginning to display the fearsome symptoms of its false image in statist societies?

One noted commentator advocated a vigorous remedy: "Make your judges responsible. Impeach them. Impeachment of a judge would be a very healthful thing in these times."[3] That was William Howard Taft, who is not ordinarily considered a radical, speaking during the heyday of the *Lochner* Court in 1911. Taft was then President, and later became Chief Justice, the only person in our history to have occupied both of those high offices. But, while many might cheer his suggestion most heartily, Taft had forgotten the lesson of Jefferson and his Republicans in their abortive effort to remove Justice Chase through the impeachment process. History tells us that impeachment, so far at least, has not solved the problem.

Another solution is to await presidential appointments of new Justices who presumably would pay greater homage to the Constitution, and perhaps even give evidence of understanding it. But history also teaches us that presidential guesses regarding appointments to the Court cannot be counted upon to effect a lasting limitation of the Court's own power. In the long run all that new appointments can assure us is that the Court's legislating and amending urge might be held off for a more or less respectable period of mourning; but we know that the urge will recur, in some changed political atmosphere, in the guise of some novel judicial revelation, in pursuit of some new and elevated cause.

There is, of course, the alternative of constitutional amendment, a remedy which, however, requires a virtual political upheaval to accomplish. The fact that many of the supporters of Court encroachment point to amendment as a remedy, if the country does not like what is being done, bears stark (if unintended) witness to the fact that amendment is now routinely accomplished by as few as five extra-constitutional votes on the Supreme Court. To "un-amend" the damage done in this manner, we are told, we must go through the long and tortuous procedures set down in the Constitution as its legitimate mode of change. But does the Constitution stack the cards against itself that badly? Is there good reason why we should continue to labor under this judicially created, and politically impossible, impediment?

Another possibility would be to inaugurate a movement requiring that Supreme Court Justices be subject to a vote of reconfirmation, or retention, after a given number of years on the bench. This is a practice which has been widely adopted among the States, most notably in California, where a successful effort to unseat the Chief Justice and two Associate Justices has gained national attention. The complaint against such a system predictably would be that a periodic vote of affirmation would interfere with the independence of the Court. The question, however, is not primarily one of independence, but of responsibility. When judges refuse to be bound by the terms of a written constitution, and in particular when they feel free to revise such a constitution at will, they have forsaken their claim to complete independence, for the reason that they have repudiated the expected judicial responsibility upon which that claim is based. To adopt any system of reconfirmation for Justices of the United States Supreme Court would, of course, require a constitutional amendment. Perhaps the introduction of such an amendment, and the debate which it would entail in Congress, in the media, and among the states and the people would prove therapeutic, whatever the fate of the amendment might be in simply drawing our attention to fundamental issues.

The power of judicial review, as affirmed by Chief Justice Marshall in *Marbury v. Madison,* contemplated for the Court the relatively modest role of border policeman, yet there is evidence that Marshall himself may have sensed that he had created a potential monster. We have seen the vitriolic denunciation of the Taney Court by Abraham Lincoln, and the equally vehement condemnation of the waning *Lochner* Court by Franklin Roosevelt. And we know that Marshall's own Court was involved in the earliest of these political counterattacks against an invading judiciary, after Thomas Jefferson and his Republicans had defeated the Federalists in 1800, and the embittered Federalists had sought to offset their political loss by entrenching themselves in the courts. The central thrust of that political counterattack, the attempt to remove Justice Samuel Chase by impeachment, ended in the dramatic Senate trial in which the attempt failed by only a few votes. It had been a close call for Justice Chase, and for the Court. In the thick of the trial, with the outcome still uncertain, Chief Justice Marshall became fearful for the independence of the judiciary, and in a letter to Chase made an unexpected suggestion.

Marshall proposed that when a judge renders "a legal opinion contrary to the opinion of the legislature," instead of resorting to the recourse of impeaching and removing such a judge, "impeachment should yield to an appellate jurisdiction in the legislature." That means that certain Supreme Court decisions should be appealed to Congress. Nor did Marshall leave any doubt but that he meant what he said. Such a course, he observed, would allow a "reversal of those legal opinions deemed unsound by the legislature," and "would certainly better comport with the mildness of our character than a removal of the Judge who rendered them unknowing of his fault."[4]

When Marshall's great biographer, Albert J. Beveridge, came across the letter containing this proposal, he could hardly believe it: "Marshall thus suggested the most radical method for correcting judicial decisions ever advanced, before or since, by any man of the first class. Appeals from the

Supreme Court to Congress! Senators and Representatives to be the final judges of any judicial decision with which a majority of the House was dissatisfied!" Beveridge could scarcely contain himself. "Had we not the evidence of Marshall's signature to a letter written in his well-known hand, it could not be credited that he ever entertained such sentiments. They were in direct contradiction to his reasoning in *Marbury v. Madison,* utterly destructive of the Federalist philosophy of judicial control of legislation." As though to assure himself that he had really read it, Beveridge included a facsimile of the letter in his biography, *The Life of John Marshall.*[5]

Marshall's suggestion was most certainly written in a desperate hour for the Court, and unquestionably does not represent what Marshall would have preferred in the Court's relationship with Congress. Its intriguing aspect, however, is that Marshall appears to have perceived no constitutional impediment to congressional review. Nor was the idea of legislative review novel in the country in Marshall's time. When the Constitution was written there were many who would have lodged appellate judicial power in the Senate. In Great Britain the upper house of Parliament, the House of Lords, was (and still is) the final appellate body for legal questions. In the American Articles of Confederation the Continental Congress was assigned wide authority in hearing judicial appeals. Some of the newly formed States, after the Declaration of Independence became effective, also adopted the British model, though most chose to create separate and distinct court systems. The opposition to legislative appellate jurisdiction was based upon a particular view of the law and the courts, and was capsulized by Alexander Hamilton in Federalist No. 81.

The view of Hamilton, and of others who felt as he did, was based on the assumption that courts would remain courts. His arguments are directed towards objections to legislative bodies overturning *jury findings,* or to their reversing *ordinary findings of law.* There was no thought of the possibility that courts might interfere with legislation, as they did during the *Lochner* era, or that they might themselves legislate, as they do now. On the contrary, Hamilton argued that particular "misconstructions and contraventions of the will of the legislature" by the courts "can never be so extensive as to amount to an inconvenience, or in any sensible degree to affect the order of the political system." This would, in Hamilton's view, be prevented by "the general nature of the judicial power, from the objects to which it relates, from the manner in which it is exercised, from its comparative weakness, and from its total incapacity to support its usurpations by force." These were the assumptions underlying the rejection of legislative review of judicial decisions.

Hamilton believed that any remaining difficulties in controlling the judiciary would be easily remedied through the constitutional power of impeachment. He did not live to discover how ineffective the impeachment power was to be. He was killed in the infamous duel with Aaron Burr only weeks before the trial and acquittal of Justice Samuel Chase in the United States Senate, a trial presided over, in his capacity as Vice President, by Burr.

Chief Justice Marshall did not again advance the extreme remedy of legislative review to counter judicial abuse, and the idea has been rejected in the American legal tradition. Of perhaps equal significance is the fact that Marshall, after fastening the concept of judicial review into our constitutional system in *Marbury v. Madison,* never again invoked the doctrine to invalidate an Act of Congress. It may well be that he had come to fear the possible consequences of his invention—that if judicial review did become a monster run amok, the Court would be cut down and destroyed, and with it the independence of the judiciary. For Marshall, judicial restraint was the better alternative, and he stated the principles of restraint in powerful language.

The difficulty remains that, rather than the restraint of a John Marshall, we have labored under the boundless expansionism of a Chief Justice who could ask, of a position being advanced before the Court, not if it was constitutional, but if it was "good." One wonders, even after the bald nature of such transgression has been exposed, how so vast an expropriation of unauthorized power could have gone unnoticed. The truth of the matter is, at last, becoming apparent. What the Court has been doing has not gone unnoticed at all. Not really. What has occurred is that Congress has willingly acquiesced in what the Court has done. The reason is simple enough—the policies implemented by judicial fiat have been favored by liberal congressional elements, and by their allies in the academies and the media. Although these forces could not have implemented such policies by forthright legislative action, they have been able to impede efforts to thwart or reverse their implementation as effected by the judiciary.

Irving Kristol observes that the non-elected judiciary "could not wield such power without the consent, overt or tacit, of our elected representatives. It is common for many of these representatives to talk out of both sides of their mouths—to indicate dissent from judicial or administrative decisions while obstructing any legislative effort to reverse or limit them." In exposing the root and thrust of this drive, Kristol says that, "Such hypocrisy is most common among liberal politicians—they made this revolution, after all, or at least did not oppose it." To Kristol, this "helps explain the conservative drift of popular opinion" as a consequence.[6]

Thus, for example, a "liberal" Senator from a Catholic state might posture, wail, and protest at the Court's abortion decisions, yet escape his responsibility with a sly wink in the direction of the Court, and a shrug of the shoulders towards his outraged constituents. After all, what can he do? "It's the Constitution—the Court said so." As Joseph Sobran has put it, "In the era of liberal hegemony in Congress and the media [the Court] pulled a daring series of judicial coups simply because it knew it could get away with it; could count on congressional acquiescence and favorable publicity for each of its 'historic' decisions."[7]

Malcolm Richard Wilkey, former Judge of the Court of Appeals for the District of Columbia Circuit, shares the view that Congress is culpable as well as the Courts. "Congress is paralyzed . . . It no longer performs the role set for it in the Constitution: to make the fundamental policy choices for the nation. Consequently, the federal courts now make many of those choices." The judicial activist does this, Judge Wilkey observes, "while, of course, dissembling obeisance to the theory of the separation of powers by keeping on his robe."[8] Joseph Sobran reminds us that, as seen by the Framers, the "whole philosophy of government holds that power must be checked by power, one institution restraining another reciprocally. The Constitution clearly provides for this; only Congress isn't willing to assume its role in the process."[9]

Thus it is the *joint irresponsibility* of the Supreme Court *and* the Congress which has allowed a revolutionary political agenda to become the law of the land, an agenda which surely could never have survived either the legitimate political process of congressional enactment or that of constitutional amendment. As the responsibility—or irresponsibility—of Congress for a rising judicial tyranny becomes apparent, the question of whether Congress should, or ought, to accept responsibility for redress cannot be avoided. It can be argued that the courts have become so accustomed to wielding political power, that only political surgery can promise a cure for the disease. Some members of Congress have sought to address the issue by introducing bills to withdraw jurisdiction from the

Supreme Court in particular areas, such as abortion, school prayer, or busing.

Article 3, Section 2, of the Constitution provides (with qualifications which are not here relevant) that "the Supreme Court shall have appellate Jurisdiction, both as to Law and Fact, with such Exceptions, and under such Regulations as the Congress shall make." The Supreme Court itself has unequivocally recognized that the power of Congress to make "Exceptions" and to impose "Regulations" upon its appellate jurisdiction is a complete and plenary power.

The most dramatic example of this was that of the Mississippi newspaper editor, McCardle, discussed in an earlier chapter, whose case had been argued before the Supreme Court but not yet decided, when Congress, over the veto of President Andrew Johnson, voted to rescind the jurisdiction of the Court to proceed further. In its opinion in the case, *Ex Parte McCardle,* handed down in 1869,[10] the Court ruled that its authority to render a decision had been abrogated by Congress, and that it no longer had jurisdiction over the matter.

Under the principle of *Ex Parte McCardle* it would be constitutionally possible for Congress to withdraw all appellate jurisdiction from the Supreme Court, and to leave it with only the original jurisdiction provided for in the Constitution. Nor would such a result have surprised Chief Justice Marshall. Marshall had expressed himself unequivocally as to the power of Congress, under the provisions of Article 3, Section 2, to provide "Exceptions" and "Regulations" in regard to the appellate power of the Supreme Court. He had told the Virginia ratification convention in 1788 that, "These exceptions certainly go as far as the legislature may think proper for the interest and liberty of the people."[11]

Marshall expounded further on the subject in writing the opinion for the Court in *United States v. More,* in 1803.[12] The appellate jurisdiction of the Supreme Court was first delineated in the Judiciary Act of 1789, which did not provide appellate jurisdiction in criminal cases. The question in *United States v. More* was whether, in this circumstance, the Supreme Court *had* appellate criminal jurisdiction. Marshall held that it did not, for the singular reason that such jurisdiction was *not mentioned* in the Act of 1789. Without a *specific congressional grant* of such jurisdiction, Marshall was saying, there could be none. Commenting on the *More* case, New York attorney and author C. Dickerman Williams emphasizes the far-reaching implications of that holding. He observes that Marshall was "satisfied that

Congress could exclude from the Supreme Court's consideration [even] claims by an accused that his rights under [the Bill of Rights] had been violated in the trial court."[13] The *More* opinion may seem surprising in this day and age, yet the essence of that opinion has been repeatedly affirmed in the Court's decisions over the years.

The Supreme Court has held that "this Court exercises no appellate power unless it is conferred by act of Congress;"[14] that its appellate jurisdiction "is wholly a creature of legislation;"[15] that what its appellate powers "shall be, and to what extent they shall be exercised, are and always have been, proper subjects of legislative control;"[16] and, as recently as 1943, that, "Our appellate jurisdiction is defined by statute."[17] Thus, it is not only in the post-Civil War case of *Ex Parte McCardle*—as is sometimes supposed—that the Court has determined that the existence of its appellate jurisdiction lies solely within the power of Congress.

A fundamental, and potentially highly therapeutic, exercise of that power by Congress would be to withdraw jurisdiction of the Supreme Court to interpret or enforce the Fourteenth Amendment. A major crime of the Justices has been to contravene the great central purpose of the Constitution, which is to prevent concentration of power, hence, to prevent despotism. In large part the Court has done this through the Fourteenth Amendment, and through the mischief or its "incorporation" doctrine related to the Amendment.

The main force of such decisions has been directed, not against the national government, or against Congress, but against the states. In so doing, the Court has been the engine, and the knowing engine, of a massive gathering of power in Washington. New and undreamed of functions have been created to administer newly invented "rights." More critically, the vitality of the great countervailing power against centralism, federalism and the federal system, has been sapped, and its purpose threatened. Presumably this type of encroachment could be prevented in the future by altering or withdrawing the Court's appellate jurisdiction in regard to the Fourteenth Amendment.

Whether it has been busing children to distant schools because of their race; prohibiting prayer in schools; disallowing state aid to religious schools; the life and death questions of abortion and capital punishment; or any of the remainder of the radical social agenda which the Court has thrust upon the country over three decades, the basis has been almost entirely in the Fourteenth Amendment—and in but *four words* of that

Amendment at that. A constitutional revolution has been built out of "due process" and "equal protection" in the relatively simple provisions of the Fourteenth Amendment that, "No State shall . . . deprive any person of life, liberty, or property, without the due process of law; nor deny to any person within its jurisdiction the equal protection of the laws."

It required centuries for the reluctant promise of King John in Magna Carta, to respect the law in dealing with his subjects, to become enforceable "due process of law," so that all persons might be treated equally before the law. The Fourteenth Amendment was designed to insure that the newly freed slaves would be afforded such protection. Professor Lino Graglia puts the matter in sharp perspective in observing that, "As important as the due process clause is, it has absolutely nothing to do with, say, the power of New York State to limit the working hours of bakers or of Texas to restrict the availability of abortion." Professor Graglia asserts bluntly that, "The Supreme Court's decisions to the contrary cannot in any intellectually respectable sense be said to represent interpretations of the clause." Indeed, "So blatant are these violations that some of the Supreme Court's most important decisions can hardly be discussed in public without provoking open laughter."[18]

The truth of such observations is being grasped by many who have heretofore taken the Court at its word, and been willing to follow its dictates. But the fact is that the decisions which constitute its recent revolution are poorly, even ridiculously, argued, and stand only because few, as yet, have analysed their content with the acumen of Professor Graglia, and of others who truly care for the Constitution, apart from the "constitutional law" which the Court has sought to attach to it. It may well be that selective withdrawal of jurisdiction by Congress, particularly in regard to the Fourteenth Amendment, will ultimately be required to redress the constitutional imbalance which has occurred.

A serious objection to any sort of removal of jurisdiction is that it is a hit and miss, piecemeal, even meataxe, device, which removes jurisdiction in entire areas where, in general, courts should operate, depriving us of avenues of redress which have been, and ought to remain, primarily judicial. So plenary is the power of Congress in regard to the appellate jurisdiction of the Court, however, that carefully crafted legislation could very likely establish desirable limits on the Court, and at the same time preserve judicial jurisdiction where it ought to apply.

A strong argument can be made, in any event, that effective steps towards a meaningful external check upon illicit judicial power can be initiated only by Congress, whether it be selective withdrawal or regulation of jurisdiction, impeachment, or some form of constitutional amendment limiting the Supreme Court's authority, or subjecting Justices to limited terms or a vote of reconfirmation on a periodic basis. An effort along any of these lines would, at last, be a healthy admission by Congress of its joint culpability in the Court's revolutionary transgressions, whatever the final outcome.

Any doubt about the complicity of Congress in these matters, or about the depth to which politics has infected the law, was conclusively laid to rest by the conduct of the United States Senate in the confirmation hearings of Judge Robert Bork, as was any prospect of an early congressional remedy. Here was a candidate who had demonstrated as large and deep a grasp of constitutional principles as almost any judge in this century, and who had repeatedly articulated the fundamental requirements of a constitutional system based in law and democracy. Yet it was these very qualities which made him a deadly threat to the revolutionary forces in the country who wish to repudiate the Constitution and its principles in favor of some other order, which they are loath to reveal, or even admit. But the threat posed by Judge Bork was clear enough. With animal cunning and sub-reptilian morality, the radical forces manned their battle stations.

"Robert Bork's America," proclaimed Senator Ted Kennedy, would be tormented by midnight police raids, segregated lunch counters, back alley abortions, and courthouse doors "locked on the fingers of millions of citizens." This remarkable salvo was fired immediately following Judge Bork's nomination, just prior to the Fourth of July weekend. Such an instantaneous response was felt to be necessary lest too many Senators, perceiving the high qualifications of the nominee, were to signal their early support. As Senator Kennedy later expostulated to the *Boston Globe,* "The statement had to be stark and direct so as to hold people in their places until we could get material together."[19] An unprecedented delay of over two months was set before hearings would begin in order for Senate Democrats to marshal their forces and search for ammunition. Opponents opened what they, themselves, characterized as a "war room" in the basement of the Senate office building in which the hearings were to be held, and mounted a "blitz" of media ads distorting Judge Bork's record beyond recognition, in an effort to destroy him by portraying him as morally insensitive and intellectually dishonest.

Columnist Norman Podhoretz observed several months later that only one side, the side opposing Bork, was aware that there was a war going on. Those supporting Bork seemed not to notice until they had been "blown out of the water."[20] Polls were conducted to discover what issues might most easily be exploited against the Judge. Particularly sensitive, the polls revealed, were questions of privacy and minority rights. False charges of impending "bedroom break-ins" were designed to appeal to the general population, while Senator Kennedy tirelessly gathered black support by raising fears of "opening old wounds" through repeated telephone calls to the South from his Cape Cod summer retreat at Hyannisport. Senator Joseph Biden later confessed that, at first, "We couldn't find anybody who wanted to weigh in with a fist fight," but persistent calling wore resistence down.[21]

The charges levelled through the media and in the Judiciary Committee were unprincipled, mean, and false. Each was answered thoroughly and patiently by the candidate, most not once but many times. For example, Judge Bork's main objection to the general right of privacy, as stated by the Court in *Griswold v. Connecticut*, was that it was without limit or defini-tion. No one answered his observation that Congress would never legislate such an ambiguous principle, or that there is "plenty of privacy" in the Constitution already, including guarantees found in the First, Fourth, and Fifth Amendments. His similar refutation of fraudulent charges concerning "sterilization of workers," free speech, due process and others was lost in the weeks of repetitious distortions, insinuated and explicated over and over again, after each had been logically and judicially disproved. The changes penetrated, stuck, proliferated, and came to displace the reality of Judge Bork's judicial philosophy. The smear became the fact to many who did not pay close attention to the process, or who may not have well understood the qualifications for judicial office. Little lies became familiar, accumulated, sapped at the foundations of the truth, and at last congealed, as intended, into the Big Lie designed to destroy the victim.

Even a big lie must be kept sufficiently inflated. A Harris poll reported fifty-seven percent opposed to Judge Bork's confirmation. Milton Fried-man and a colleague demonstrated that this poll was based on biased questions, designed to elicit the negative response.[22] To suppress any dissent from the radical line among blacks the staff of Senator Howard Metzenbaum resorted to intimidation of witnesses, warning one black professor that if he testified, he would be ridiculed through intense ques-tioning outside the field of his expertise; while another black, a woman, was told that if she testified for Bork a boycott of the national company of which she was a director would be instituted.[23]

Against this background, one watched the proceedings of the Judiciary Committee with an unfolding sense of ineluctable tragedy. And still, as the storm gathered and broke over the chambers of the Committee, not the candidate himself, his supporters on the Committee, or the President who had nominated him seemed even slightly aware of the lethal cloud engulfing them. The Big Lie was answered with fact and logic, bit by bit, case by case, and, to the honest mind, convincingly. But the fury was not of logic, dispassion, fairness, or reason; it was of venom, hatred, and calculated fear. Both the candidate and his supporters allowed themselves to be sucked into a vortex of repetitious trivia, and lost their bearing on the great constitutional principles being methodically battered and destroyed. In the year of the Constitution's 200th birthday, we witnessed the label "extremist" smeared over a nominee to the Supreme Court because he advocated taking that document seriously!

Behind the thin patina of "senatorial courtesy" it was apparent from the beginning that the Judge was playing against the house, and that the dice were loaded. At one point, in response to a charlatan's tirade by Senator Kennedy, raising the specter of Jim Crow laws, the Judge responded with dignity, and suppressed anger, that, "If those charges were not so serious, the discrepancy between the evidence and what you say would be highly amusing." The tirade made the media and stirred the mob; the restrained judicious response died in committee. At no point did even the White House itself summon the insight or courage to turn the proceedings against those who have been using the courts to advance a radical agenda for thirty years, those who were then in the act of defaming a man who they feared in their bones—and with good reason—would be capable of effectively exposing their game if confirmed to the Court. That was what the fight was all about. It was a fight for the guts of the republic.

When all was lost, at least so far as Judge Bork was concerned, one White House spokesman summed up the blind impotence of the Judge's supporters, if unwittingly: "I plead guilty to underestimating the opposition," he wailed; "I thought it was going to be a fair fight."[24] As the *Wall Street Journal* put it, "The affair reminded the White House that to win a political boxing match, you must step into the ring."[25]

In order to perfume the proceedings with a semblance of respectability, reasons, of sorts, had to be advanced for defeating the man who former

Chief Justice Burger termed one of the best qualified for the Supreme Court in the last half century. The "extremist" and "right wing ideologue" charges were not entirely convincing in the face of the candidate's learned, reasoned, and modulated responses during questioning by the Committee. But that was alright, for by then the virus of fear and distortion had done its work. Senator David Pryor put the case for the inquisition with unctuous, if disingenuous, simplicity. He charged that Judge Bork had "polarized America," and had become "the most diversive nominee to have his name before the Senate in modern times."[26] So completely had passion displaced principle that to Republican Senator John W. Warner the constitutional issue was totally lost. "I searched the record. I looked at this distinguished jurist, and I cannot find in him the record of compassion, or sensitivity and understanding of the pleas of the people to enable him to sit on the highest Court of the land." Senator John C. Danforth, a bit more perceptive, and considerably more candid, stated simply that, "What has happened to Robert Bork is wrong. The man's been trashed in our house. Some of us helped generate the trashing, others yielded to it, but all of us are accomplices."[27]

To lend perspective to the spectacle, it is worth a few moments to recall the background and qualities of some of those responsible for the trashing. We have in these backgrounds a dead woman at the bottom of a pond, an elaborate coverup, and a Senator whose "most extensive legal experience centers on the law of inquest;"[28] a Senator forced to return a "finder's fee" of $250,000 taken for placing a couple of telephone calls; a Senator forced to withdraw from the presidential race for admitted plagiarism; and a Senator forced to resign from the Senate Intelligence Committee for leaking classified national security documents. Those are some of the qualities we know of. One may wonder what else might emerge from the senatorial closets were the other gentlemen of the Committee, or of the Senate, subject to anything like the treatment accorded Judge Bork.

During the whole process no effective attempt was made to expose or to attack the hidden agenda of Judge Bork's enemies. Their slogans included "privacy," "fundamental rights," "equal dignity," and similar inviting concepts. But many of the groups holding these apparently benign views are the same ones who would exploit the Court to move towards a radical-extremist transformation of the country. Examining the programs of these groups, Terry Eastland, Director of Public Affairs for the Justice Department, concluded that their agenda "is really about securing constitutional

protection for homosexual conduct, prostitution and use of illicit drugs . . .
the abolition of the death penalty, further extension of the abortion liberty
. . . legalization of the distribution of child pornography, elimination of
restrictions on the production and sale of obscenity, and expulsion of
legislative chaplains and traces of religion from public life."[29]

The academic point man for the Bork assassination was Harvard Law
professor Laurence Tribe. Others, such as Philip Kurland and Kathleen
Sullivan, their eyes gleaming at the prospect of Caesar's fall, joined lustily
in thrusting their own swords into the dying flesh. These academics
represent the school of thought which speaks of "noninterpretivism,"
"nonoriginalism," the "principled decisions of judges," "social conscience," the "impassioned claims of citizens," and such other touchstones of "constitutional" exposition, rather than the imperatives of the
document itself. No one can honestly read the Constitution to justify an
agency of government exercising arbitrary, self-generating, and self-judg-
ing authority. But that is what the Supreme Court has come to be over the
past thirty years, and that is what Judge Bork's opponents want it to
continue to be.

Nor is this a harmless academic scam; it is a profound and revolutionary
challenge to ordered liberty, which cannot be hushed or hidden forever,
even by academic artifice. Judge Bork knows this, and those who destroyed
his nomination fear that knowledge. Speaking before the Philadelphia
Society in April of 1987, before he was nominated to the Court, Judge
Bork asked, "If the Constitution is not law, what authorizes a judge to set at
nought the judgment of the representatives of the American people? If the
Constitution is not law, why is the judge's authority superior to that of the
President, Congress, the armed forces, the departments and the agencies,
and that of everyone else in the nation? Why should anybody obey us? No
answer exists."[30]

The *Wall Street Journal* has suggested that, "If a Robert Bork cannot be
confirmed, some objection would be found to John Marshall himself." In
an uncharacteristically bitter mood, the same editorial concluded that,
"Washington, D.C. is a city lying in the gutter, wallowing in hypocrisy. It
has become a bizarre sinkhole of character assassination and smirking self-
righteousness."[31] Even this may be too light a judgment. The fight against
Judge Bork—its qualities, its tactics, its participants, and its results—
leaves no doubt that vital principles are under attack. Those who joined in
the slaughter of Bork wittingly (and in some cases no doubt unwittingly)

have shown themselves to be the enemies, not just of Judge Bork, or even of President Reagan or Attorney General Meese, but enemies of the Constitution and the rule of law.

At the core of this assault is a libertine-radical-socialist-statist attack on the American order, root and branch. We face nothing less than a revolutionary challenge to our constitutional system. The war did not end with the elimination of one judge, but only intensified. The Battle of Bork did, however, considerably clarify the fact of the war, and what it is about. Norman Podhoretz drew a stark perspective, stressing that beyond the immediate goal of destroying Bork himself "there was a longer-range goal as well—to delegitimize the entire philosophy of judicial restraint for which Bork stands by smearing it as a cynical cover for racism, sexism and hostility to individual rights." This, Podhoretz prophesied, is "nothing less than a war to the death."[32]

The bitter, frightening, and tragic irony of all this is that it has been the Supreme Court itself, over the past three decades, which has taught us to make politics of the law. It has written the agenda of often shrill minorities into the Constitution as legitimate principles of that document, and has whetted the appetites of even more strident elements for similar dispensations. Thus the Court, in large part, has brought down upon itself this revolution against everything for which it should stand and fight. It has been the Court itself, certainly with the complicity of Congress, but in the forefront the Court, which has led us to witness the shameless absence of honor, dignity, or honesty in the means used in the United States Senate to defeat a good and honorable man. Even the skeptical must now recognize how deeply into the roots of law the infection of politics has penetrated.

Chief Justice Harlan Fiske Stone once observed of Supreme Court Justices that "the only protection against unwise decisions, and even judicial usurpation, is careful scrutiny of their action, and fearless comment on it."[33] Unfortunately, some three decades of scrutiny and comment did very little to improve the wisdom, or reduce the usurpation, of the Warren and Burger Courts. The Burger Court did not reverse, or even reexamine to any significant degree, a single major decision of the Warren Court's social agenda. And it was, after all, the Burger Court, not the Warren Court, which perpetrated, and perpetuated, perhaps the worst constitutional miscarriage of all—*Roe v. Wade*. What we observed in these two judicial eras was a bitterly ironic affirmation of another observation of Chief Justice Stone that "the only check on our power is our own self-restraint!"[34]

The truth of the matter is that none of the suggested remedies to right judicial wrongs is entirely convincing. Yet, the balance between law and government, between *gubernaculum* and *jurisdictio,* is in danger of being irretrievably lost. We must recognize that if the Constitution can be changed whenever the Supreme Court sits, we have no Constitution. By what principles are we to be governed? Where is the sanctuary of freedom to be found? Perhaps the most important need of all is to save the courts from themselves—and for the American people. The functions performed by *courts as courts* are absolutely essential to the existence of a free society. They can be performed by no other agency.

For all of the possible permutations of the debate, the essential problem remains relatively simple. It is a question of respect for law, and of devotion to the Constitution. It is a question of good faith. Those who manipulate the Constitution for their own ends know perfectly well what they are doing, while the veil of legal sophistry by which they have sought to conceal their true views and aims has become tattered and transparent. The Courts are not behaving at all as the American people expect them to behave, and that fact is emerging irrepressibly into the public conscience.

An aspect of twentieth century relativism is that individuals possessed of power are no longer subject to any reliable check on the exercise or expansion of that power. The constraints of the Church, and with them the precepts of morality, have been loosened, and may ultimately fail entirely. The belief that subject matter and discipline are the bulwark of education has faded. The authority of the family has been dissipated. Hitherto accepted principles of morality are repudiated. In the maelstrom which has resulted the law of the Constitution might conceivably have served as a bedrock of stability. Had we, by chance, been blessed with great jurists among members of the Supreme Court, such as Marshall, a Story, or a Learned Hand, our constitutional history might have been quite different.

As it was, the Warren Court, and then the Burger Court, joined with enthusiasm, and with little or no evident awareness of the probable consequences of their actions, the "social engineers" who want to change society, and, implicitly, the nature of the human species in the process. In these circumstances it may as well be admitted, however reluctantly, that none of the instruments available for reforming the Supreme Court, and restoring to its decisions a pattern of law and thought conforming to the splendid history out of which our written Constitution was formed, show promise of enduring success. We must concede that patches and bandages are the best that can be hoped for.

And so, despite what history teaches us to expect over the long term, the only real prospect for near term improvement is the appointment of a type of Supreme Court Justice, and of judges in the lower courts, who are cut of a different cloth from the activists who subvert and repudiate our constitutional heritage. There is no infallible litmus test, and no guarantee that the apparent proclivities of an individual appointed to the bench can, with confidence, be projected into his or her judicial opinions, as many a President has learned to his dismay and anger. But with due care the odds can be improved.

What is to be sought after is not anyone with a program or a policy. What is required is not new Justices of a "conservative" agenda, designated to counteract the liberal-socialist agenda of their predecessors. The whole problem we have been dealing with arises from judges indulging their predilections and philosophies instead of conscientiously attempting to understand and apply the Constitution. We need no more of that. With a new Chief Justice, and other changes on the Court, there still remains the opportunity for a new departure.

What is wanted of new Justices of the Supreme Court, and of judges in every court in the land, are individuals who have given some thought to the uncertain birth of law, and to the difficult struggle to fashion constitutional restraints on power; who grasp the liberating wonder of the social contract; who are humble before the fragility of these precious concepts; who revere the institutions which embody the law; who perceive clearly the difference between legal authority and governmental power; who know that freedom rests upon a dependable rule of law; who are aware how fleeting and elusive the era of law and freedom has been in human history; who recognize, in pride and humility, that the Constitution which they are privileged to have inherited may very well remain the "last best hope on earth" for a free and honorable existence; and who approach with awesome respect the knowledge that, if now lost to the lures of unrestrained power, foreign or domestic, liberty under law may never be regained.

As the American Constitution enters its third century, the fate of that great document is shrouded in doubt. The challenge is clear enough, and emanates from powerful forces in American society. The open question is whether, "We, the People," considering the alternatives, do or do not wish to reaffirm our desire to "secure the Blessing of Liberty to ourselves and our Posterity," and to rejuvenate and respect the constitutional structure agreed upon two centuries ago to that end.

FOOTNOTES

Frontispiece
Plato, *The Republic*, Book VI.
Thomas Jefferson, letter to Jarvis, 1820, quoted in *Thomas Jefferson on Democracy*, Saul K. Padover (ed.), Mentor 1949, p. 64.

1. An Outline of Abuse
1. See note Frontispiece.
2. See note Frontispiece.
3. Richard E. Morgan, *Disabling America—The "Rights Industry" in Our Time*, Basic Books, 1984.

2. The Pit, the Smoke, and the Oracle
1. *Marbury v. Madison*, 5 U.S. 137 (1803).
2. Raoul Berger, *Government by Judiciary*, Harvard University Press, 1977, pp. 358–359.

3. A Slave and the Forbidden Fruit
1. *Dred Scott v. Sandford*, 60 U.S. 393 (1857).
2. *Marbury v. Madison*, 5 U.S. 137 (1803).
3. Raoul Berger, *Government by Judiciary*, Harvard University Press, 1977, p. 222.
4. Wallace Mendelson, "The Politics of Judicial Activism," *Emory Law Journal*, vol. 24, 1975, pp. 48–49.
5. William H. Rehnquist, "The Notion of a Living Constitution," *Texas Law Review*, vol. 54, 1976, p. 702.
6. Carl Brent Swisher, *American Constitutional Development*, Houghton Mifflin Co., 1943, p. 519.
7. *Ibid.*, p. 251.

4. Louis Lochner's Bakery
1. *Dred Scott v. Sandford*, 60 U.S. 393 (1857).
2. *Lochner v. New York*, 198 U.S. 45 (1905).

255

3. Raoul Berger, *Government by Judiciary,* Harvard University Press, 1977, p. 196, n. 11.
4. *Ibid.,* p. 194.
5. *Adkins v. Children's Hospital,* 261 U.S. 525, 570 (1923), dissenting.
6. For a summary of legislation invalidated by the Supreme Court, see Stephen L. Wasby, *The Supreme Court in the Federal Judicial System,* Holt, Rinehart and Winston, 1978, pp. 39–40.

5. Louisiana Train Ride

1. *Plessy v. Ferguson,* 163 U.S. 537 (1896).
2. *Dred Scott v. Sandford,* 60 U.S. 393 (1857).

6. Civil Rights, Judicial Wrongs

1. *Brown v. Board of Education,* 347 U.S. 483 (1954).
2. Raoul Berger, *Government by Judiciary,* Harvard University Press, 1977, p. 118.
3. *Ibid.,* p. 129, n. 47.
4. *Ibid.,* pp. 118–120.
5. *Ibid.,* pp. 120–121.
6. Wallace Mendelson, "The Politics of Judicial Activism," *Emory Law Journal,* vol. 24, 1975, p. 60.
7. *Plessy v. Ferguson,* 163 U.S. 537 (1896).
8. Archibald Cox, *The Role of the Supreme Court in American Government,* Oxford University Press, 1976, p. 57.
9. *Op. cit.,* note 2, p. 245.
10. *Adkins v. Children's Hospital,* 261 U.S. 525, 570 (1923).
11. *Op. cit.,* note 2, p. 289, n. 24.
12. *Dred Scott v. Sandford,* 60 U.S. 393 (1857).

7. Reading, Writing, and Judicial Arithmetic

1. *Brown v. Board of Education,* 347 U.S. 483 (1954).
2. *Green v. County School Board,* 389 U.S. 1003 (1968).
3. *Alexander v. Holmes,* 396 U.S. 19 (1969).
4. *Swann v. Charlotte-Mecklenburg Board of Education,* 402 U.S. 1 (1971).
5. *Keyes v. School District No. 1, Denver, Colorado,* 413 U.S. 189 (1973).
6. *Dayton Board of Education v. Brinkman,* 444 U.S. 887 (1979). *Columbus Board of Education v. Penick,* 444 U.S. 887 (1979).
7. *Armour v. Nix,* 446 U.S. 931 (1980).
8. *Los Angeles Times,* May 13, 1980, Part I, p. 1.
9. *Nolan Estes v. Dallas NAACP,* 444 U.S. 1040 (1980).
10. United States Commission on Civil Rights, Clearing House Publication 43, June 1973.
11. Thomas Sowell, *New York Times Magazine,* August 8, 1976, p. 14.
12. *Los Angeles Times,* December 5, 1980, Part I, p. 1.
13. *Los Angeles Times,* October 21, 1980, Part I, p. 24.

14. *New York Times*, July 8, 1979, IV 2:3.
15. *Op. cit.*, note 11, p. 15.
16. *Harper's*, February 1981, pp. 26–29.
17. William Raspberry, *Oregonian*, June 26, 1981, p. C 11.
18. Richard E. Morgan, *Disabling America*, Basic Books, 1984, p. 73.
19. Jennifer L. Hochschild, quoted in *The New Republic*, March 11, 1985, p. 37.
20. *Crawford v. Board of Education of the City of Los Angeles*, 458 U.S. 527 (1982).
21. *Washington v. Seattle School District No. 1*, 458 U.S. 457 (1982).
22. *Wall Street Journal* (Western edition), July 12, 1982, p. 16.
23. *Wall Street Journal* (Western edition), April 16, 1987, p. 24.
24. Charles E. M. Kolb, *Wall Street Journal* (Western edition), January 5, 1988, p. 22.

8. Judicial Gerrymander

1. *Williams v. Mississippi*, 170 U.S. 213 (1898).
2. *Guinn v. United States*, 238 U.S. 347 (1915).
3. *Lane v. Wilson*, 307 U.S. 268 (1939).
4. *Nixon v. Herndon*, 273 U.S. 536 (1927).
5. *Smith v. Allwright*, 321 U.S. 649 (1944).
6. *Terry v. Adams*, 345 U.S. 461 (1953).
7. *Colegrove v. Green*, 328 U.S. 549 (1946).
8. *South v. Peters*, 339 U.S. 276 (1950).
9. *Baker v. Carr*, 369 U.S. 186 (1962).
10. *Gray v. Sanders*, 372 U.S. 368 (1963).
11. *Wesberry v. Sanders*, 376 U.S. 1 (1964).
12. *Kirkpatrick v. Preisler*, 394 U.S. 526 (1969).
13. *Lucas v. Colorado General Assembly*, 377 U.S. 713 (1964).
14. Robert Bork, "Comments," *The Judiciary in a Democratic Society*, Leonard J. Theberge (ed.), Lexington Books, D. C. Heath & Co., 1979, p. 110.
15. Michael M. Uhlmann, "The Supreme Court and Political Representation," Theberge, *Ibid.*, p. 92.
16. *Ibid.*, p. 94.
17. Raoul Berger, *Government by Judiciary*, Harvard University Press, 1977, pp. 68–69.
18. *Baker v. Carr*, 369 U.S. 186, 323 (1962).
19. John W. Finley, Jr., "The Courts and Affirmative Action," Theberge, *op. cit.*, note 14, p. 124.
20. *Gray v. Sanders*, 372 U.S. 368, 381 (1963).
21. *Reynolds v. Sims*, 377 U.S. 533, 555 (1964).
22. *Op. cit.*, note 15, p. 100.
23. Wallace Mendelson, "The Politics of Judicial Activism," *Emory Law Journal*, vol. 23, 1975, p. 62.
24. Robert B. McKay, "Reapportionment: Success Story of the Warren Court," *Michigan Law Review*, 1968, pp. 230–231.
25. Nathan Glazer, "Towards an Imperial Judiciary," *The Public Interest*, Fall 1975, pp. 120–121.

26.   Timothy G. O'Rourke, *The Impact of Reapportionment,* Transaction Books, New Brunswick, N.J., 1980, pp. 151, 159.
27.   *Karcher v. Daggett,* 462 U.S. 725 (1983).
28.   M. Stanton Evans, *Washington Times (National Edition),* May 17, 1985, p. 3B.
29.   Robert J. Van Der Veld, "One Person-One Vote Round III: Challenges to the 1980 Redistricting," *Cleveland State Law Rev.,* vol 32, 1983–4, p. 606, n. 180.
30.   *Davis v. Bandemer,* 470 U.S. 389 (1986).

9.   To Be or Not To Be

1.   Shakespeare, *Hamlet,* Act III, Scene 1.
2.   *Roe v. Wade,* 410 U.S. 113 (1973).
3.   For a sensitive discussion of these issues see Mary Anne Warren, "On the Moral and Legal Status of Abortion," *The Monist,* vol. 57, 1973.
4.   *Roe v. Wade,* p. 142.
5.   *Ibid.* p. 143.
6.   *Griswold v. Connecticut,* 381 U.S. 479 (1965).
7.   *Ibid.* p. 484.
8.   Ruggero J. Aldisert, "The Role of the Courts in Contemporary Society," *University of Pittsburgh Law Review,* vol. 38, 1977, p. 442, n. 16.
9.   John Hart Ely, "The Wages of Crying Wolf: A Comment on *Roe v. Wade,*" *Yale Law Journal,* vol. 82, 1973, pp. 933, 947.
10.   *Harris v. McRae,* 448 U.S. 297 (1980); *William v. Zbaraz,* 448 U.S. 358 (1980).
11.   Roger Simon, *Los Angeles Times,* July 4, 1980, Part II, p. 5.
12.   *City of Akron v. Akron Center for Reproductive Health,* 462 U.S. 416 (1983); *Planned Parenthood v. Ashcroft,* 462 U.S. 476 (1983); *Simopoulous v. Virginia,* 462 U.S. 506 (1983).
13.   John T. Noonan, Jr., "A Pragmatic Politician's Parody of Solomon," *Human Life Review,* vol. IX, no. 3, Summer 1983, p. 5.
14.   *Thornburgh v. American College of Obstetricians and Gynecologists,* 471 U.S. 1011 (1986).
15.   Charles Dickens, *Oliver Twist,* Chap. 51.

10.   Beat the Rap

1.   *Mapp v. Ohio,* 367 U.S. 643 (1961).
2.   Norman M. Robertson, "Reason and the Fourth Amendment—the Burger Court and the Exclusionary Rule," *Fordham Law Review,* vol. 46, 1977, p. 173.
3.   *Draper v. United States,* 358 U.S. 307, 318 (1959).
4.   *Weeks v. United States,* 232 U.S. 383 (1914).
5.   *Wolf v. Colorado,* 338 U.S. 25 (1949).
6.   *Gitlow v. New York,* 268 U.S. 652 (1925).
7.   *Palko v. Connecticut,* 302 U.S. 319 (1937).
8.   *Illinois v. Gates,* 462 U.S. S. 1237 (1983).
9.   *Coolidge v. New Hampshire,* 403 U.S. 443 (1971).

10. *United States v. Montgomery,* 561 F.2d 875 (D.C. Cir. 1977).
11. *People v. Minjares,* 24 Cal. 3d 410 (1979).
12. *Ibid.,* n. 2.
13. Charles G. Douglas, III, "State Judicial Activism—the New Role for State Bills of Rights," *Suffolk University Law Review,* vol. xii, 1978, p. 138.
14. *People v. DeFore,* 242 N.Y. 13, 150 N.E. 585 (1926).
15. *Stone v. Powell,* 428 U.S. 465, 500–501 (1976).
16. *San Francisco Chronicle,* February 9, 1981, p. 20.
17. *United States v. Calandra,* 414 U.S. 338, 348 (1974).
18. *Nix v. Williams,* 467 U.S. 431 (1984).
19. *U.S. v. Leon,* 463 U.S. 1206 (1984).
20. *Massachusetts v. Sheppard,* 464 U.S. 889 (1984).
21. Richard E. Morgan, *Disabling America,* Basic Books, 1984, p. 103.
22. William Tucker, "Bring Back the Jury," *The American Spectator,* August 1986, pp. 18ff.

11. Obscenity in Law and Fact

1. *Rosenfeld v. New Jersey,* 408 U.S. 901 (1972).
2. *Gooding v. Wilson,* 405 U.S. 518 (1972).
3. *Stromberg v. California,* 283 U.S. 359 (1931).
4. *Brown v. Louisiana,* 383 U.S. 131 (1966).
5. *Tinker v. Des Moines School District,* 393 U.S. 503 (1969).
6. *New Rider v. Board of Education,* 414 U.S. 1074 (1974).
7. *People v. Cowgill,* 396 U.S. 371 (1970).
8. *Smith v. Goguen,* 415 U.S. 566 (1975).
9. *U.S. v. O'Brien,* 391 U.S. 367 (1968).
10. *Regina v. Hicklin,* L.R. 3QB 360 (1868 Eng.).
11. *Roth v. United States* and *Alberts v. California,* 354 U.S. 476 (1957).
12. *Ginzburg v. United States,* 383 U.S. 463 (1966).
13. *Jacobellis v. Ohio,* 378 U.S. 184 (1964).
14. *Redrup v. New York,* 386 U.S. 767 (1967).
15. *United States v. Reidel,* 412 U.S. 351 (1971).
16. *Stanley v. Georgia,* 394 U.S. 557 (1969).
17. *Miller v. California,* 413 U.S. 15 (1973).
18. *Paris Adult Theatre v. Slaton,* 413 U.S. 49 (1973).
19. *Schad v. Mount Ephraim,* 452 U.S. 61 (1981).
20. *Marsh v. Alabama,* 326 U.S. 501 (1945).
21. *Amalgamated Food Employees Union 590 v. Logan Valley Plaza,* 391 U.S. 308 (1968).
22. *Lloyd Corporation v. Tanner,* 407 U.S. 551 (1971).
23. *Scott Hudgens v. N.L.R.B.,* 424 U.S. 507 (1975).
24. Phillip Kurland, "1970 Term: Notes on the Emergence of the Burger Court," *The Supreme Court Review,* University of Chicago Press, 1971, p. 265.
25. Howard Ball, *Judicial Craftsmanship or Fiat?,* Greenwood Press, 1978, p. 136.
26. Benjamin A. Richards, "The Historical Rationale of the Speech-and-Press Clause of the First Amendment," *University of Florida Law Review,* vol. xxi, 1968, p. 209.

27. *Ibid.*, p. 215.
28. *Prudential Ins. Co. v. Cheek,* 259 U.S. 530 (1922).
29. *Gitlow v. New York,* 268 U.S. 652 (1925).
30. *Palko v. Connecticut,* 302 U.S. 319 (1937).
31. Raoul Berger, *Government by Judiciary,* Harvard University Press, 1977, p. 272.
32. George Gilder, "Why I Am Not A Neo-Conservative," *National Review,* March 5, 1982, p. 220.
33. *Los Angeles Times,* September 17, 1981, Part V, p. 14.
34. *New York v. Ferber,* 458 U.S. 747 (1983).
35. William Simon, *A Time for Truth,* Reader's Digest Press, McGraw-Hill Book Company, 1978, p. 234.
36. Archibald Cox, *The Role of the Supreme Court in American Government,* Oxford University Press, 1976, pp. 45–46.
37. John Hart Ely, "Towards a Representation-Reinforcing Mode of Judicial Review," *Maryland Law Review,* vol. 37, 1978, p. 477.

12. The Virulence of Arrogance

1. *Goldberg v. Rostker,* 509 F.Supp. 586 (1980).
2. *Rostker v. Goldberg,* 448 U.S. 1306 (1980).
3. Wallace Mendelson, "The Politics of Judicial Activism," *Emory Law Journal,* vol. 24, 1975, p. 60.
4. Theodore Eisenberg and Stephen Yeazell, "The Ordinary and the Extraordinary in Institutional Litigation," *Harvard Law Review,* vol. 93, 1980, pp. 509–511.
5. Owen M. Fiss, "The Supreme Court 1978 Term," *Harvard Law Review,* vol. 93, 1979, pp. 29, 31, 34.
6. Arthur Selwyn Miller, *Toward Increased Judicial Activism: The Political Role of the Supreme Court,* Greenwood Press, 1982, pp. 271, 305.
7. Archibald Cox, *The Role of the Supreme Court in American Government,* Oxford University Press, 1976, pp. 35–36.
8. Phillip B. Kurland, "Facing the Reality of a Political Court: A Critical Analysis," *The Supreme Court in American Politics,* David F. Forte (ed.), D. C. Heath & Co., 1972, p. 93.
9. *Ibid.*, p. 94.
10. J. Skelly Wright, "The Role of the Supreme Court in a Democratic Society—Judicial Activism or Restraint?," *Cornell Law Review,* vol. 54, 1968, pp. 27–28.
11. Walter Berns, "The Least Dangerous Branch, But Only If . . . ," *The Judiciary in a Democratic Society,* Leonard J. Theberge (ed.), D. C. Heath and Co., 1979, p. 15.
12. Frank M. Coffin, "The Frontier of Remedies: A Call for Exploration," *California Law Review,* vol. 67, 1979, p. 992.
13. Peter Brimelow and Stephen J. Markman, "Supreme Irony," *Harper's,* October 1981, p. 18.
14. *Ibid.*, pp. 18–20.
15. *Ibid.*, p. 18.
16. *Ibid.*, pp. 19–20.

13. The Madhouse and the Judge

1. *Wyatt v. Stickney,* 325 F.Supp. 781, 785 (M.D.Ala. 1971).
2. *Wyatt v. Stickney,* 344 F.Supp. 373 (M.D.Ala. 1972).
3. Nathan Glazer, "The Judiciary and Social Policy," *The Judiciary in a Democratic Society,* Leonard J. Theberge (ed.), Lexington Books, D. C. Heath & Co., 1979, p. 73.
4. *Youngberg v. Romeo,* 457 U.S. 307 (1982).
5. Jonathan Brant, "Pennhurst, Romeo, and Rogers, The Burger Court and Mental Health Law Reform Legislation," *The Journal of Legal Medicine,* vol. 4, 1983, p. 348.
6. *Holt v. Sarver,* 300 F.Supp. 825 (E.D.Ark. 1969).
7. *Holt v. Sarver,* 309 F.Supp. 362 (E.D.Ark. 1970).
8. *Finney v. Arkansas Board of Correction,* 505 F.2d 194 (8th Cir. 1974).
9. Frank M. Coffin, "The Frontier of Remedies: A Call for Exploration," *California Law Review,* vol. 67, 1979, p. 983.
10. *Inmates of Suffolk County Jail v. Eisenstadt,* 360 F.Supp. 676, (D.Mass. 1973).
11. *Inmates of Suffolk County Jail v. Kearney,* 573 F.2d 98 (1st Cir. 1978).
12. *Op. cit.,* note 9, p. 988.
13. *Op. cit.,* note 3, p. 72.
14. *Wright v. Rushen,* 642 F.2d 1129 (1981).
15. *Hudson v. Palmer,* 463 U.S. 1216 (1984).
16. *Block v. Rutherford,* 465 U.S. 1411 (1984).
17. *Bolling v. Sharpe,* 347 U.S. 497 (1954).
18. *Hobson v. Hansen,* 269 F.Supp. 401 (D.D.C 1967).
19. Lino A. Graglia, "The *Brown* Cases Revisited," *Benchmark,* vol. 1, no. 2, March–April 1984, p. 26.
20. Donald L. Horowitz, *The Courts and Social Policy,* The Brookings Institution, 1977, pp. 106–170.
21. Raoul Berger, *Government by Judiciary,* Harvard University Press, 1977, pp. 428–430.
22. *Op. cit.,* note 3, pp. 77–80.
23. Charles G. Douglas, III, "State Judicial Activism—the New Role for State Bills of Rights," *Suffolk University Law Review,* vol. xii, 1978, p. 1134.
24. Frank M. Johnson, Jr., "The Role of the Judiciary with Respect to the Other Branches of Government," *Georgia Law Review,* vol. II, 1977, pp. 474–475.

14. The Court Turns Up the Pressure

1. *Furman v. Georgia,* 408 U.S. 238 (1972).
2. *Gregg v. Georgia,* 428 U.S. 153 (1976).
3. Frank G. Carrington, *Neither Cruel nor Unusual,* Arlington House, 1978, p. 162.
4. See Carrington, *ibid.,* for a detailed discussion of the *Furman* and *Gregg* cases, each of which, when argued, was accompanied on the Court's docket by several similar cases from other states.
5. Clement E. Vose, "Interest Groups, Judicial Review, and Local Government," *Pressure Groups in American Politics,* H. R. Mahood (ed.), Scribner, New York, 1967, p. 271.

6. Luther Harmon Zeigler and G. Wayne Peak, *Interest Groups in American Society* (2d ed.), Prentice Hall, Engelwood Cliffs, N.J., 1972, p. 201.
7. *Brown v. Board of Education*, 347 U.S. 483 (1954).
8. Richard Y. Funston, *Constitutional Counterrevolution?*, John Wiley & Sons, 1977, p. 33.
9. Zeigler and Peak, *op. cit.*, note 6, p. 200.
10. *Missouri ex rel Gaines v. Canada*, 305 U.S. 337 (1938).
11. *Sweatt v. Painter*, 339 U.S. 629 (1950).
12. *Op. cit.*, note 5, pp. 271–272.
13. *Ibid.*, pp. 272, 274.
14. *Engel v. Vitale*, 370 U.S. 421 (1962).
15. *McCollum v. Board of Education*, 333 U.S. 203 (1948).
16. *Lemon v. Kurtzman*, 411 U.S. 192 (1971).
17. *Jaffree v. The Board of School Commissioners of Mobile County*, 553 F.Supp. 1104 (1983).
18. *Wallace v. Jaffree*, 472 U.S. 38 (1985).
19. *Massachusetts v. Mellon*, 262 U.S. 447 (1923).
20. *Doremus v. Board of Education*, 342 U.S. 429 (1952).
21. *Engel v. Vitale*, 370 U.S. 421 (1962).
22. *Abington Township School District v. Schempp*, 374 U.S. 203 (1963).
23. *Luther v. Borden*, 48 U.S. 1 (1849).
24. *NAACP v. Button*, 371 U.S. 415 (1963).
25. *Ibid.*, p. 425.
26. Ruggero J. Aldisert, "The Role of the Courts in Contemporary Society," *University of Pittsburgh Law Review*, vol. 38, 1977, pp. 458–459.
27. *Ibid.*, p. 458.
28. Martin Shapiro, "The Supreme Court and Freedom of Speech," *The Supreme Court in American Politics*, David Forte (ed.), D. C. Heath & Co., 1972, p. 39.
29. Martin Shapiro, "The Courts v. The President," *Journal of Contemporary Studies*, vol. iv, 1981, pp. 5–14.
30. Richard E. Morgan, *Disabling America, The "Rights Industry" in Our Time*, Basic Books, 1984, p. 62.
31. *Ibid.*, pp. 186–187.
32. Karen O'Connor and Lee Epstein, "The Role of Interest Groups in Supreme Court Policy Formation," *Public Policy Formation*, Robert Eyestone (ed.), JAI Press, 1968, p. 68.
33. *Ibid.*, p. 78.
34. *Ibid.*, p. 77.

15. Social Fallout

1. *Brown v. Board of Education*, 347 U.S. 483 (1954).
2. *Los Angeles Times*, September 19, 1980, Section I, p. 3.
3. *Chicago Sun Times*, August 8, 1979, p. 4.
4. *Los Angeles Times*, June 4, 1979, Part I, p. 3.

5. *Eastbay Today*, January 12, 1981, p. A6.
6. *Los Angeles Times*, June 16, 1981, Part I, p. 2.
7. *Los Angeles Times*, February 9, 1981, Part I, p. 1.
8. *Los Angeles Times*, January 20, 1981, Part II, p. 4.
9. *Los Angeles Times*, August 8, 1980, Part II, p. 1.
10. Edward Donnerstein, *New York Times*, September 30, 1980, Sec. III, p. 1.
11. U.S. Department of Justice, Attorney General's Commission on Pornography, Final Report, June 1986.
12. *Wallace Mendelson*, "The Politics of Judicial Activism," *Emory Law Journal*, vol. 24, 1975, p. 62.
13. Thomas Sowell, "A Black Conservative Dissents," *New York Times Magazine*, August 8, 1976, p. 14.
14. *Los Angeles Times*, August 29, 1980, Part 1-A, p. 1.
15. Richard Y. Funston, *Constitutional Counterrevolution?*, John Wiley & Sons, 1977, p. 323.
16. Charles G. Douglas, III, "State Judicial Activism—The New Role for State Bills of Rights," *Suffolk University Law Review*, vol. xii, 1978, p. 1148.
17. Ruggero J. Aldisert, "The Role of the Courts in Contemporary Society," *University of Pittsburgh Law Review*, Vol. 38, No. 3, 1977, pp. 456–457.
18. *Los Angeles Times*, March 2, 1981, Part I, p. 3.
19. *Salt Lake Tribune*, February 23, 1981, p. A9.
20. *San Francisco Chronicle*, March 14, 1981, p. 36.
21. *Los Angeles Times*, March 13, 1981, Part I, p. 1.
22. *Washington v. Seattle School District No. 1*, 454 U.S. 890 (1983); *Crawford v. Board of Education of the City of Los Angeles*, 458 U.S. 527 (1983).
23. *San Francisco Examiner & Chronicle*, November 5, 1967, p. 8B.
24. Raoul Berger, *Government by Judiciary*, Harvard University Press, 1977, p. 329.
25. Robert Bolt, "A Man for All Seasons," *Laurel British Drama: The Twentieth Century*, Robert W. Corrigan (ed.), Dell, 1965, p. 395.

16. Courts under Siege

1. *Los Angeles Times*, Nov. 21, 1980, p. 3.
2. *Marbury v. Madison*, 5 U.S. 137 (1803).
3. Wallace Mendelson, "The Politics of Judicial Activism," *Emory Law Journal*, vol. 24, 1975, p. 45.
4. *Dred Scott v. Sandford*, 60 U.S. 393 (1857).
5. *Op. cit.*, note 3, pp. 48–49.
6. William H. Rehnquist, "The Notion of a Living Constitution," *Texas Law Review*, vol. 54, 1976, p. 702.
7. *Ex Parte McCardle*, 74 U.S. 506 (1869).
8. Carl Brent Swisher, *American Constitutional Development*, Houghton Mifflin Co., The Riverside Press, Cambridge, 1943, p. 326.
9. *Op. cit.*, note 3, p. 50.
10. *Lochner v. New York*, 198 U.S. 45 (1905).

11. *Op. cit.,* note 3, p. 50.
12. *Ibid.*
13. Theodore L. Becker and Malcom M. Feeley (eds.), *The Impact of Supreme Court Decisions,* Oxford University Press, 1973, pp. 39–41.
14. *Brown v. Board of Education,* 347 U.S. 483 (1954).
15. *Op. cit.,* note 3, p. 63.
16. Charles G. Douglas, III, "State Judicial Activism—the New Role for State Bills of Rights," *Suffolk University Law Review,* vol. 12, 1978, p. 1139.
17. *Wall Street Journal* (Western edition), Aug. 29, 1984, at 22.
18. *Wall Street Journal* (Western edition), July 22, 1986, p. 30.
19. *Assembly v. Deukmejian,* 30 C.3d 638 (1982); *Legislature of the State of California v. Deukmejian,* 34 C.3d 658 (1983).
20. *San Francisco Chronicle,* September 23, 1984, p. B11.
21. Patrick B. McGuigan, *Judicial Notice,* July/August 1986, p. 19.
22. Alexis de Tocqueville, *Democracy in America,* Vintage Books, 1955, vol. 1, p. 157.

17. The Social Contract

1. Robert Ardrey, *The Social Contract,* A Delta Book, Dell Publishing Co., 1970, p. 97.
2. *Ibid.,* p. 358.
3. *Ibid.,* p. 3.
4. *Ibid.,* p. 95.
5. Thomas Hobbes, *Leviathan,* Part I, Chapter XIII.
6. Vernon Louis Parrington, *Main Currents In American Thought,* Harcourt Brace, 1927, 1930, vol. 1, p. 328.
7. Edward S. Corwin, *The "Higher Law" Background of American Constitutional Law,* Cornell University Press, 1955, p. 65.
8. John Hart Ely, "Towards a Representation-Reinforcing Mode of Judicial Review," *Maryland Law Review,* vol. 37, 1978, p. 472.
9. *Ibid.*
10. James Madison, *Federalist No. 51.*
11. Raoul Berger, *Government by Judiciary,* Harvard University Press, 1977, p. 413, n. 20.

18. The Process of Restraint

1. Raoul Berger, *Government by Judiciary,* Harvard University Press, 1977, pp. 366–367.
2. *Ibid.,* p. 297.
3. *Ibid.,* pp. 297–298.
4. *Gibbons v. Ogden,* 22 U.S. 1 (1824).
5. *Ibid.,* pp. 188–189.
6. J. Skelly Wright, "The Role of the Supreme Court in a Democratic Society—Judicial Activism or Restraint?," *Cornell Law Review,* vol. 54, 1968, pp. 27–28.

7. Archibald Cox, *The Role of the Supreme Court in American Government*, Oxford University Press, 1976, pp. 117–118.

19. Gubernaculum and Jurdisdictio

1. *The American Spectator*, January 1984, p. 46.
2. Paul Johnson, *Modern Times*, Harper & Row, 1983, p. 623.
3. *Ibid.*
4. William Kristol, " 'They Disdain to Conceal Their Views and Aims': The New Candor in the Law Schools," *Benchmark*, vol. 1, No. 6, 1984, p. 13.
5. *Ibid.*, p. 17.
6. *Ibid.*, p. 20.
7. John Hart Ely, "Toward a Representation-Reinforcing Mode of Judicial Review," *Maryland Law Review*, vol. 37, 1978, p. 485.
8. William H. Rehnquist, "The Notion of a Living Constitution," *Texas Law Review*, vol. 54, 1976, p. 699.
9. *Marbury v. Madison*, 5 U.S. 137, 170 (1803).
10. *Ibid.*, p. 176.
11. *Ibid.*, pp. 176–177.
12. *Ibid.*, pp. 179–180.
13. Raoul Berger, *Government by Judiciary*, Harvard University Press, 1977, p. 307.
14. Luther Harmon Zeigler and G. Wayne Peak, *Interest Groups in American Society*, (2nd ed.), Prentice Hall, Englewood Cliffs, N.J., 1972, p. 185.
15. Charles Howard McIlwain, *Constitutionalism, Ancient and Modern*, Cornell University Press, 1947.
16. *Ibid.*, p. 140.
17. *Ibid.*, p. 146.

20. Liberty under Law?

1. *Osborne v. Bank of United States*, 9 Wheat. 738, 866 (1824).
2. Carl Brent Swisher, *American Constitutional Development*, Houghton Mifflin Co., The Riverside Press, Cambridge, 1943, p. 773.
3. Raoul Berger, *Government by Judiciary*, Harvard University Press, 1977, p. 414.
4. Albert J. Beveridge, *The Life of John Marshall*, Houghton Mifflin Co. (4 vol.), 1916, vol. 3, p. 177.
5. *Ibid.*, p. 178.
6. Irving Kristol, *The Wall Street Journal* (Western Edition), July 25, 1985, p. 18.
7. Joseph Sobran, "A Naive View," *Human Life Review*, Winter, 1983, p. 14.
8. Malcolm Richard Wilkey, "Judicial Activism, Congressional Abdication, and the Need for Constitutional Reform," *Harvard Journal of Law & Public Policy*, Summer, 1985, pp. 504–505.
9. *Op. cit.*, note 7.
10. *Ex Parte McCardle*, 74 U.S. 506 (1869).
11. C. Dickerman Williams, "Congress and the Supreme Court," *National Review*, February 5, 1982, p. 109.

12. *United States v. More,* 7 U.S. 159 (1803).
13. *Op. Cit.,* note 11, p. 110.
14. *Barry v. Mercein,* 46 U.S. 103 (1847).
15. *Daniels v. Railroad Co.,* 70 U.S. 250 (1865).
16. *The Francis Wright,* 105 U.S. 381 (1881).
17. *Stephan v. United States,* 319 U.S. 423 (1943).
18. Lino Graglia, "A Theory of Power," *National Review,* July 17, 1987, p. 35.
19. *Human Events,* Nov. 7, 1987, p. 3.
20. Norman Podhoretz, *Savannah Morning News,* October 10, 1987, p. 4A.
21. *Op. cit.,* note 19.
22. Milton Friedman and Gerhard Casper *Wall Street Journal* (Western Edition), October 21, 1987, p. 32.
23. *Wall Street Journal* (Western Edition), October 20, 1987, p. 38.
24. *Human Events,* November 7, 1987, p. 4.
25. *Wall Street Journal* (Western Edition), October 29, 1987, p. 26.
26. *Washington Times,* October 2, 1987, p. A11.
27. *New York Times* (National Edition), October 24, 1987, p. 8.
28. *Wall Street Journal* (Western Edition), September 24, 1987, p. 26.
29. *Wall Street Journal* (Southwest Edition), October 27, 1987, p. 32.
30. *National Review,* August 28, 1987, p. 36.
31. *Wall Street Journal* (Western Edition) November 9, 1987, p. 24.
32. *Op. cit.,* note 20.
33. *U.S. v. Butler,* 297 U.S. 1, 79 (1936), dissenting.
34. *Ibid.*

TABLE OF CASES

INDEX

269